Fighting Corruption
in Developing Countries

Fighting Corruption in Developing Countries

Strategies and Analysis

Edited by Bertram I. Spector

Kumarian
Press, Inc.

Fighting Corruption in Developing Countries: Strategies and Analysis

Published in 2005 in the United States of America by Kumarian Press, Inc., 1294 Blue Hills Avenue, Bloomfield, CT 06002, USA

Production and interior design by Jennifer Boeree, Scribe
Copyedited by Chris Curioli
Proofread by Dale Rohrbaugh, Scribe
Index by Paul Kish
The text of this book is set in Adobe Garamond 10.3/12.3

Printed in Canada by Transcontinental Printing.

∞:The paper used in this publication meets the minimum requirements of the American National Standard for Information Sciences—Permanence of Paper for printed Library Materials, ANSI Z39.48-1984.

Library of Congress Cataloging-in-Publication Data

Fighting corruption in developing countries : strategies and analysis / edited by Bertram I. Spector.
p. cm.
Summary: "Presents a sector-by-sector analysis of corruption in developing countries written by experts that address nine sectors: education, agriculture, energy, environment, health, justice, private business, political parties and public finance. Concludes with policy-oriented suggestions for eliminating corruption. Written for students, researchers, and practitioners" —Provided by publisher.
Includes bibliographical references and index.
ISBN 1-56549-202-1 (pbk. : alk. paper)
1. Bureaucracy—Corrupt practices—Developing countries.
2. Administrative agencies—Corrupt practices—Developing countries.
3. Corruption—Developing countries. 4. Corruption—Developing countries—Prevention. I. Spector, Bertram I. (Bertram Irwin), 1949–
HN980.F54 2005
364.1'323'091724—dc22

2005000405

14 13 12 11 10 09 08 07 06 05   10 9 8 7 6 5 4 3 2 1   First Printing 2005

For Sam and Naomi
and
hope for a well-governed world

Contents

Part 2. Applied Analyses

The cover art and the artwork accompanying each chapter were drawn by political caricaturist Boris Pertsev of Tomsk, Russia, originally for the newspaper "Tomskiy Vestnik."

List of Tables

Chapter 12

Chapter 13

List of Figures

Foreword

During the past decade, corruption has been of increasing concern to those toiling in relative obscurity on governance issues. Part of the push came from within donor agencies, convinced that a failure to address corruption was at least one factor in the poor performance of first-generation public administration and civil service reforms.

More demand came, however, from citizens living in many developing countries confronted with endemic corruption in their government, universities, and businesses. Frustration mounted as press outlets provided more information on corruption but no evidence of anyone being held accountable. Civil society organizations, such as Transparency International, took root and spread throughout the globe, linking up with other coalitions. Governments tentatively moved to respond. By the late 1990s, donor, citizen, and government efforts to address corruption were expanding.

In 2002, however, the attention paid to corruption by policymakers increased significantly. Even as corruption had percolated to the top of the governance agenda, governance itself rose to the top of the development agenda and beyond. Today, effective governance is recognized as a *sine qua non* for development and poor governance, in turn, as a contributing factor to poverty, conflict, and state failure, with repercussions for global security.

How did this happen? One place to start the story is with the aid effectiveness debate. Influential research by Burnside and Dollar in the late 1990s argued that aid had been effective in countries with good policies, good governance, and less corruption, but tended to have little or no effect on growth in countries with weak policies and high corruption.[1] Daniel Kaufmann and other colleagues at the World Bank developed new measures of governance with broad country coverage and were able to demonstrate significant links between governance and a range of development outcomes.[2]

In March 2002, US President George W. Bush announced his intention to establish the Millennium Challenge Account to reward developing countries that are "ruling justly, investing in their people, and encouraging economic freedom." Efforts to control corruption would, he announced, be the single "hard hurdle" to be cleared before performance in other areas would be considered.[3] Two weeks later, heads of state from developed and developing countries announced the Monterrey Consensus—a "new partnership" in which developing countries would commit themselves to "sound policies, good governance and the rule of law" and developed countries would, in turn, provide greater resources for development.

According to the new US National Security Strategy issued in September 2002, "[t]he events of September 11, 2001, taught us that weak states, like Afghanistan, can pose as great a danger to our national interests as strong states" because "poverty, weak institutions, and corruption can make weak states vulnerable to terrorist networks and drug cartels within their borders."[4] Currently, several countries and multilateral donors are developing strategies to address weak states that emphasize the links between corruption, poor governance, and weak states.

With this backdrop, the US Agency for International Development (USAID) began preparation of new regional and global strategies to address corruption that would scale up anticorruption efforts, integrating anticorruption into USAID's development efforts across all sectors. Much of the research compiled in this volume was commissioned by USAID as inputs to development of this new strategy.

USAID's first objective was to broaden the conversation beyond governance specialists to engage all key sectors affected by corruption. The sector papers compiled in Part 1 of this volume were very helpful in doing so. I hope they will also be helpful for individuals who want to understand how corruption relates to their particular area of focus and what approaches might be within their manageable interest. For governance and anticorruption specialists, these sector snapshots may help to broaden their understanding of corruption and demonstrate additional entry points for addressing it.

In some cases, the sectoral reviews helped to highlight new issues affecting multiple sectors. One example involved police forces. The papers, based on interviews with a wide range of development professionals, indicated that police corruption imposed tremendous costs not only on the administration of justice but also on agriculture (increased cost of getting products to market), the environment (weak enforcement of environmental protections), private sector development (restraint on trade within and across borders), and state legitimacy (police are the "public face" of the state for many citizens). It became clear that USAID's limited congressional authority to work with police forces constrained its ability to address the impacts of corruption on development.

Conflict, gender, corruption—these are all issues that affect multiple sectors and they raise challenges for specialized organizations. Management Systems International's (MSI) work on the sectoral dimensions of corruption is a useful beginning for discussing the issues in general terms. Patterns of corruption vary significantly, however, across and within countries and local knowledge will always be essential.

The second part of the volume pulls together pieces of research, many of which were also commissioned by USAID. "Learning Across Cases" by Bertram I. Spector, Michael Johnston, and Phyllis Dininio contributes to a small but vitally important literature attempting to evaluate the success of various types of anticorruption interventions. Much more work of this kind is needed, despite the many methodological challenges. Omar Azfar's empirical work on the relationship between corruption and health and education outcomes shines light on a relatively neglected dimension of corruption—its impacts on service delivery. In comparison, significantly more work has been done on the impacts of corruption on economic growth and democratic consolidation. Phyllis Dininio's chapter on recorruption reminds us that countries do not travel along a constant trajectory from more to less corrupt, nor do they reach a plateau where efforts to prevent, detect, and sanction corruption are no longer necessary. These safeguards need to become institutionalized.

Today, anticorruption and good governance are receiving considerable attention by policymakers around the world. This attention is vitally important but it needs to manifest itself in concerted action, diplomacy, trade and aid conditionality, additional aid resources, and additional knowledge to combat corruption. This book makes an important contribution on the knowledge side, and more knowledge helps reformers make the case for more resources.

But we also need to align expectations with reality. If, as the World Bank estimates, the corruption "industry" generates more than US$ 1 trillion in bribes per year, then what magnitude of resources are needed to contain and reduce it? If aid is not effective in corrupt policy environments, then how can aid be employed to make policy environments less corrupt, particularly in weak states? When the state and key segments of the economy have been "captured" by corrupt interests, how can this stranglehold be broken? There is no shortage of difficult questions in the corruption field. This book dares to wade into these waters and offers us new ideas, understanding, and knowledge.

In highly corrupt countries, the governments that must lead anticorruption efforts often have the most to lose if these efforts are successful. That has been the key constraint to date. Nonetheless, as described above, political leaders have indicated a greater awareness of the importance of controlling corruption and, more broadly, building governance. Important shifts in incentive structures and attitudes are also taking place in the global business environment. Finally, despite collective action challenges, Open Society Institute President Aryeh Neier has argued that the anticorruption movement now emerging may have potential comparable to that realized by the human rights movement and the environmental movement during the past twenty-five years.[5] Already a history of corruption and/or a failure to address it has brought down several governments. Corruption will never be eliminated, but fortunately for all of us, that is not the goal. Even modest, incremental reductions in corruption can have large impacts on income, health, education, poverty, and other key development outcomes. Small gains are real gains, and that is one of the important themes of this book.

Madalene O'Donnell
Former Senior Anti-Corruption Advisor at the USAID Democracy and Governance Office and, currently, at the Center on International Cooperation, New York University
October 1, 2004

Notes

1. See Craig Burnside and David Dollar, "Aid, Policies, and Growth," The American Economic Review, vol. 90(4), pages 847–868, September 2000. See also William Easterly, Ross Levine and David Roodman, "Aid, Policies, and Growth: Comment," The American Economic Review, June 2004, vol. 94; Craig Burnside and David Dollar, "Aid, Policies, and Growth: Reply," The American Economic Review, June 2004, vol. 94, no. 3.

2. Daniel Kaufmann, Art Kraay, Pablo Zoido-Lobotón, Governance Matters (World Bank Policy Research Working Paper 2196) October 1999.

3. Remarks by U.S. President George W. Bush on Global Development, Inter-American Development Bank, March 12, 2002: http://www.whitehouse.gov/news/releases/2002/03/2002 0314-7.html.

4. Introduction to the National Security Strategy of the United States of America, September 2002.

5. Aryeh Neier, "Rooting Out Corruption to Allow Democracy to Grow," Open Society News, Summer/Fall 2003.

Acknowledgments

The research undertaken by the contributors was conducted under two contracts from the United States Agency for International Development (USAID) to Management Systems International (MSI), an international development consulting firm based in Washington, DC. I express my appreciation to Madalene O'Donnell who promoted the idea of a sectoral approach to fighting corruption and to Sarah Elizabeth Jones and Dennis Wendel for their support of innovative applied analytical studies in this area. All of this work was conducted within the calm and peaceful waters of MSI, where Larry Cooley and Marina Fanning have provided safe haven for the anticorruption practice area to grow and prosper. Thanks also go to Stephen Schwenke for his skillful coordination of the sectoral study and to Helen Grant-Glaze for administering that effort. Finally, I am extremely grateful to James Lance, Editor and Associate Publisher at Kumarian Press, who has been an enthusiastic supporter of this book project, and to Katherine Sepponen who helped edit the final manuscript and integrate the bibliography across the entire volume.

The views expressed in this book are those of the authors' alone and should not be attributed to the sponsoring agencies, the United States Agency for International Development, or the US government.

Acknowledgments

Acronyms

ADR	Alternative dispute resolution
BPDB	Bangladesh Power Development Board
BPI	Bribe Payers Index
CAO	Citizen advocate office
CMS	Central medical stores
CPI	Corruption Perceptions Index
DESA	Dhaka Electricity Supply Authority
DFID	Department for International Development
DHS	Demographic and health survey
DPP	Democratic Progressive Party
EDL	Essential drug list
EIA	Environmental Impact Assessments
EMIS	Education management information system
FDI	Foreign direct investment
FOI	Freedom of information
GAVI	Global Alliance for Vaccines and Immunization
GDP	Gross domestic product
GFATM	Global Fund to Fight AIDS, Tuberculosis and Malaria
ICAC	Independent Commission Against Corruption (Hong Kong)
ICRG	International Country Risk Guide
IFPMA	International Federation of Pharmaceutical Manufacturers Associations
IMF	International Monetary Fund
IP	Integrity pact
IV	Instrumental variable
KACA	Kenya Anticorruption Authority
KMT	Kuomintang
LDP	Liberal Democratic Party
MERC	Middle East Regional Cooperation Program
MSI	Management Systems International
NEAT	National Elementary Aptitude Test
NGO	Nongovernmental organization
NHA	National health accounts
OECD	Organization for Economic Cooperation and Development
OLS	Ordinary Least Squares
PAG	Petroleum Advisory Group
PETS	Public expenditure tracking survey

POSE	Point-of-service evaluation survey
PRI	Institutional Revolutionary Party
PVO	Private Voluntary Organization
QSDS	Quantitative service delivery survey
RPM	Rational Pharmaceutical Management
SAI	Supreme audit institution
SDP	Service delivery point
UMNO	United Malay National Organization (Malaysia)
UNDP	United Nations Development Program
USAID	United States Agency for International Development
VAT	Value added tax
WHO	World Health Organization
WRI	World Resources Institute
WWF	World Wildlife Foundation
ZANU-PF	Zimbabwe African National Union-Popular Front (Zimbabwe)

Chapter 1

Fighting Corruption

Bertram I. Spector

Is corruption in government incurable? In many countries, rampant personal greed seems to be correlated with the assumption of public office. Unofficial payments seem to be the only way for low-paid government workers to get by. Higher level officials appear to use their influence for the benefit of their family and friends rather than for the public good. In the private sector, the only way to build a business seems to involve paying speed money (bribes that facilitate faster processing of applications or documents) or giving kickbacks to bureaucrats. In some instances, special interests seem to be capable of "buying," or capturing, influential public officials on a sustained basis to ensure that the goals of such entities are satisfied ahead of the public's interests. This is referred to as "state capture." Ordinary citizens, too, cannot seem to get quality public services without providing gifts or paying bribes. And society, in general, appears to tolerate these practices, providing a nurturing environment for sustained corruption. People and society just cannot see their way out of the predicament.

If we look at trends in several quantitative indicators of corruption, our skepticism about dealing successfully with this problem is reinforced. The Transparency International (TI) Corruption Perceptions Index ranks 70 percent of 133 countries as below the median score, and 90 percent of all developing countries in the sample score less than the median score. But pervasive corruption is shown to be a frequent characteristic of both rich and poor countries (TI, 2003). The 2002 TI Bribe Payers Index portrays very high levels of bribery by corporations in both developing and industrialized countries (TI, 2002). According to the World Bank's 2002 governance indicators, thirteen of the twenty most populous countries rank below the world average in their ability to control corruption (Kaufmann, Kraay, and Mastruzzi, 2003).

A cynic might look at these highly pessimistic findings and conclude that containing corruption is an entirely unrealistic goal—certainly too difficult to achieve within the short or medium term. However, activities and reforms have been initiated in countries around the world that have made a difference. These initiatives have targeted particular programs and sectors. They have focused on changing processes at different levels of government. They have attacked petty corruption, grand corruption, and state capture. And they have been initiated by various types of stakeholders—government, civil society, business, and the media. Consider these scenarios.

- Citizen Advocate Offices (CAOs) have been established in four regions of Russia—Vladivostok, Irkutsk, Samara, and Tomsk—providing legal support services to victims of alleged corruption and excessive bureaucracy on a *pro bono* basis. There has been a continuous high public demand for their legal services, demonstrated by hundreds of grievances being registered every month. Many grievances deal with housing, employment, and pensions, where bureaucrats demand bribes or stand in the way of citizens obtaining what they legally deserve. Assistance has also been offered to entrepreneurs who are frequently harassed and extorted by inspectors and police and victimized by court decisions that are not enforced. CAO lawyers have been successful in resolving many of these corruption cases in favor of abused citizens either administratively or in court. For example, citizens were reinstated in their jobs after being dismissed unlawfully, public services were delivered that were not previously provided as intended, police misconduct was exposed and officers reprimanded, irregularities and nepotism were exposed in the Army Housing Administration, passport agency officials were sanctioned for extorting citizens, and unlawful fines levied by tax inspectors against businesses were repealed by the Arbitrage Court.

- In Uganda, only 13 percent of funds allocated for textbooks and supplies were reaching local schools. To fix the problem, all fund transfers to district education offices were published in newspapers and broadcast on the radio. As well, each primary school was required to post a public notice of all funds received. Within three years, 90 percent of nonsalary funds provided by the central government were reaching the schools.

- Latvia's anticorruption reforms of its revenue administration included an important citizen oversight activity. In addition to a major reorganization of the State Revenue Service tax and customs functions, including strengthened internal controls, a Vigilance Unit was established, operating independently of the financial police, to monitor adherence to the ethics code, conduct disciplinary hearings, develop incentives to foster integrity, and monitor declarations of income and assets by public servants.

- In 1999, a huge corruption scandal was exposed involving the chief executive of the Lesotho Highlands Water Project and twelve of the biggest dam-building companies in the world. The companies were accused of paying bribes to win lucrative dam-building and engineering contracts. Within the year, the chief executive was convicted of thirteen counts of bribery and sentenced to eighteen years in prison for taking more than $2 million in bribes.

- Before the South Korean national elections in April 2000, civil society watchdogs published blacklists of candidates and parties tainted with corruption. The press provided additional investigative reporting and disseminated the blacklists. Their activity had a major influence on the election outcome.

- In Kenya and Niger, donor-assisted health care financing projects have developed management systems and incentives to reduce opportunities for corruption in the procurement and distribution of pharmaceuticals. Local budgeting and cost recovery systems, strong financial control systems, and inventory control systems have been instituted, improving accountability and transparency.

- In Thailand, an election can be revoked and candidates disqualified if they or their campaign staff engage in corruption or vote-buying. Because the dismissal of politicians from parliament reduces a party's delegation and hence its voting power, such regulations increase incentives for strict party control over candidate behavior and clean election campaigns.

- Regional Accounts Chambers in Russia are important government oversight agencies charged with managing public spending, ensuring financial accountability, and strengthening public institutions. Their audits can detect fraud and abuse. A computer-based tracking system was developed and implemented to ensure timely follow-up when irregularities are uncovered.

All of these, and many more, successes were conceived of and accomplished by governments and their civil societies, usually with the technical assistance of international development consultants.[1] No one would be bold enough to say that corruption is gone in these countries as a result of these initiatives, but some sources of abuse have been closed, cynical attitudes have been reversed, overwhelming public tolerance for corruption reduced, and, little by little, official transactions with citizens are becoming more transparent and accountable. Citizens in these communities are beginning to feel more in control of their lives, less demeaned, and more optimistic that corruption can be contained, stopped, or averted. They can see a time when corruption is not an everyday occurrence and when government is efficient and responsive to their needs.

Many positive initiatives such as these are being taken in countries around the world to reduce the opportunities and impact of all levels and types of corruption: petty, grand, and state capture. These initiatives may be small, but they are important steps in the right direction, slowly transforming cultures of systemic corruption into societies that demand greater transparency from government, strict accountability of officials for their actions, and strong enforcement of laws and regulations. None of these changes take hold overnight; they require the perseverance and commitment of political leaders, citizens, and the media over the long term to ensure not only that the legal and enforcement infrastructure is put in place to deter corrupt practices, but also that preventive reforms are widely instituted to reduce opportunities for corruption, and that the public is educated about the social costs of corruption and about legal and civil rights.

Because corruption is such a pervasive and resilient form of human behavior in all countries, these same types of anticorruption initiatives and continued societal vigilance are needed in developing and transitional states, as well as in industrialized nations, to control and contain corruption at low and manageable levels.

These initiatives also demonstrate the diversity of corruption and anticorruption strategies. Corruption is most commonly defined as *the misuse of public office for personal gain* (Klitgaard, Maclean-Abaroa, and Parris, 2000). But in the mind of the average citizen, corruption is not as abstract as this definition might suggest. It rather is seen as the extralegal and often humiliating transactions required to facilitate the delivery of government services in a wide range of sectors, including education, communal housing, justice, procurement, public finance, business, and politics. In each sector, corruption manifests itself differently and gets embedded into various sector-specific processes, which demand sector-specific solutions. But the fundamental elements of corruption—the misuse of office and the private motive—are common across all sectors.

At the core of the problem of corruption are several common but devastating misconceptions. First, there is often a basic misunderstanding of what *public service* implies. Elected or appointed officials and administrative personnel in government often fail to appreciate the special provision of their employment—they are servants of the public and are entrusted with carrying out their functions and expending public funds with the public's interest in mind. They have no ordinary job.

Second, public servants sometimes lack understanding of what constitutes a *conflict of interest*. The line between public and private can be unclear in some societies, and laws and regulations do not specify or enforce the difference well. Corruption thrives when the wealth and potential of the public sector are used without permission by those who happen to work in government. In fact, many public opinion surveys find that people generally associate corruption with illicit monetary transactions, such as bribes, kickbacks, speed money, and extortion, but not with illicit influence transactions, such as nepotism, favoritism, and misuse of public property. The general lack of understanding that abuse of influence also constitutes corruption typifies the conflict between public and private interests.

Finally, *respect for the rule of law* is often denied. It is replaced by creative approaches to "get around the system" to obtain what one needs. Corrupt practices are tolerated, not because corruption is revered, but because people cannot see a way out of the dilemma. They believe that living with corruption is their fate and that there is nothing that can be done about it. This fatalistic attitude can easily translate into a chaotic Darwinian world where the rule of law that is meant to give order to society is ignored in favor of personal incentives and motives.

* * *

Despite earlier taboos against discussing, let alone doing anything to reduce corruption, by the mid-1990s many international and bilateral donors, governments, and nongovernmental organizations were debating how to deal with the problem and were advocating for and promoting reforms. They initiated assessments of corruption, the development of adequate legal frameworks, the establishment of government institutions such as anticorruption commissions, the strengthening of law enforcement bodies, and the education of citizens about the costs and consequences of corruption (Bhargava and Bolongaita, 2003). Has this helped? Although Kaufmann (2003) found that results vary across countries, in general these decade-long initiatives have not had an appreciable impact on controlling corruption or reducing state capture. He argues that conventional approaches to fighting corruption—passing laws, creating new institutions, and conducting anticorruption campaigns—have failed to make significant inroads to control or reverse the problem. Rather, a new orientation that emphasizes external accountability—approaches that impose extensive checks and balances on public institutions and officeholders—might put sufficient demand on government to abide by the rule of law and curb corrupt tendencies.

Fighting Corruption in Developing Countries draws on lessons from past experience but, as Kaufmann does, challenges traditional approaches to contain corruption. It argues that corruption needs to be addressed by demands for reform on a *sector-by-sector basis*, and it stresses that policy decisions concerning appropriate anticorruption strategies should be informed by *knowledge-based applied analyses*.

Within a country, corruption knows no borders: it does not remain localized in particular government departments but pervades all functions where citizens and businesses transact with officials. Thus, one of the best ways to understand the spread of corruption and what can be done to control it is by analyzing its impact *sector-by-sector*. International experience has demonstrated that broad anticorruption programs may have positive, though short-term, effects on the problem while raising public awareness. However, programs that are targeted at vulnerable sectors (i.e., the education or health areas) can take hold and be sustained over the longer term. After all, policy is usually made function by function; within each function, anticorruption strategies can be more specifically targeted at root causes and enforced. Moreover, surveys demonstrate that when people think about corruption and how it affects their lives, it is by sector.

In Part 1, nine sector specialists reflect on how their sectors are vulnerable to corrupt practices and what decisions are available to control corruption and the situational constraints that need to be considered. Each chapter analyzes each sector in depth on where the vulnerabilities are, how corruption typically manifests itself, barriers to growth, international experience in dealing with these corruptive situations, and practical remedies. The nine chapters are grouped in terms of political, social, and economic functions. First, the justice sector and political parties are examined. Next, health care and education are addressed. Finally, public finance, environment, energy, agriculture, and the private sector are evaluated. An integrative analysis follows that draws out common threads and distinctive differences among these sectors.

The book continues in Part 2 with several practical applied analyses that can inform rational decision-making in fighting corruption. Chapter 12 addresses the impact of corruption on the effective delivery of health care and educational services. Using a quantitative approach, this study develops policy recommendations for reforms that would yield effective service delivery outcomes. Chapter 13 develops a meta-analytic approach so that policymakers can learn from the growing number of case studies in the anticorruption field. Rather than drawing on the idiosyncratic results of single cases, this approach informs decisions by summarizing analytically the findings across many cases under a variety of conditions. Chapter 14 addresses the very real risk of *recorruption*: the possibility that despite all efforts, corruptive forces will reverse gains achieved over time. Policy recommendations are presented on how to avert backsliding.

* * *

Corruption undermines governance, economic growth, and, ultimately, the stability of countries and regions. In an era when we are keenly attuned to the implications of state failure on conflict and terrorism, the detrimental impact of corruption on regime stability takes on important meaning. Uncontrolled corruption not only hurts the host polity but can take a toll on its neighbors as well, far and wide. Finding and sharing the best strategies that put a check on corrupt practices can in many cases be part of the preventive antidote that halts the onset of state failure and its associated maladies. Taking the threat of corruption out of the equation should eliminate one of the key facilitating factors for domestic, regional, and worldwide unrest.

If a sectoral approach to fighting corruption is most likely to yield results, as suggested by this volume, what are the operational issues that need to be addressed to get strategies implemented in a practical way?

- A sectoral orientation would mean a decentralization of the anticorruption effort, making transparent and accountable governance the direct responsibility of officials in each sectoral agency—in public energy and health agencies, for instance. Sectoral leaders, after all, should be responsible and accountable for properly governing the operations decisions and expenditure of public funds in their domains. Directing anticorruption policy from a central commission or agency would not be appropriate unless the mission of such an entity would be changed to serve as a clearinghouse and oversight institution, although establishing a permanent interagency task force might be a channel to share experience across sectoral agencies. Education, environment, and agriculture specialists, for example, would need to be trained to be sensitive to corruption vulnerabilities in their sectors and to have the tools at their command to act upon such vulnerabilities. These specialists would need sector-specific assessment tools as well to monitor the effect of their remedies and to detect new points of weakness.

- How can each sector be provided with incentive to assume these anticorruption responsibilities seriously and with vigor? Certainly, it has always been the duty of public officials in all sectors to carry out their functions ethically and in the public interest. But positive and goal-directed action can be motivated by establishing or strengthening internal controls through performance measurement. Sector leaders can be made clearly responsible for how they use sectoral budgets and meet certain measurable targets. Monitoring and evaluation systems can be designed and implemented within sectoral agencies not only to stimulate this goal-directed performance but also to provide incentives for achievement of these goals.

- External controls are often needed to ensure compliance with performance objectives and to deal with instances of misgovernance or abuse. Perhaps oversight agencies, similar to U.S. regulatory enforcement agencies like the US Office of Government Ethics with its representation in each sector, can be established to monitor transparency, accountability, and integrity sector by sector.

- Even if the job of fighting corruption is decentralized, there needs to be a way to centralize information to support the challenge. Web-based applications and databases could be implemented to facilitate information sharing across functions, programs, levels of government, and countries.

- Sector-by-sector anticorruption strategies are likely to be conducted at all levels of government—national, regional, and local. For regional and local reforms to proceed, facilitating legislation and regulation will need to be implemented at the central level first. Many of the same challenges described above regarding incentives, monitoring, and sharing of information will be repeated at each level of implementation.

- To be sustainable, strategies within each sector will have to be developed to target all levels and types of corruption—petty, grand, and state capture. Strategies will have to be found to transform the sector context to make it less susceptible to corruption vulnerabilities as well.

There are several international catalysts that will sustain the current movement toward corruption containment. For one, the US government's Millennium Challenge Account uses "control of corruption" as one of its threshold criteria for selecting countries for substantial foreign assistance (Brainard et al., 2003). For those countries that fall below the threshold on the corruption indicator, there is a strong motive to provide technical aid with the goal of improving the chances of such countries for the next selection. Thus, promoting anticorruption programs will be at the top of the agenda for those "near-miss" countries. Another catalyst is conditionality. Some loans from the International Monetary Fund and the World Bank are granted conditional on visible improvements in fighting corruption. Often, this takes the form of establishing an anticorruption commission or adopting particular legislation. Yet another tool for stimulating anticorruption programs is through the social pressure of the community of nations that adopts international treaties and conventions on the subject. There are now several global and regional conventions—the United Nations Convention Against Corruption, the Organization for Economic Cooperation and Development (OECD) Convention on Combating the Bribery of Foreign Public Officials, the Inter-American Convention Against Corruption, the African Union Convention on Preventing and Combating Corruption, and the Asia Development Bank Policy on Corruption, for example—that place specific demands and constraints on signatory countries to act against corrupt practices.

* * *

The fight against corruption is not likely ever to result in an ultimate victory but rather in more competent ways to control and contain it. This demands that countries and the international community develop more targeted and efficient strategies than they currently have based on a more reliable and insightful set of facts and propositions about what works and under what circumstances to enable policymakers to make smarter decisions. The chapters in this book offer a starting point for this renewed challenge.

Notes

1. These and other cases are described in more detail in Part 1 of this book.

PART 1

THE SECTORAL DIMENSIONS OF CORRUPTION

Chapter 2

Justice System

Mary Noel Pepys

Corruption within the justice system is generally defined as the use of public authority for personal gain that results in the improper delivery of judicial services and legal protection for citizens. Typically, the justice system includes judges, prosecutors, the police, public defenders, the private bar, court personnel, and court decision enforcement agencies, such as penal institutions. This chapter will consider corruption carried out by judges, prosecutors, the police, and court personnel within developing and transitional countries.

In a democracy based on the rule of law, the role of the judiciary, as an independent and equal branch of government, is to protect human rights and civil liberties by ensuring the right to a fair trial by a competent and impartial tribunal. All citizens are entitled to equal access to the courts and equal treatment by the investigative bodies, prosecutorial authorities, and the courts themselves, regardless of their position in society. Yet, in corrupted judicial systems, the powerful and wealthy can escape prosecution and conviction, while large segments of society are excluded from their rightful access to fair and effective judicial services.

As the ultimate decision maker and the highest governmental official within the justice system, the judge is the focal point for reducing corruption and promoting the rule of law. However, whether the judge is engaged in criminal, civil, commercial, or administrative decision-making is essentially immaterial to the root causes and forms of corruption that can potentially infect the judicial system.

Corruption in the justice system can potentially impact on all aspects of judicial oversight. Police, prosecutors, and court staff often play a role in improperly influencing the provision of judicial services, and their involvement in corruption can have a menacing impact on the entire judicial process.

Police and magistrates (judges and prosecutors) in developing countries often receive dismally low salaries and perform their duties under abominable working conditions that consist of overcrowded office space and dilapidated courtrooms. This situation can be magnified by the lack of support staff and equipment and minimal access to current laws or revisions to laws. A justice system replete with individuals who are ill-informed, underpaid, and overworked is a well-tested recipe for corruption.

Although the role of the courts is to protect the human rights and civil liberties of every citizen in a democratic country, many public opinion polls show that the public views the judicial branch as one of the most corrupt governmental institutions in their country. In several recent surveys in Southeast Europe, for example, more than half of the respondents perceive that corruption is widespread in the courts, among judges, and among the police. In Albania, 44 percent of respondents indicate that they have been extorted by judges; in Bangladesh, judicial extortion is experienced by 63 percent of the respondents.[1]

The perception of corruption is as insidious, and just as important to overcome, as corruption itself, as they both have the effect of undermining the public's trust in the justice system. Citizens are less likely to abide by the law if they believe others, particularly governmental leaders, are disobeying the law and avoiding detection and punishment. Aggrieved individuals will resort to "taking the law into their own hands" to resolve disputes rather than submit to a judicial system that is perceived to be dishonest and biased. Foreign investors will shun those countries where the judicial system has the reputation of applying the law in an inconsistent and capricious manner. In an increasingly global arena with highly competitive markets, the economic growth of countries with corrupt judiciaries, real or perceived, can be seriously retarded. Until corruption within the judicial sector is severely curtailed or eradicated, most legal and programmatic mechanisms put forth to reduce corruption in other sectors of society will be significantly undermined.

Vulnerabilities to Corruption in the Justice System

To design effectively a response to the problem of corruption, it is crucial to understand the particular vulnerabilities of the justice sector.

Underlying Causes of Corruption in the Justice System

There are several underlying causes of corruption in developing and transitional countries that tend to make their judiciaries more prone to corrupt practices, some of which are institutional and others attitudinal.

Role of Government. The government both as an institution and as a place of employment often receives little respect from the general public. Disillusioned citizens oftentimes view government leaders as placing their own self-interests above the interests of society at large. Given the fact that in many countries the historical role of government has been to promote the state's rights over citizens' rights, citizens have traditionally observed with skepticism the legitimacy of their own governmental leaders. Moreover, citizens in many developing and transitional countries often view the judicial branch, particularly judges, as an impediment to democracy rather than as a democratic check to balance federal and executive powers.

Governmental Leaders Engaged in Corrupt Behavior. Governmental leaders, including judges, prosecutors, and police, in corrupt countries often disregard the very laws, rules, and procedures they are supposed to enforce. Those governmental leaders who sidestep laws are rarely prosecuted and convicted. Thus, the average citizen in such countries considers himself foolhardy if he abides by the very system his leaders are eschewing.

System Based on Personal Influence and Contacts. When the system for receiving governmental goods and services is based on contacts rather than merit and where appointment and promotion is a product of patronage, citizens try to appease powerful individuals rather than place faith in an impotent set of laws. In countries where it is *who you know* and not *what you know*, merit-based rewards are seldom available. Acceptance and belief in the power of contacts rather than content is so pervasive in many countries that even when judicial decisions are based on merit, most citizens dismiss the decisions as the product of personal influence.

Tolerance Toward Corruption. In most countries where corruption has reached epidemic proportions, there is a high tolerance for corruption, particularly because it is viewed as the only avenue for accomplishing certain actions. In some instances, the payment of a bribe is a normal and acceptable way of doing business. Corruption is so common in certain arenas that citizens do not even view their behavior as immoral. For instance, attorneys who consider themselves law-abiding do not hesitate to pay a bribe to a court clerk to expedite a case file. Because the attorney is not interfering in the substance of the case, he does not believe any corrupt transaction has been conducted. Such an attorney overlooks the fact that his behavior can have the effect of distorting the average citizen's access to the court's procedural process.

Fear of Reprisal. Police and magistrates are often coerced into making decisions out of fear of retribution. The fear of demotion or transfer to an undesirable location or position is a powerful incentive to make unjustifiable decisions. Fear of revenge if the decision is against or in favor of an objectionable political party or ethnic group can distort the outcome as well. Being perceived as politically incorrect or unpatriotic can force police and magistrates to decide against their better judgment.

Nonjudicial Role of the Judge. Governments in many countries require judges to undertake nonjudicial responsibilities, such as serving on commissions of inquiry or assuming burdensome administrative duties. Deflecting judges from their primary judicial duties can result in severe delay in the resolution of cases. In corrupted systems, using improper influence on judges often averts such delay. The remuneration system is often deficient and does not allow for individuals to maintain an adequate standard of living. This encourages police, prosecutors, and judges to engage in corruption as a way to supplement their income instead of upholding the law.

Administrative Court Procedures. The majority of administrative procedures within the court system is inadequately monitored and creates a climate amenable to unfettered corruption. In many countries, administrative court procedures are bureaucratic, cumbersome, and confusing and are carried out by court personnel who have broad discretionary powers with little accountability.

The Focus of Corruption in the Justice System

Corruption that exists in the justice system can take place at any time beginning with the commencement of a criminal investigation or the filing of a civil lawsuit through the judicial process culminating in enforcement of the court's decision.

Corruption Within the Criminal Process. In the investigation of criminal conduct, police have wide discretionary powers, much of which goes unchecked. For a proper sum, police can suppress the filing of police reports, distort evidence and thereby ensure certain outcomes, engage in delaying tactics until evidence is lost or destroyed, and even refuse to investigate. If the alleged perpetrator is politically powerful, wealthy, or belongs to a certain ethnic group, the police can use their discretionary powers to protect them, rather than investigate. Police can also commit crime, such as rape or robbery, during the investigation of other crimes.

Even with excellent police investigation, prosecutorial discretion can thwart the lawful processing of a criminal case. Similar to the police, prosecutors can also be bribed to delay the investigation and processing of a case. Moreover, powerful government ministries can exert substantial pressure on the public prosecutor to stop prosecution. Such prosecutorial indiscretions usually go unchecked, as there are often no objective criteria for managing caseloads and prioritizing investigations that would allow unlawful acts to be identified.

Other criminal procedures such as the inconsistent issuance of summons, the unjustifiable refusal or granting of bail, discrepancies in prosecuting high profile criminal suspects versus petty criminals, unwarranted acquittals, and general disparities in sentencing give rise to the public's suspicion that corruption exists within the criminal justice system.

Corruption Within the Civil Process. In the filing of a civil lawsuit, the private citizen is typically faced with a daunting array of court procedures, many of which are complex and arcane. Often, court employees are willing to circumvent the administrative process for a price. Due to their numerous responsibilities, which receive little oversight by court administrators, court personnel are in a position to manipulate the rules and procedures as best suits them. They may accelerate or delay a case without detection. They may "lose" the case file and then "find" it after the citizen gives them a gift. They may also influence the assignment of cases or allow access to a judge for a fee.

In many cases, lawyers do not hesitate to seek out those court employees who knowingly and expertly engage in corrupt, unsupervised administrative tasks in exchange for an illicit fee, as they know there is a low risk of being detected. For those litigants who do not have legal representation and can barely pay the legitimate fees, let alone the illicit payments of bribery, equal access to justice is denied.

Ineffective Enforcement of Judgments. Civil or criminal lawsuits that emerge unscathed from the judicial process can still be subject to corruption during the enforcement phase. Bailiffs can extort payments from losing parties to ignore the judgment. Even reputable bailiffs can unwittingly create difficulties during the enforcement phase due to imprecise and confusing or even contradictory judgments. Police who object to the judge's conviction of an individual can refuse to incarcerate the guilty. Even financial institutions that are required by a judicial decision to levy the account of a powerful or wealthy individual can refuse to do so. Such defiant behavior stems from acute disrespect for the judicial system.

Forms of Corruption Within the Justice System

Much of this corruption occurs outside the public eye and often between only two individuals, both of whom are engaged in the illegal conduct and each benefiting from it. Consequently, the various forms of corruption within the justice system are difficult to expose and challenging to prove, which impedes prosecution of the corrupt behavior.

Financial, Political and Societal Pressures. One of the most common forms of corruption within the police and judiciary is the payment of a bribe, either sought after by the police or magistrate or offered by the accused, the litigant or lawyer as an inducement to make certain decisions. For the payment of a fee, police and magistrates can alter the substance of the outcome. Judges can also affect the procedural process of a case (i.e., continually adjourn a case until a fee is paid).

Illicit remuneration comes in many forms. Governmental leaders, particularly those who wield immense power over the judicial system, are in a position to offer tangible benefits such as housing, cars, and vacations to those magistrates who curry favor by tacitly agreeing to rule in favor of the leader's desires. In some cases, magistrates can become accustomed to a higher standard of living and, when facing retirement, can increase their demands to maintain the same lifestyle after leaving office.

Apart from receiving an illicit fee payment or material possessions, magistrates may also benefit from succumbing to political pressure by obtaining professional advancement. Responding favorably to those who have undue influence on the judicial system or who have power or powerful connections can result in promotion or other professional benefits to the magistrate.

During the Soviet regime, "telephone justice," that is, directives by senior governmental officials concerning pending cases, was not uncommon; it continues today to a lesser degree. Ministries with historical power over the judiciary are accustomed to exerting pressure on the judicial branch and are reluctant to relinquish their control. Evidence of such political pressure is substantiated by the disproportionate number of decisions favoring the executive branch and powerful local enterprises, particularly those with direct political or financial connections to the government.

Other sources of pressure include family members or friends who seek "favors" from magistrates. Due to their personal relationship with a magistrate, close associates can expect certain outcomes. Doing favors for family and friends is such an ingrained behavior in many cultures that magistrates do not often believe it affects their role as impartial arbiters. Rather than reveal the conflict of interest and seek disqualification, magistrates often submit to the pressure without compunction.

Pressure Within the Justice System. Another insidious form of corruption comes from within the justice system itself. Chief police officers, prosecutors, or judges can exert significant administrative authority over their subordinates. By the simple act of assigning an investigation to a certain police officer or a case to a certain prosecutor or judge, the outcome of the investigation or case can be determined.

In some courts, the senior judge reviews the decisions of the other judges to assure the "correctness" of their opinions. Although the purpose of the review may be to seek accuracy of the facts and law, such internal pressure can have the effect of ensuring that judges comply with the senior judge's position in order to maintain good relations and secure their favor.

Responses to Corruption in the Justice Sector

Assessment of Corruption

An independent assessment of corruption involving all stakeholders (e.g., parties to a civil dispute include the accused, the victim, police, prosecutor, defense counsel, private bar, judges, court personnel, and court decision enforcement agencies, including penal institutions) is essential before any systematic response to eradicating corruption can be developed and implemented. Evidence of corruption, and not just suspicions or popular belief, is required in order to assess effectively the nature of the problem and develop a framework of anticorruption policies.

False Assumptions and Allegations of Corruption. One of the major issues that needs to be broached when developing a response to corruption is the public's perception of corruption. In countries where corruption is endemic, where the public views government with disrespect, where governmental leaders reputedly engage in serious corruption, and where contacts and not content determines the outcome, citizens typically perceive any unfavorable decision to be the product of corruption. Citizens in such countries refuse to believe that unfavorable judicial decisions are based on merit. Incompetent attorneys exacerbate the problem, masking their own shortcomings by convincing their clients that the case was lost because the other party paid a bribe to the magistrate. It is not uncommon for attorneys who are unscrupulous to seek a bribe from their client under false pretenses, claiming the judge demanded it for a favorable outcome when in fact the illicit fee remains with the attorney. If the outcome is unfavorable, the attorney's defense is simply that the bribe was not sufficient.

Judicial Leadership in Assessing and Combating Corruption. Reform-minded and respected leadership of the police and magistracy within the justice system must not only be involved in assessing corruption but also, and more importantly, in determining the priorities and sequencing of reforms. Corruption within the justice system is multifaceted and multilayered and to be effectively opposed must have committed leadership.

Institutional and Attitudinal Reforms

The responses to corruption can be grouped into two categories, institutional and attitudinal. In general, anticorruption reforms must:

- Limit the authority of decision makers within the justice system and those who have control over the justice system.
- Reduce the unfettered discretion of administrative office-holders within the justice system.

- Strengthen the transparency and accountability of all who are involved in the justice system.
- Improve the terms of employment within the justice system, including appointment, remuneration, working conditions, and training.
- Transform societal attitudes toward justice system corruption.

In particular, the following reforms have real potential for curbing corruption.

Increase Independence of the Judicial Branch. The judiciary must fiercely guard its independence in order to balance powers equitably among the branches of government. To insulate magistrates from political influence, the judicial branch, rather than the executive branch, must control or at least have oversight authority of its administration and budget. Additionally, the budget for the justice system must be at a level that allows for effective and efficient administration of justice.

Role of Judicial Councils. Judicial councils that are independent from the justice ministry can be helpful in securing judicial independence by assuming the responsibility for appointing and promoting judges. Judicial councils usually substitute for the traditional authority of the president or parliament in making judicial appointments. When properly used, judicial councils are less bureaucratic and less politicized and can achieve more efficient results than the government. During the past fifteen years, numerous Latin American countries have created judicial councils that have developed impressive track records for independence (Hammergren, 2002).

Enhance Prosecution Capability of Public Prosecutor. The autonomous role of the public prosecutor in fighting corruption must be strong in order to investigate effectively government officials (including judges) and powerful private individuals. Additionally, the criminal code must allow for prosecution and conviction not only with direct evidence of bribery but also with circumstantial evidence, such as possessing wealth that is unexplained by employment and other lawful activities. Until the public observes that corrupt behavior by governmental leaders and private individuals is not tolerated within the justice system, corruption within other sectors of society will continue.

In Latin America, efforts have been underway to strengthen the prosecutor's office. For instance, in Colombia, the attorney general was granted significant investigative powers to fight corruption, which he used successfully to prosecute senior governmental officials and drug lords. In Honduras, an office of the general prosecutor against corruption was established and sufficiently funded, which allowed the general prosecutor to expose successfully corruption in the military. In India, the supreme court took a leadership role in exposing political kickbacks and was rated as one of India's most trusted institutions (USAID, 1999).

Appointment, Promotion, Dismissal. The system for appointments, promotions, and dismissals must be transparent and based on due process procedures to reduce nepotism and political patronage within the employment process. Objective and merit-based standards must be applied to each applicant for appointment and promotion.

Competitive examinations that are transparent should be established as the standard tools to distinguish the competent from the well connected. The Republic of Georgia, with the assistance of foreign donors, required all sitting judges to pass a rigorous examination resulting in numerous judges being forced out of office. Competitive examinations, however, can only be effective if the demand exceeds the supply.

Term of Appointment. To shield judges from external influence and to reduce the opportunities to succumb to political pressure and favoritism, the term of office for judges must be lengthy, if not lifetime, to increase job security and stability and to enhance the personal resolve to avoid governmental pressure. Within a system of lifetime appointments, there must be substantial and visible accountability mechanisms, which ensure that judges do not take advantage of their positions.

Increase Salary and Enhance Working Conditions. It is very difficult to combat corruption within the justice system when magistrates and police are paid considerably lower wages than individuals in the private sector and comparable government offices. The salary discrepancy between comparable individuals within different branches of government reflects the disrespect the executive and legislative branches have toward the judicial branch. Although there is often governmental rhetoric in many countries about the importance of an independent judiciary, low judicial salaries prove otherwise.

Increasing the income of magistrates and police aids in eliminating the necessity to supplement their paltry income with bribes. Although it may not necessarily reduce the incentive for corruption, at least a respectable salary gives the perception that the government regards the judiciary to be equal with the other two branches. It should be noted that a significant increase in compensation across the board for judges and law clerks in Venezuela, Ecuador, and Argentina (78, 89, and 130 percent, respectively) may have reduced corruption but did *not* affect the perception of corruption in these countries during the period 1991–1999 (UNDP, 2001).

In Bosnia, a precondition of the international community to assist in eradicating corruption within the judiciary was to require the government to increase significantly the wages of judges. As of 2002, judges in Bosnia receive US$900-$1,800 monthly, while judges in Serbia receive only US$200-$350 monthly (ABA/CEELI, 2001, 2002). Although it is too soon to ascertain the impact that increased compensation has had on the ethics of judicial decision-making in Bosnia, the international donors anticipate that higher wages will reduce corruption.

Improving the working conditions of magistrates, particularly judges, so that their environment is conducive to thoughtful deliberation is essential to ensuring that judicial decisions are of sound reason. Many judges within corrupt judiciaries share offices, often four judges to a small room, with malfunctioning office equipment and limited support staff. Better working conditions will not only assist in improving the quality of their decision making but also increase their professional prestige.

Declare Assets. One approach for combating corruption, as well as the perception of corruption, is the requirement that all magistrates and police disclose their assets and the assets of close family members prior to taking office, periodically throughout their tenure, and upon departing from office. In order to be effective, such declarations must be verified and monitored on a regular basis by an independent official. The requirement to declare assets exposes those justice officials whose lifestyles are in noticeable contrast to their salary.

Enhance Professionalism. In many countries, there is a serious lack of professionalism in the courts; magistrates do not appreciate the solemnity of their profession, of the trial procedure, of written evidence and oral testimony, or of judicial decisions that are based solely on the facts and the law. An effective weapon against corruption is an education and training system in which magistrates develop an in-depth understanding of the law. Often, magistrates succumb to pressure because their knowledge of the law and its application is faulty and unsound. A government-sponsored system for the education and training of magistrates on substantive and procedural legal matters prior to assuming their roles and a comprehensive curriculum that enables magistrates to be continually educated and trained during their term in office is essential to enhancing judicial accountability.

In numerous countries in Central and Eastern Europe as well as the former Soviet Union, foreign donors, with the assistance of the local ministry of justice and the judges' association, have created judicial training centers that have successfully trained new judges as well as sitting judges throughout the country. Judicial training centers in Latvia, Albania, Bulgaria, and Moldova are examples of such assistance.

Enforce Codes of Ethical Conduct. In order to strengthen the integrity of magistrates and police and to reduce cronyism within the judicial system, a code of ethical conduct is crucial. Such codes, when rigorously enforced, oblige magistrates and police to become accountable for their actions and decisions. If magistrates are seen to prosecute "their own" for inappropriate behavior, the public's respect for prosecutors and judges increases, provided these instances are properly covered by the media.

In Albania, comprehensive training regarding the ethics code for midlevel police officers was conducted throughout the country by a nongovernmental organization (NGO) under a US Agency for International Development

(USAID) grant. Not only did the training reinforce an understanding of appropriate ethical conduct by the police, but it also reestablished the linkage and sense of mutual responsibility between the police and the civil society it is meant to protect.

Ensure Immediate Access to the Laws. Systematic distribution of all laws and amendments to laws to every magistrate is an essential component of a comprehensive program combating corruption. Lack of legal knowledge about the prevailing laws and regulations and lack of immediate access to such legal doctrines can result in incorrect rulings, part of which may be based solely on the ignorance of the magistrate. Additionally, an unsuspecting magistrate who is subject to improper external or internal influence has little legal defense when he or she is without timely access to the laws and their amendments.

Random Case Assignment. In countries with corrupt judiciaries, case assignment is usually within the jurisdiction of a powerful authority that can manipulate the assignment to guarantee the outcome of certain court decisions. On the surface, purposeful assignment can be defended, particularly if the assignment is based on the experience, expertise, or workload of magistrates, but such systems can be susceptible to abuse. If possible, the distribution of cases should be random and, under all circumstances, not influenced by any person concerned with the outcome of the case.

Publication of Judicial Decisions. One of the most effective responses to eliminating corruption within the justice system, one that not only reduces corruption but also the perception of corruption, is the publication of judicial decisions. In numerous countries, often in civil law countries, judicial decisions are not traditionally published nor are there verbatim court transcripts, as lower court decisions do not have the weight of precedence. Thus, where there are inconsistent applications of the law or where there is an indefensible ruling, it is difficult to ascertain and establish such facts, as judicial decisions are not made available to the public.

It is not uncommon for several judges sitting on the same bench to apply the law differently to similar fact patterns or, more insidiously, for an individual judge to apply the law differently across cases with similar fact patterns. Without verbatim court transcripts or published decisions, such discrepancies are difficult to detect. Publication of judicial decisions that are well reasoned and that properly apply the applicable law to the facts can protect the innocent judges while exposing the guilty ones.

Vigorous Enforcement of Judicial Decisions. In many countries, more than half of the judicial decisions are not enforced. The delay or even absence of court decision enforcement gives rise to the public's disrespect for the judicial system. Much of the enforcement problem is due to a lack of sufficient resources. Yet, when those resources do exist and individuals or institutions defy the court's decision by refusing to enforce it, vigorous sanctions must be imposed.

Alternative Dispute Resolution. An essential component of a multifaceted response program to reduce corruption within the judiciary is alternative dispute resolution (ADR). Alternative dispute resolution is a process by which the plaintiff and defendant attempt to reach a settlement outside the courtroom, either through arbitration, mediation, or civil settlement.

Alternative dispute resolution reduces the monopolistic nature of state-sanctioned judicial services by providing alternative methods to obtain a resolution through the private sector. Through effective application of ADR, case delay can significantly be reduced in the courts. Chile, Ecuador, and Uganda have implemented ADR mechanisms that have resulted in a reduction in case delay and court-related corruption (Buscaglia 2002).

Increase Transparency and Accountability of the Administrative Process. Due to the complexities of administrative procedures, there is a significant level of administrative discretion given to court personnel. This confused environment entices not only court staff to seek illegal payment for services but also a willingness on the part of the court user to pay them. Court administrative procedures must be streamlined and easily understood by all so that arbitrary decision-making by court staff is reduced. Uniformity and transparency in the administrative process significantly diminish the capacity of court personnel to obtain illicit payments.

The institutional accountability of the justice system must ensure that public resources are fairly allocated and used efficiently for their intended purposes. Court staff must be personally accountable for performing their roles and responsibilities in compliance with all applicable rules, regulations, and standards of ethical conduct. Salaries and promotion for all court personnel must be based on clearly enunciated performance standards.

Enhance Transparency and Efficiency of Case Management Systems. A case tracking system is essential in order to enhance the transparency of court administration. Computerization of court files can significantly reduce the labor-intensive workload of court personnel, particularly those who are still handwriting their work or compiling case files, while enhancing the quality of judicial administration. Furthermore, the use of tamper-proof software can prevent documents or case files from being "lost" or "found" for a fee.

Computerization not only strengthens case management but also increases the transparency of court proceedings by providing court users with an opportunity to observe the consistent, or inconsistent, application of temporal standards to each case filed. In several courts in Bulgaria, most notably the supreme administrative court, the court record system has been computerized, allowing litigants and their attorneys to access public court records and track each case through its resolution. Users of the supreme administrative court's Web site may learn the date of filing of each case, the location of the file, and the length of time a particular file has been at each judicial station (Supreme Administrative Court of the Republic of Bulgaria, 2004).

Role of the Bar Associations. Anticorruption measures for the judicial system do not rest solely within the court structure. Frequently overlooked is recognition by the bar that it contributes to the corruption of the judiciary by acting as a conduit between the litigant and the magistrate. Bar associations have the responsibility to expose and reduce bribery within the justice system by imposing strict sanctions against any of its members who engage in corrupt judicial practices.

Role of Law Faculties. The culture for bribing decision-makers begins at a very young age. In law faculties in those countries where corruption is endemic, it is not uncommon for students to bribe school administrators and law professors for admission, to receive passing grades, or ultimately to graduate from the law faculty.

The legal education system must adequately compensate academics to minimize their incentive to receive illicit payments. Furthermore, courses on ethics must be required so that law students who become the future lawyers and judges of the country no longer rely on manipulating the system but rather learn how to succeed within it.

Role of Civil Society. Civil society can assist in reducing corruption within the justice system by enhancing public awareness of court procedures and citizens' rights while also creating pressure on the government for reform. Nongovernmental organizations can play an important role in developing an accurate image of the judiciary by offsetting the negative image often presented by the state and the press, which leads to the perception of corruption.

In Latvia and Albania, NGOs, in conjunction with court officials, developed and distributed to the public law pamphlets that clearly outline the public's rights and obligations under certain laws and the process for filing and adjudicating cases. Nongovernmental organizations can also be useful in ferreting out corruption by engaging in court monitoring. In Croatia, an NGO was successful in exposing magistrates who were not abiding by judicial procedures during war-crime trials of public individuals.

In Ukraine, Russia, and Albania, citizen advocate offices (CAOs) specializing in providing legal support to victims of alleged corruption and excessive bureaucracy have been established under USAID grants (Management Systems International, 2003). Publicity of their establishment produced hundreds of requests for legal help with issues of corruption, indicating a pent-up demand in society for a trusted and independent source of legal assistance. The CAOs have been extremely effective not only in representing individual claimants, either through court proceedings or administrative solutions, but also in identifying those institutions or groups of officials in which corruption is endemic by analyzing trends in grievances. Through their independence and objectivity, the CAOs have quickly achieved legitimacy not only among the public, but with judicial authorities as well. For example, in Albania, a tripartite commission was established to expedite the investigation and prosecution of corruption cases that included the

CAO, the general prosecutor, and the minister of state in charge of anticorruption programs.

Role of the Press. News reporters who cover the courts and who are ignorant of the law and judicial procedures can nourish the public perception of a corrupt judiciary by inaccurately reporting false allegations of judicial misconduct. Reporters who do not understand judicial rulings or decisions may misinterpret a judge's reasoning and thereby distort the motive of the judge. Such reporters grossly misuse their power as the gatekeeper of public information. Those reporters who routinely cover the courts must be educated in the law and about court procedures and must recognize their responsibility to be factually correct. Further, they must have access to court records and court press officers who can enhance their understanding of court rulings and decisions.

Conclusions

Most anticorruption responses are institutional and are, indeed, essential to eradicating corruption within the judiciary. But the ultimate response, without which corruption will never be eradicated, is societal. Clearly, one's behavior is shaped by the threat of apprehension, conviction, and punishment, but one's personal ethics and moral values are the fundamental incentives for sound decision-making.

Reforms must focus on one's personal ethics and the societal attitude toward ethical behavior. There must be a common belief in society that ethics matter. Ethical behavior must be rewarded, and the rewards must exceed the risks of engaging in corrupt behavior.

Although unethical behavior may benefit individuals and companies, the country always suffers. There must be a societal awakening to the deleterious effects corruption has on the economic and political growth of a country. In this regard, public leaders who are reform-minded must lead public campaigns exhorting anticorruption reforms.

Notes

1. See, for example, the following surveys: *Regional Corruption Monitoring* (2002): *Diagnostic Surveys of Corruption in Romania* (2001); *Corruption in Slovakia* (2000); *Corruption in Bangladesh Surveys* (2002).

Chapter 3

Political Parties

Verena Blechinger

Both in industrialized democracies and the developing world, political parties are often seen as central to the corruption problem. Discourses on corruption and anticorruption strategies have identified parties as key actors who sometimes abuse their powerful position in the political system to extort bribes, supply their members and supporters with lucrative positions in the public sector and related corporations, shape political and economic institutions for the benefit of affiliated interest groups, or channel public resources into the hands of party leaders, members, or supporters.

Party corruption is especially problematic in newly democratizing and developing countries where political and economic institutions are not yet secure. The redistribution of public assets, which is a necessary part of democratic transition, is often disturbed by corruption. In the long run, party corruption and related scandals can undermine public trust and lead to voter cynicism and disillusionment with the political system, thus threatening the viability of democracy. Long-term high-level corruption may also provide a powerful incentive for political parties to secure political power, thus producing authoritarian regimes, one-party monopoly states, and nondemocratic governments. The prospect of gains from corrupt practices might also tempt opposition parties to try to overthrow democratically elected governments or might make existing governments more resistant to further democratization.

Although current international anticorruption regimes such as the Organization for Economic Cooperation and Development (OECD) Convention on Combating Bribery of Foreign Public Officials in International Business Transactions have not yet included party corruption into their frameworks, US and international policymakers and anticorruption NGOs, such as Transparency International, point out the importance of dealing with party corruption, especially with regard to political contributions (see, e.g., Transparency International, 2000).

Although corrupt parties can stall or even destroy democratization processes, political parties that are not distorted by corruption but that are part of a well institutionalized and competitive political framework can play a vital role in democracies and perform valuable political and social functions. Parties provide a link between citizens and government. They mobilize voters on behalf of certain goals and interests, select and train candidates for public office, organize election campaigns, send representatives to parliament, organize legislatures, formulate political agendas and policies, manage policy processes and steer or, as opposition parties, monitor government activities. By publicizing and promoting their programs, parties also provide voters with substantial information about current political issues, the general workings of government, and citizens' democratic rights. Thus, they actively contribute to voter education and human development and can function as builders of social capital. This role of political parties can become even more important in transitional states that are in the process of defining and stabilizing the rules and institutions of democratic government and market economies.

Manifestations of Corruption in the Area of Political Parties

Elections and Election Campaigns

Election campaigns are costly. Parties and candidates need money to print posters, brochures, and leaflets or to pay for TV and radio advertisements to make their message known to voters. They have to pay staffers and equipment to organize and run campaigns and to finance campaign-related travel of candidates and party leaders. Therefore, campaign finance is an important issue in political competition. In their struggle to win, parties and individual candidates often try to outspend each other, and under financial pressure, both candidates and party leaders might be willing to accept payoffs or illegal donations offered by wealthy donors in exchange for promises of future favors.

In developed and transitional countries alike, politicians are tempted to spend as much money as possible on their campaigns, often in excess of official campaign spending limits. In Japan, for example, election laws prescribe a limit for the amount of money candidates can spend during the campaign period. The spending limit depends on the number of registered votes per seat and the total voter population of the electoral district. In the 1980s and early 1990s, candidates of the long-term ruling Liberal Democratic Party (LDP) exceeded the legal limit by at least six times and as much as thirteen times (Fukui and Fukai, 2000, pp. 23–24). Most of these funds come from corporate donations. The workings of the illicit system were illustrated, for example, in the course of investigations of the 1992–1993 Sagawa Transport scandal. In order to secure a good position in the deregulating transport sector in Japan, the company Sagawa paid about 2.5 billion yen (approximately US$25 million) in illegal campaign donations to 200 Diet members and leading local politicians of the LDP and opposition parties (Kikuchi, 1992). Similarly, in India, legal limits of campaign expenditures are regularly exceeded by ten to fifteen times the allotted amount (*Loksatta Times,* 2001, p. 3).[1] In South Korea, almost all candidates exceed the legal limit on campaign expenses of approximately 90 million won (around US$112,000) per candidate. During the April 2000 National Assembly elections, Korean media reported that candidates had to spend about 3 billion won (about US$3.75 million) to win their local constituencies (*Korea Herald,* 2000). Routine violation of legal spending limits suggests that more than laws are required to control politician and party behavior and to minimize excessive campaign spending.

In political systems with weak party competition, or in states with long-term one-party rule and party control over the public sector and society, parties also might be tempted to extort contributions from businesses. Under authoritarian rule until 1993, political fund raising in South Korea crossed the borderline to extortion. All South Korean presidents during this period, from Park Chung-Hee to Roh Tae-Woo, set up private foundations and forced big business to pay regular contributions as membership fees in proportion to their revenues. Those who refused encountered problems when applying for government credit, licenses, or business loans, and they also could expect regular tax audits by financial authorities whose personnel were often appointed on the basis of their party connections. Similarly, regular campaign contributors could expect lenient treatment of their tax declarations (Koh, 1996; Kim, 1997; Moran, 1999).

To fill their campaign chests, parties not only accept donations from wealthy donors or extort them from the business community but often also demand contributions from individual candidates and parliamentarians. Although the payment of contributions to one's own party can be seen as a politician's legitimate support for building a strong party organization and thus an investment in the party's future, they come close to corruption and extortion when they are demanded in the context of candidate selection and nomination for national or regional elections or as the "price" for a promising ranking on a party's list of candidates. Similarly, it is a corrupt practice when party leaders extort contributions from candidates by threatening to remove their names from the party proportional list, to assign them to a less secure constituency, or if they offer to switch names on the party list in return for donations. We can also consider it corruption when party leaders demand donations from party members as a prerequisite for promotion within the party hierarchy or for eligibility for party leadership. In South Korea, for example, from 1961 to 1993, candidates on the proportional lists of both the ruling and opposition parties were ranked according to their contributions to the party (Chon, 2000, pp. 71–77). Another form of party corruption in this context is the regular collection of a portion of a parliamentarian's salary by party leaders as "contribution" in return for party support at election times.

Another manifestation of corruption in the area of political parties is vote buying. In transitional countries, and especially in countries where patronage is an important social factor, voters may expect presents and gifts from parties and candidates prior to elections and then make their decision on the basis of the amount and quality of such gifts. Once such a tradition has been established, voters are also likely to demand gifts in exchange for votes. In Thailand, for example, vote buying has been a major problem for years, and it is still a widespread practice despite repeated reform efforts. Especially in poor rural areas, voters actively sell their vote to the highest bidder. In the 1996 election, parties and candidates would try to buy individual votes or sometimes even buy "wholesale" votes of families or whole villages. In return, party representatives would offer cash, sometimes clipped to campaign literature, food, clothing, and other gifts. Officials estimate that prior to the 1996 elections, Thai politicians spent about

US$1 billion on vote buying (*New York Times*, 1996, 1998). Thai parties also actively pay bribes to candidates of rival parties at election time. In order to win a majority in national or local elections or to increase their number of seats in parliament, Thai parties make it a practice to offer bribes of up to US$720,000 to candidates who are willing to switch parties (*Bangkok Post*, 2000; *New York Times*, 1996).

In this context, the first democratic elections in a country are generally high stake occurrences and, accordingly, the temptation for corrupt activities is likely to be high. In the initial stages of democratic transition, party systems are still rather weak, and the relationship between civil society and political parties is not yet fully established. For parties, the potential rewards for victory in the first election are very high. They include the opportunity to shape the country's political and economic institutions, thus ensuring future benefits for the party's supporters and the chance to enter the next elections as incumbents. Given these high stakes, parties face increased pressures to engage in corrupt transactions. Similarly, party supporters hope to invest as much money as possible to make sure that the winner of the first election will advance their interests. Foundational elections also attract increased attention from foreign interests such as neighboring governments or transnational corporations that are interested in favorable political conditions and a friendly business climate. In South Africa, for example, prior to the 1999 elections, Nelson Mandela revealed that his party had received donations in the tens of millions of US dollars from foreign governments such as Saudi Arabia, Indonesia, the United Arab Emirates, and Malaysia (*Business Day*, 1999). For all these reasons, even if elections and party systems are new in transitional countries, the opportunities for party corruption we see in developed countries can equally apply in the developing world, and even more so in the first election.

Party Activities in Parliament

Politicians who have won a seat in parliament are eager to produce and work in support of policies that benefit their supporters and shape political and social development according to their parties' preferences. Their performance in parliament may be monitored and evaluated by voters. If voters are content with their representative's performance in parliament, he or she usually has a good chance to be voted into office again. On the other hand, if voters do not actively monitor a politician's conduct, or if there is a lack of competition so that voters do not have many alternatives to choose from, and if reelection thus is very secure no matter how a politician performs, there is a strong chance that he or she will engage in corrupt activities. The same is true for political parties.

Parties whose behavior in parliament is not monitored by an active opposition or by informed voters, and parties that are very secure in their hold on power, are more likely to indulge in extralegal means of amassing personal wealth and exercise of power. The longer such a state of noncompetition lasts or the greater the degree of noncompetition, the more corruption can be expected. In extreme cases, we might see parties that either act on behalf of any group ready to pay the appropriate sum or demand fees and kickbacks for public contracts, government loans, or licenses. To various degrees, such corruption can be found, for example, in the Institutional Revolutionary Party (PRI) in Mexico, the United Malay National Organization (UMNO) in Malaysia, or the Kuomintang (KMT) in Taiwan. It is also significant that recently, some of these parties have either been forced out of power or have voluntarily changed political conditions that allow increased party competition.

Although we thus can expect corruption from parties that are facing little competition, on the other hand, we may also see corruption on the side of those that are likely to lose their hold on power or whose leaders are not allowed to run for reelection by their country's electoral system. In countries with a weak party system, a high level of party fluctuation, and a high turnover in government, politicians and parties might face the prospect of losing power after just one term in office, independently of how they perform. Consequently, they might be more likely to use their offices to maximize personal profit for party leaders and to channel as many benefits as possible to supporters, family, and friends. Party members in parliament also might be tempted to serve the interest of their parties' leaders in the hopes of securing a future appointment elsewhere. One example of a country with high incidence of corruption and an electoral system based on the principle of "non-reelection" is Mexico. Members of the two chambers of the Mexican parliament are not allowed to seek reelection immediately after their first term in office, and for the president, the law prohibits reelection. Bribery has long been widespread throughout Mexican politics, and the 1997 scandals surrounding former president Carlos Salinas and members of his family indicate a tendency among many Mexican politicians to maximize profit during their term in office (Morris, 1999).

A third factor that might lead to corruption in the context of party activity in parliament is party discipline (Rose-Ackerman, 1999, p. 129). A strong party leadership that controls the activities of all party members in parliament can use its authority to further democracy and political and economic development, and to benefit the public good. However, party leaders might also decide to support the agendas of wealthy organized interests or certain social groups in exchange for payoffs and pressure party members in parliament to support this agenda. In Japan, the long-term ruling Liberal Democratic Party used to relocate political decision-making from parliament into party committees. Diet members would decide in their party committees what position to take on certain issues. In parliament, party members mostly voted unanimously along party lines. Often, business and interest group representatives were present at such committee meetings and party leaders made it a habit to introduce young Diet members to interest group representatives to cultivate mutually advantageous relationships (Blechinger, 1998, pp. 249–251).

Party leaders may also use party discipline to suppress criticism from party members of corrupt activities. In Zimbabwe, for example, leaders of the ruling party Zimbabwe African National Union-Popular Front (ZANU-PF) have led denunciation campaigns against party members who publicly spoke out against corruption of the party leadership, thus preventing these key party members from being selected to stand for re-election on the party list (*Indian Ocean Newsletter*, 1999).

Party Control over State Resources and Redistribution

Ruling parties shape political agendas and institutional and economic development and also monitor the bureaucracy, control the distribution and management of public resources, and supervise the activities of public corporations. Parties in government play an important role in shaping the relationship between state and society and between wealthy interests and power.

The magnitude of party competition and party control over state institutions and society is important for developing corrupt structures. The more control a party has over state institutions and society, and the lower the level of party competition, the higher is the risk for corrupt behavior. In countries with strong party control over state institutions and society, parties might be tempted to abuse their influence to secure private gain for party members and supporters. Similarly, in noncompetitive systems (i.e., in one-party dominant systems or communist states where a single political party monopolizes control over government, the economy, and public life), the ruling party may face a low risk of losing power even if it engages in corrupt transactions. On the other hand, in liberal democracies with high party competition, a clear separation of power, leadership accountability and functioning checks and balances, as well as a vibrant civil society, corrupt actors face a higher risk of exposure and, consequently, of being driven out of power, thus keeping corruption at bay.

One extreme case of a monopoly party in a noncompetitive system was the former Soviet Union. The authority of national and local party officials was not limited to the allocation of government resources or to personnel decisions in government and state-owned enterprises. The party's power reached into all levels of economic activity. Informal networks that traded contacts to influential party officials or strategic knowledge became a valuable "good" in corrupt transactions; in other words, "information about who, how, and where was the lifeblood of economic and political survival" (Wedel, 2001, p. 3).

Similarly, autocratic parties whose leaders do not allow opposition parties, often use their power monopoly to exploit public resources and to manipulate state institutions for the accumulation of personal profit for themselves and their supporters. Zimbabwe under the rule of President Robert Mugabe and his party, the Zimbabwe African National Union-Popular Front (ZANU-PF), for example, has been suffering from widespread corruption, illegal confiscation of land, and party-induced violence (*Financial Times,* 2001; Taylor, 2002).

Multiparty systems with active party competition can generally be considered less vulnerable to corruption. Party competition provides voters with an alternative when they do not approve of the ruling party's politics and it thus prevents parties from extortion. However, even multiparty systems run the risk of suffering from corruption when major parties politicize society and take control over important sectors of business and public life. Under such conditions, a change in government might indicate who is "in" and who is "out," but might no longer provide voters with an alternative. The case of Italy illustrates this corruption regime. The Clean Hands investigation in the early 1990s proved that Italian political parties had managed to politicize and control all aspects of public life, from the bureaucracy to public enterprises to civil society. Corrupt exchanges took place no matter which party was in government (see DellaPorta and Vannucci, 1999). Another example of a multiparty system with a high amount of party control over state institutions and society and related frequent incidents of corruption is India.

Corruption is also likely in states where formerly strong monopoly parties get weakened during the process of political and economic transition. In the post-Communist countries in Eastern Europe, the weakening of the Communist Party's power monopoly and the erosion of the centralized party-dominated state provided new incentives for corruption. All over Eastern Europe, albeit in varying degrees, former high-ranking party officials (*nomenklatura*) used their connections and insider knowledge to rig privatization bids, secure cheap government loans, and acquire resources for themselves and their associates. Corruption is further stimulated by the continuing loyalties of state bureaucrats to their long-established personal ties to current or former party and government officials, thus impeding the formation of new state institutions and free market economies. Reformed communist and newly established democratic parties are often part of such corrupt networks, especially in cases where party leaders owe their party's survival to the support and funding of powerful oligarchic groups (O'Rourke, 2000; Karatnycky, 2001; Wedel, 2001).[2] Similarly, in Mozambique after independence, the ruling party, Frelimo, controlled society and all economic activities for about one decade. In the context of privatization in the early 1990s, numerous corruption cases came to light of how Frelimo party officials and cabinet members used their inside knowledge of government to secure interests in profitable state enterprises for themselves, party supporters or their family members (Harrison, 1999, pp. 543–544). Corruption in these formerly communist countries therefore limits the resources available to newly founded democratic parties, making it difficult to establish a stable and competitive party system.

China and Vietnam are cases where there still is no party competition, but party control over society is weakening due to economic liberalization and the gradual entry of private business activities. In these countries, the decrease of the party's monopoly on power provides an opportunity for local actors, usually lower ranking party officials who are often underpaid and autocratic, to get involved and to spread corruption even further (Ma, 2001, pp. 145–147). Similarly, corruption spread in the Philippines when national government was decentralized in 1992 and opportunities for patronage evolved for local officials (*Business World*, March 2001).

The vacuum left by weakening party institutions in former monopoly-party states also offers opportunities for organized crime. As recent cases from Russia, Ukraine, Vietnam, and other countries demonstrate, organized crime in post-communist societies acts both as a "business partner" of political corruption networks, paying bribes to high-ranking politicians and bureaucrats to facilitate illegal activities, and as a "substitute" for state and party institutions, taking over formerly party-controlled functions such as conflict mediation or private security (Shelley, 1995; O'Rourke, 2000).

As illustrated above, in order to understand fully corruption in political parties, we have to address both party competition and the level of party control over state institutions and society. Parties have to be understood as links between state and society and between wealth and power. Their activities relate both to the political world and to society, and similarly, party corruption affects both spheres.

Parties in postcolonial states face one more temptation for corrupt behavior. Before independence, the awarding of contracts and the distribution of public funds was a monopoly of colonial officials. Once in power, newly established parties are confronted with strong business counterparts who are often willing to offer bribes to keep their position as government contractors. Many parties in postcolonial states were founded with the intention to enhance representation of previously disadvantaged or sidelined interests. Becoming aware of the opportunities related with their newly won power, political parties often "perpetuated the colonial system rather than modifying it" (Ruzindana, 1997, p. 134). Widespread party organizations used the money gained in corrupt transactions for the building of political organizations that offered housing, food, and jobs to refugees from rural poverty or conflict in exchange for votes, thus ensuring their future position in power and laying the roots for future corruption (see, e.g., *Africa News Service*, September 2001). Especially in transitioning countries with insecure political and economic institutions, such forms of patronage and clientelism are common. Patronage structures can be seen as a means for parties to build and maintain an organizational base that can be activated during election campaigns. For local supporters who are often poor and do not have other avenues with which to access political decision-making processes and public goods and services, patronage networks are sometimes the only way to receive basic services. Examples of clientele and patronage networks can be found throughout Africa and Latin America. In the literature on corruption and development, the case of Nigeria is especially well documented (see, e.g., Brownsberger, 1983; Balogun, 1997). Whenever there are political appointments, greater transparency and free media organizations provide opportunities to check excesses.

Strategies and Measures to Eliminate Corruption

To eliminate corruption in political parties, institutional redesign is important. Generally, the risk of corruption is higher in political systems where representative processes structured to enforce government accountability are weak and where there are limited or no political mechanisms to dismiss government officials that engage in corrupt activities. In order to eliminate corruption in political parties, reforms have to address both the governing regime with which parties interact and internal party governance. Parties can even lead the transition to greater democracy, because democratic parties can be role models for former monopoly parties, as can be seen from recent developments in Taiwan. On the other hand, democratic reforms and economic development are likely to fail if influenced by corrupt parties. Therefore, the structure of parties is critical for improving democracy in transitional countries.

Restructuring Party Authority

Strategies in this area should have two aims. First, measures are needed to facilitate the development of a competitive liberal democratic regime. Such measures may include limitations on monopoly party authority and incentives to increase civil liberties and tolerate opposition formation. On the other hand, in countries with weak party systems, measures might be necessary to strengthen the authority and organization of political parties to enable a competitive party regime. Such strategies include the creation of legislation to define the scope of activities and authority of political parties, the introduction of public funding for party activities, and campaign finance legislation to control campaign spending and to ensure equal standards for party competition. Second, party restructuring also has to address internal party democracy. Measures include the creation of rules for transparent and competitive party leadership elections and candidate nomination procedures, the provision of incentives for party leaders to pursue nonfactional policies, and the introduction of codes of conduct for party members, along with internal party financial checks and balances.

Changing the External Framework of Party Activity

Party laws are crucial in framing the context in which political parties operate. Party laws regularly cover party registration, finance, and general operation. They provide legitimacy to party activities while, at the same time, defining party responsibilities and introducing government bodies empowered with oversight and enforcement. Many transitional countries do not have specific party legislation and only refer to party activities in election laws, such as the Philippines, or have introduced party laws only recently, such as South Korea (1987, amended in 2000), Cambodia (1997), Indonesia (1999), or Nepal (2001) (for details, see Thornton, 2001, pp. 6–8). To create a solid institutional base for party competition and to underline the important role parties play in democratic politics and to thus reduce opportunities for corruption, it is important that party laws do not only focus on parties as organizers of election campaigns, but as important pillars of democratic politics whose activities go beyond election campaigning. Otherwise, risks are high that parties act within the bounds of law during the campaign period, but engage in corrupt transactions all other times.

Public funding for political parties can be a valuable means to support the development of competitive political parties and to ensure transparency and fairness in election campaigns. By making parties less dependent on large campaign contributors, public funding can also stimulate more policy-oriented activities by party leaders. Public funding is common in advanced industrialized democracies in Western Europe and in Eastern European postcommunist states and has recently also been introduced to transitional countries in Africa and Asia.[3] Public subsidies succeed in stabilizing party systems and in supporting the development of party organizations. On the other hand, experiences from industrialized countries with a long tradition of public subsidies have shown that public funding does not always produce a reduction in campaign spending. In the case of Japan, for example, the Law on Public Funding for Political Parties originally stated that public subsidies should not exceed two thirds of the amount a party receives in contributions in the previous year. To ensure that they would receive the whole amount they were entitled to as per their share of the vote in the last elections and their number of seats in parliament, Japanese parties have started increasing fund-raising campaigns, an effect contrary to the intentions of the law (Blechinger, 2000, pp. 540–541).

Another step toward a more competitive environment for political parties is the creation of campaign finance legislation. The introduction of contribution limits for campaign donors or of expenditure limits for general party activities and campaign spending, can reduce the unfair distribution of political funds and increase equality in political competition. Moreover, public disclosure of funding sources provides voters with additional information about the linkages between parties and interest groups, and thus increases transparency in the political system. Both spending limits and disclosure rules are rather frequent in both industrialized democracies and transitional countries, however, in many countries, these regulatory restraints have little effect because they are either not enforced or contain loopholes (see, e.g., Alexander and Shiratori 1994; Nassmacher, 2001; Pinto-Duschinsky, 2002). Almost every democracy in the world faces problems of excessive campaign spending, independent of the shape of campaign finance legislation. Although the types of spending might differ, with a focus on expensive TV and radio advertising in industrialized nations, and higher cost for campaign vehicles and gifts for voters in patrimonial systems, the general trend to spend as much money as possible on election campaigns seems to be true for both industrialized countries and the developing world. Spending limits for campaigns are often not enforced or, in countries with very rigid election campaign laws such as Japan, parties tend to evade spending limits by spending most of their campaign funds before the start of the official campaign period.

Three lessons can be learned: first, it is important to introduce campaign finance regulations at an early stage in political development. Second, campaign finance regulations seem to be more efficient if they not only cover the campaign period, but the general activities of political parties outside of the campaign period, thus contributing to equal opportunities among parties and reducing incentives for corruption. Third, spending limits work more efficiently in combination with disclosure. A high degree of transparency in political finance reduces the opportunity for parties to build secret campaign chests and slush funds. The details of such regulations need to be shaped according to the context of individual countries. Whereas, for example, the United States fully discloses the names and addresses of all donors to political campaigns, such a practice might have negative consequences for donors in states where monopoly parties control public institutions and society, especially when donations are made to opposition parties. In such contexts, it might be more useful to strengthen intermediate control bodies such as electoral commissions.

Strengthening Internal Party Democracy

To participate efficiently in competitive democracy and to maintain legitimacy with voters, parties need internal democratic structures. Measures in this context include the introduction of party statutes that regulate membership, leadership and candidate selection, codes of conduct for party officials and candidates, disclosure of party finances and assets, and a system of internal party checks and balances. To improve intraparty democracy, rank and file members should be involved in the elections of party leaders. Similarly, transparent procedures for candidate selection and nomination can reduce opportunities for corruption.

Disclosure of income, assets, and other information useful for the prevention of corruption, and ties to certain firms or interests, both of the party as a political body and of party leaders, are an important means to raise the risks for politicians in case they engage in corrupt activities. It also enables voters to understand who their representatives are, what social forces are supporting a party, and what policies and interests the party stands for. However, as with campaign finance and anticorruption legislation, disclosure laws can only be effective when monitored independently.

Especially for newly established parties in transitional states, it might also be important to raise awareness for corruption and related issues. In traditional societies, for example, party members might see it as their duty toward their supporters to provide benefits in the form of patronage and clientelism. As part of anticorruption work, training seminars and discussions for party members and candidates can play an important role. The Democratic Party of Thailand and the Philippine LDP have recently implemented such initiatives (Thornton, 2002, p. 11). In recent years, and under the influence of anticorruption organizations such as Transparency International, parties in several countries, such as, most recently, Pakistan, pledged not to engage in and to confront corruption (*Agence France Press*, September 2002). However, such pledges are often related to election campaigns and if their implementation is not monitored by party members and misbehavior does not produce sanctions, their efficiency might not go beyond campaign rhetoric.

Finally, it has to be noted that in competitive political systems, parties might be willing to introduce voluntarily internal reforms if confronted with a successful competitor. A good example for such voluntary reforms as a reaction to electoral defeat is the KMT in Taiwan. After the Democratic Progressive Party (DPP) defeated the long-term ruling KMT in the last presidential election, and after opinion polls showed that Taiwanese voters preferred "clean" political parties, the KMT leadership initiated a program of internal party reform and restructuring (Thornton, 2002, p. 14).

Improve Accountability

To increase further transparency and accountability, party restructuring should be combined with anticorruption legislation and the creation of independent anticorruption watchdogs, such as independent electoral commissions or parliamentary ethics committees that regulate and police party corruption.

Many countries have introduced anticorruption laws in recent years (for Asia, see, e.g., Thornton, 2002). Such legislation usually prescribes harsh punishment for corrupt activities of politicians, bureaucrats, and business representatives. Punitive measures, however, are only effective when they are implemented and enforced. When the judiciary does not actively prosecute violations of anticorruption laws and trials are dragged out for years, anticorruption legislation remains toothless. A strengthening of the judiciary, both through legal reform that prioritizes corruption cases and intense training to improve investigators' and prosecutors' skills and awareness of corruption, must accompany anticorruption laws. Moreover, anticorruption laws are useless when parliamentarians are protected from prosecution by immunity, as is the case, for example, in Mexico (Economist Intelligence Unit, 2002). To make anticorruption laws more powerful, it might be useful to partially revoke politicians' immunity in corruption cases.

A second strategy to improve accountability is the strengthening of checks and balances within government, for example through the creation of "watchdog" institutions that monitor government and party activities. The creation of monitoring and auditing institutions in government and of anticorruption committees in parliament, however, can only be effective if they have jurisdiction to prosecute and sanction misbehavior, and if they are independent. Independence can be achieved by ensuring, for example in the statutes of such institutions, that committees must represent all parties in parliament, thus preventing them to be used as tools in political infighting.

Realign Incentives

Politicians are most likely to engage in corruption when there is a low risk to be prosecuted, punished, or to lose their seat in parliament as a consequence of voter displeasure with their conduct. Similarly, parties are less likely to engage in or support corrupt leaders or their activities when such behavior is punished at the ballot box. To prevent corruption, it is therefore necessary to increase the risks. One strategy is to revoke an election and to disqualify candidates if they themselves or their campaign staff engage in corruption or vote buying, as it is practiced, for example, in Thailand (*Bangkok Post*, November 2000). Because the dismissal of politicians from parliament reduces the party's number of seats, such regulations increase the incentives for party leaders to control candidate behavior and promote "clean" election campaigns. This is especially true in competitive systems, as it can be expected that a party tainted by corruption will have reduced chances to get its candidate elected in an ensuing by-election. In addition to punitive measures, activities by donor organizations to raise awareness for corruption as a problem in political party systems, for example, through regional seminars about "best practices" or training for party officials, can provide valuable incentives for party leaders to keep corruption at bay. In transitional countries, political and economic development and the survival of parties in government often depend on foreign aid and investment. If good governance, transparency, and accountability are considered favorable elements in the evaluation of a country's application for grants, trade credits, loan guarantees, and investment, party leaders might be more likely to change their behavior accordingly. This might be even more the case in an international arena where "clean politics" contribute to the prestige of government.

Change Attitudes and Mobilize Political Will

Civil society and a free press play a crucial role in anticorruption activities in the area of political parties. In the industrialized and the developing world, voter awareness of corruption and their discontent with corrupt politicians are increasing. Cases of political corruption and bribery bring voters to the streets in protest, and NGOs that fight corruption are gaining influence. Along with information disclosure and transparency, an informed public is the best means to prevent corruption. If politicians and party leaders know that their activities are closely watched and chances of exposure are high, they might refrain from corrupt activities. Moreover, as in the case of Taiwan and also in the recent elections in South Korea, if parties can win elections on the basis of their anticorruption program and transparent and democratic party organization, other parties might follow their example, thus instigating change in the party system. In the South Korean national elections in April 2000, civil society groups that published "blacklists" of candidates and parties tainted with corruption had a strong influence on the election outcome (Chon, 2000; Park, 2000). The press multiplied this effect by reporting about the blacklists and providing further background information.

Voter education campaigns, along with financial and organizational support for civil society groups, are crucial elements of anticorruption policies. Regional and local seminars about good governance and best practices for civil society organizations that educate voters might be a suitable strategy to increase awareness of corruption.

Notes

1. For more information on campaign finance and corruption in India, see http://www.loksatta.org. Loksatta ("People Power") is a NGO devoted to clean elections.

2. For local variations of corruption between the postcommunist states in Eastern Europe, see Karatnycky (2001).

3. For an overview, see, for example, Pinto-Duschinsky's study of the 143 countries ranked as "Free" or "Partly Free" by the latest Freedom House rankings. He found that 59% of these countries have a system of public subsidies for political parties (Pinto-Duschinsky, 2002, pp. 76–80).

Chapter 4

Health Care

Taryn Vian

Development economists agree that health is an essential goal of development and a country need not have high income to achieve better health (Sen, 1999). In the health sector, the government plays an important role in promoting equitable access to services, assuring sustainable financing for health objectives and preventing the spread of disease. But too often, governments fail to perform these functions, leading to inadequate and unequal access, poor quality of care, and inefficient services. In many cases, government failure is linked to corruption.[1]

Corruption has been defined as the abuse of public roles and resources or the use of illegitimate forms of political influence by public or private parties (Johnston, 1997, p. 62).[2] Corruption in health may involve bribes from a private supplier to win a government procurement contract, misappropriation of public resources for private gain, or government employees who extort under-the-table payments from patients.

The health sector is particularly vulnerable to corruption for several reasons, including the diversity of services and outlays, the scale and expense of procurement, and the nature of health care demand. There are many kinds of processes and expenditures occurring in the health sector, from expensive construction and high-tech procurement, with attendant risks of bribery, collusion and *ex post* corruption, to frontline services being offered within a provider-patient relationship marked by imbalances in information and inelastic demand for services (Lewis, 2000).

The resulting corruption in health care can have great social costs. In many countries, economic conditions since the late 1980s have resulted in less government financing for health services, which in turn has translated into ruptures in supply of medicines and inadequate (or nonpayment) of salaries for health workers. Within this environment, corruption becomes a survival strategy for government workers and patients alike. As health services fail, people end up having to pay out-of-pocket for services that are supposed to be free, with the burden falling disproportionately on the poor (Killingsworth, 1999, pp. 152–163; Lewis 2000; World Bank, 2001a).

Different countries can have divergent perceptions about corruption, given their history and the balance of political and economic opportunities and interest groups (Johnston, 1997). For example, studies have shown that the health sector is seen as one of the least corrupt sectors of government in several Latin American countries, even though up to 40 percent of patients reported having to make informal payments to receive care (Di Tella and Savedoff, 2001). Yet in Central Europe, survey respondents consistently pointed to hospitals as one of the most corrupt government institutions, with 81 percent reporting that they need to offer gifts to hospital doctors in order to obtain services to which they were legally entitled (Miller, Grodeland, and Koshechkina, 2001). Strategies for preventing corruption within a given country must consider these kinds of differences.

Research to document the costs of corruption in the health sector, and especially to test strategies for corruption prevention, is scarce. Some recent studies have documented the problem of informal economic activity or informal payments of health workers, defined as payments received that are outside of official policy, as will be discussed later in the chapter. Even so, it is interesting to note that this practice is often not called corruption, though it clearly fits the definition of abuse of public roles or resources. In part, this reflects the fact that corruption is not yet widely recognized among health professionals as a controllable problem or one that can be openly discussed.

Problems of Corruption and Health

Table 4.1 presents some of the major health areas and processes that are vulnerable to corruption, describing the types of problems that are likely and the outcomes that result.[3]

Table 4.1. Types of Corruption in the Health Sector[4]

Area or Process	Types of Corruption and Problems	Indicators or Results
Construction and rehabilitation of health facilities	• Bribes, kickbacks, and political considerations influencing the contracting process • Contractors fail to perform and are not held accountable	• High cost, low-quality facilities and construction work • Location of facilities that does not correspond to need, resulting in inequities in access • Biased distribution of infrastructure favoring urban- and elite-focused services, high technology
Purchase of equipment and supplies, including drugs	• Bribes, kickbacks, and political considerations influence specifications and winners of bids • Collusion or bid rigging during procurement • Lack of incentives to choose low cost and high quality suppliers • Unethical drug promotion • Suppliers fail to deliver and are not held accountable	• High cost, inappropriate or duplicative drugs and equipment • Inappropriate equipment located without consideration of true need • Substandard equipment and drugs • Inequities due to inadequate funds left to provide for all needs
Distribution and use of drugs and supplies in service delivery	• Theft (for personal use) or diversion (for private sector resale) of drugs/supplies at storage and distribution points • Sale of drugs or supplies that were supposed to be free	• Lower utilization • Patients do not get proper treatment • Patients must make informal payments to obtain drugs • Interruption of treatment or incomplete treatment, leading to development of antimicrobial resistance
Regulation of quality in products, services, facilities, and professionals	• Bribes to speed process or gain approval for drug registration, drug quality inspection, or certification of good manufacturing practices • Bribes or political considerations influence results of inspections or suppress findings	• Sub-therapeutic or fake drugs allowed on market • Marginal suppliers are allowed to continue participating in bids, getting government work • Increased incidence of food poisoning

Table 4.1. (continued)

Area or Process	Types of Corruption and Problemsi	Indicators or Results
Regulation of quality in products, services, facilities, and professionals (*continued*)	• Biased application of sanitary regulations for restaurants, food production, and cosmetics • Biased application of accreditation, certification or licensing procedures and standards	• Spread of infectious and communicable diseases • Poor-quality facilities continue to function • Incompetent or fake professionals continue to practice
Education of health professionals	• Bribes to gain place in medical school or other pre-service training • Bribes to obtain passing grades • Political influence, nepotism in selection of candidates for training opportunities	• Incompetent professionals practicing medicine or working in health professions • Loss of faith and freedom due to unfair system
Medical research[5]	• Pseudo-trials funded by drug companies that are really for marketing • Misunderstanding of informed consent and other issues of adequate standards in developing countries	• Violation of individual rights • Biases and inequities in research
Provision of services by front-line health workers	• Use of public facilities and equipment to see private patients • Unnecessary referrals to private practice or privately owned ancillary services • Absenteeism • Informal payments required from patients for services • Theft of user fee revenue, other diversion of budget allocations[6]	• Government loses value of investments without adequate compensation • Employees are not available to serve patients • Reduced use of services by patients who cannot pay • Impoverishment as citizens use income and sell assets to pay for health care • Reduced quality of care from loss of revenue • Loss of citizen faith in government

Two areas where there is great potential for corruption and where corruption is a recognized concern in most countries are procurement of drugs and equipment, and informal economic activities engaged in by health providers (e.g., informal payments, private practice on government time, etc.).[7] The rest of the chapter will focus on what is known about these two areas, which have a critical impact on health status.

Procurement and Management of Medicines, Equipment and Supplies

Outside of salaries, pharmaceuticals represent the largest category of recurrent health expenditure in most government budgets. The total value of pharmaceuticals changing hands in the developing world is estimated at US$44 billion (Woodle, 2000, pp. 121–129). Government budgets make significant contributions to public sector drug financing, often allocating 20 percent to 50 percent of the government health budget to procure drugs (Falkenberg and Tomson, 2000, pp. 52–58). Medical equipment is also an area where large sums of money may be involved and corruption is a danger.

In this section, drug and equipment supply issues are discussed according to the functional areas of selection, promotion, procurement, and distribution, showing where corruption is likely to occur and what options exist for prevention (Management and Sciences for Health, 1997, pp. 450–463).[8]

Selection

In the past 25 years, many countries have adopted drug policies and essential drug lists in an effort to limit the selection of drug products. By limiting choice, essential drugs lists (EDLs) of generically named products help health systems to achieve expanded access to a smaller number of appropriate drugs (World Health Organization, 2002). About 150 countries have essential drugs lists (Reich, 2000, pp. 1979–1981). The movement toward essential drugs lists has been critical in helping countries increase the objectivity and transparency of the pharmaceutical selection process.

Recent efforts of the World Health Organization (WHO) have promoted changes in the composition of the committees that develop and modify essential drugs lists. In the past, national expert committees made decisions about drug lists based on WHO principles for designating essential drugs, the WHO "model list," and country preferences for certain products. One danger in this type of process is the potential for members of the selection committee to have a conflict of interest, or to be susceptible to bribes. More recently, WHO is urging countries to develop EDLs starting from evidence-based clinical treatment guidelines, rather than expert opinion (Laing, Hogerzeil, and Ross-Degnan, 2000, pp. 13–20). This trend will help strengthen transparency and limit the discretion of the national committee. While essential drug lists and selection processes also exist at other levels of the health system, they are usually less well developed.

Promotion

Unethical promotion of medicines is a significant problem, not only in developing countries but also throughout the world. Studies have shown that industry hospitality (e.g. all expense-paid trips to luxury resorts), gifts, and free samples all can affect physicians' judgment (Mick, 1991, pp. 662–664; Orlowski and Wateska, 1992, pp. 270 –273; Chren and Landefeld, 1994, pp. 684–689; Wall and Brown, 2002, pp.594–599). Other potential causes of conflicts of interest include physicians who have financial stakes in pharmaceutical or medical device companies, or receive honoraria for speaking engagements, referrals, or participation in clinic-based research (Coyle, 2002, p. 397). The pharmaceutical industry is "not merely a provider of drugs, but…a substantial purveyor of information and persuasion," according to a recent report published in *The Lancet* (Dulces, 2002, pp. 1682–1684). In 1999, the industry spent US$8 billion on direct sales visits to physicians and exhibits at medical conferences (Coyle, 2002, p. 396).

WHO and the International Federation of Pharmaceutical Manufacturers Associations (IFPMA) have created ethical guidelines on medicine promotion (World Health Organization, 1988), though the effectiveness of such guidelines is not well established. It is often difficult to tell when marketing ends and corruption begins. For example, there is anecdotal evidence of influence used during development of WHO clinical guidelines on hypertension. An additional problem is pharmaceutical companies promoting clinical trials that are really for marketing purposes (Coyle, 2002, p. 400).

One option used in US hospitals to make drug selection processes more transparent is the Pharmacy and Therapeutics (P&T) Committee, a multidisciplinary group that recommends policies regarding selection and use of drugs, as well as assists with continuing education of medical staff on matters related to drugs (Heemink, 1999). Indicator-based assessments and monitoring are other ways to promote rational selection and supply management by providing objective and comparable indicators that can be used to detect unusual differences in practices compared to standards, holding managers more accountable (Rational Pharmaceutical Management Projects, 1995; Brudon, Rainhorn, and Reich, 1999). Programs to monitor corruption, such as the Drug and Commodity Transparency Program proposed for the US Agency for International Development (Duncan, 2002, pp. 5–6), may also help increase awareness of the problem and could help reduce corruption by increasing the risks of exposure.

Table 4.2 summarizes anticorruption measures for drug selection and promotion and their likely effects.

Table 4.2. Drug Selection and Promotion: Anticorruption Measures

Action	Likely Effects
Promotion of essential drugs lists (EDLs) at national and subnational levels	Limits influence of interest groups Limits discretion of drug selection committees
Using standard treatment guidelines as a basis for EDL	Promotes transparency and accountability
Enforceable codes of ethics in marketing promoted through trade and professional associations	May reduce unethical promotion activities
Pharmacy & therapeutic committees at facility level	Provides vehicle for public oversight, increasing accountability
Indicator sets and indicator-based assessments, monitoring programs like the Drug and Commodity Transparency Program	Detects unusual selection and purchasing patterns in comparison with needs Comparative data, benchmarking, and public dissemination of information can increase transparency, incentives and motivation

Procurement

New trends in the financing of health commodities may have an impact on corruption. These trends have included increasing use of "basket financing" mechanisms whereby donors and the government pool their resources for financing health services, increased use of development bank credits and loans, and the introduction of global funds for specific commodities such as vaccines and tuberculosis (TB) or HIV/AIDS drugs (Vian and Bates, 2002). These developments allow recipient agencies more opportunity to manage and disburse external resources within government systems, along with national budget allocations. With more money flowing through government systems, there are greater potential gains from corrupt procurement and distribution practices. Several authors have noted a lack of government capacity for managing procurement processes for health commodities (Bates, 2000; Kaddar, 2000; Woodle, 2000, pp. 121–129).

Drug regulation and quality assurance are also problems for some countries, and failure to enforce quality standards has resulted in a surge in counterfeit drugs in some parts of the world (Association of International Pharmaceutical Manufacturers, 2001). The regulatory process for "fast-tracking" approval and licensing of drugs may be influenced by bribes. In addition, drug inspection is a process that is susceptible to corruption. Two specific areas that are worth special attention include methods of payment for inspectors and the public release of inspection findings.

Klitgaard (2000) notes three types of corruption that are especially likely in procurement: collusion in bidding, leading to higher prices; kickbacks from contractors/suppliers, which reduce competition and influence selection; and bribes to officials responsible for regulating performance of the winning contractor, resulting in possible cost overruns and low quality. Studies of competitive contracting as a way to improve efficiency in government have noted that strong public management skills are required to write specifications, and supervise and measure contract performance (Mills, 1998, pp. 32–40; Abramson, 2001, pp. 404–411). Although competitive contracting in theory results in more efficient provision of services, it requires preconditions such as an adequately sized private sector, strong government, and sophisticated procedures for financial analysis and information management.

In health-related procurements, particular problems may arise in the specification of needs, as some medical equipment will require very technical specifications. Government officials concerned with procurement may not have the expertise to set these specifications. If the specifications are made too detailed and rigorous, it may limit competition, but if the specifications are too loose or vague, there may be more discretion for officials and therefore more opportunity for bribes to influence the selection. Procurement of consumable commodities can present an added danger for corruption because it is difficult to document whether the drugs or supplies were delivered (Rose-Ackerman, 1999). Klitgaard (2000) notes that important conditions must be in place to fight corruption in procurement, including a well delineated civil service system (merit-based and adequately paid) and law enforcement services that can investigate problems. These conditions point to the need for health services to work with overall national-level anticorruption and good governance programs.

Bribes, bid-rigging and other types of corruption can vary according to the type of procurement process followed; for example, open tender, restricted tender, negotiated competition, or direct procurement (Management Services for Health, 1997). With open tender, corruption can occur when confidential information on what different suppliers have bid is selectively shared, allowing some bidders inside information. There can also be corruption in the adjudication of tenders, where the assessment of quality and reliability are unfair and influenced by bribes. With negotiated competition there can be opportunities for extortion and bribery during the back-and-forth price discussions with firms.[9] And although direct procurement is effective with known and reliable suppliers, it requires excellent market intelligence (up-to-date price information) and is often expensive.

The World Bank and WHO both promote a move from open tender to restricted-tender with pre-qualification of suppliers (Laing,1999, pp. 51–57; World Bank, 2002a). Here, corruption tends to happen during the prequalification process; with firms paying bribes to get on the list of approved bidders or to restrict the length of the list (Rose-Ackerman, 1999, p. 64). The World Bank recently produced a procurement manual providing specific guidance for procurement using World Bank credits and loan funds, and WHO has produced a separate manual for procurement of vaccines (World Health Organization, 1998; World Bank, 2000f). USAID has assisted governments in Moldova and Zimbabwe to improve need estimation and procurement operations (Woodle, 2000, pp. 125–126). Yet, more interventions are needed to promote good procurement practices, including hands-on job training, professional development, and systems redesign assistance.

Activities that can help promote transparency in procurement include the development and dissemination of performance-ratings of suppliers, and readily available and current price information. International agencies or individual countries could maintain rosters of bidders with information on past performance ratings (Rose-Ackerman, 1999, p. 64). A more limited "white list" of reliable and prequalified suppliers is another way to share market intelligence. Price lists such as the MSH International Price Guide (Management Sciences for Health and the World Health Organization, 2001) and a WHO Web page with links to web sites with medicine pricing information (World Health Organization, n.d.) put downward pressure on prices bid by suppliers and help to reduce opportunities for bribes. Table 4.3 summarizes anticorruption measures and their effects for drug and equipment procurement.

Table 4.3. Drug and Equipment Procurement: Anticorruption Measures

Action	Likely Effects
Technical assistance to help develop governments' capacity to manage competitive procurements	Limits and clarifies authority of government officials Promotes competition
Changes in how procurement officers and quality inspectors are held accountable or paid	Provides better incentives, linked to performance
Public disclosure of inspection findings	Increases transparency
Rosters with performance ratings or white lists of suppliers, greater availability of price information	Improves accountability by increasing access to information Limits discretion

Distribution

In the past, most countries used central government procurement offices and central medical stores (CMS) to purchase and distribute commodities. The health reforms in the 1980s and 1990s have created more variations on this theme, most including some elements of privatization or contracting services.

These new initiatives have been designed to improve efficiency, though in theory, they may reduce the monopoly power of government and therefore prevent corruption as well. Some countries that have implemented these changes—with mixed results—include Tanzania, Zambia, and Ghana (Vian and Bates, 2002). It will be especially important to evaluate these structures from the point of view of preventing corruption.

Transportation systems are an essential part of supply distribution and are used for direct health services delivery as well. Corruption can occur when vehicles are appropriated for personal use (transporting goods to market, for example), and when fuel is stolen or diverted for non-health related uses. Recent work has documented innovative control systems to measure efficiency and effectiveness of transportation systems, also recommending public contracting of private services, or internal transfer pricing systems as ways to increase accountability (Nancollas, 1999; Abt Associates, 2001).

Finally, the problem of theft, diversion and resale of drugs has been documented in many countries (Killingsworth, 1999; McPake 1999, pp. 849– 865; Lewis, 2000; Di Tella and Savedoff, 2001). Corruption at this level may include:

- Theft without falsification of records (i.e. physical inventory does not match recorded stock)
- Drugs dispensed to "ghost patients"
- Drugs recorded as dispensed to real patients who do not receive them
- Drugs dispensed to real patients who pay for them and the health care provider keeps the funds, contrary to government policy.

Analyzing data from health centers in Uganda, McPake et al. (1999) estimated that more than two-thirds of drugs meant for free distribution through the public sector were lost due to theft and "leakage." An estimated 68 percent to 77 percent of revenues from formal user charges were misappropriated or pocketed by workers. McPake et al. believe that these practices contributed to observed low rates of utilization due to shortages of drugs and reduced financial accessibility. The authors also noted stories of deaths and abuse resulting from services withheld from people who could not afford to pay. Although mostly unverifiable, these accounts were seen to demonstrate a profound lack of trust between the community members and health workers. It is unclear whether the effects documented by McPake et al. are typical of formal user fee systems in other countries besides Uganda. This is an important area for further study.

USAID projects that have focused attention on the management systems and incentives needed to prevent these types of corruption include the bilateral Kenya Health Care Financing project, the Niger Health Sector Support Program, and systems-building activities of the Rational Pharmaceutical Management (RPM) and RPM Plus projects. Local budgeting and cost recovery systems with strong financial control systems that may reduce problems and inventory control systems associated with essential drugs programs may also be effective. But these efforts only provide technical solutions; to create incentives to implement these solutions may require additional actions such as involvement of community oversight groups or public dissemination of information to raise the risks of corrupt behavior. In Kenya, clarifying the role of District Health Management Boards and providing training for Board members helped increase accountability (Collins, 1996). Letters of commendation and national awards ceremonies were also used to provide praise and recognition for employees who achieved good program results (Collins, 1996).

Table 4.4 summarizes health reforms and changes that have been implemented and their possible impact on corruption prevention.

Table 4.4. Drug Distribution: Health Reforms with Anticorruption Effects

Action	Likely Effects for Preventing Corruption
Central medical stores reforms to privatize and introduce business-like incentives	Clarifies lines of authority Increases accountability and incentives
Transportation contracting and resource management systems, transfer pricing	Increases accountability and improves incentives
Improved drug management logistics information systems, indicator-based assessments	Increases accountability where systems are used (not just a technical solution, but requires the will to implement)
Financial management system	Increases accountability where systems are put into use
Local health boards, community oversight	Limits discretion Improves accountability and transparency

Informal Economic Activity of Health Personnel

Besides drug and equipment procurement and management, another key point of vulnerability to corruption is health services personnel at the service delivery point (SDP) level. Health officials in many governments are paid meager salaries, with few rewards for exceptional performance. Political patronage and delays in decision-making due to lack of local authority for personnel decisions make it difficult for managers to reward staff for good performance or sanction nonperformers (Martines and Matineau, 1998, pp. 345–358). Penalties for corruption, if they exist at all, are rare. Under these conditions, many workers engage in other economic activities during working hours or pursue opportunities for private gain through public service, including the practice of informal payments.

It should be noted that opinion is mixed on this topic: some condemn the practice of under-the-table payments and call on governments to put a stop to it, while others express sympathy and acknowledge that this is a necessary strategy for survival during times of economic crisis. Governments and medical professional associations may provide mixed messages about the acceptability of such practices, as has been documented in Hungary (Lewis, 2000). This ambivalence creates a difficult environment for policy making. Yet, as Lewis (2000) makes clear, tacit acceptance of informal payments "reduces [the government's] effectiveness as manager of the overall system, and undermines its credibility as both guarantor and regulator of the health care system."

Recent literature has begun to document the growing problem of under-the-table payments for supposedly free health care services and other illicit economic activities engaged in by health workers (e.g., various drug theft or diversion schemes described above, using public facilities to engage in private medical practice, working less than full-time at a full-time public job, etc.). Studies have documented these problems in Uganda (McPake, 1999, pp. 849–865), Eastern Europe and Central Asia (Delcheva, Balabnova, and McKee, 1997, pp. 89–100; Lewis, 2000), Russia (Feeley, Sheimann, and Shiskin, 1999), Bangladesh (Killingsworth, 1999; Gruen, 2002, pp. 267–279), Vietnam (Bicknell, Beggs, and Tham, 2001, pp. 412–420), and Latin America (Di Tella and Savedoff, 2001).

Lewis (2000) defines informal payments as "payments to institutions or individuals in cash or in kind made outside official payment channels for services that are meant to be covered by the public health system."[10] These types of payments are increasingly common: in Commonwealth of Independent States (CIS) countries, more than 60 percent of those surveyed reported making informal payments, while in Armenia the figure topped 90 percent (Lewis, 2000). McPake et al. (1999) observed that informal payments were sometimes five to ten times as high as formal user charges in Uganda. In Bolivia, 44 percent of doctors surveyed in municipal hospitals reported that informal payments occur "always" (Gray-Molina, Perezde Rada, and Yanez, 1999).

One problem in documenting this type of corruption is that it is difficult to draw the line between bribes and gift giving, the latter of which may be a culturally accepted practice for creating "webs of relationships based on mutual obligations." (Werner, 2000, pp. 11–22) For example, in Kazakhstan the word *syilyq* refers to feast gifts and counter-gifts from host to guest given during a feast; however, it also may be used to refer to a watch or suit given to a doctor in exchange for better medical treatment (Werner, 2000, pp. 11–22). In Kyrgyzstan, 55 percent of respondents thought it was permissible for a doctor to receive gifts from patients (Ilibezova, 2000). In Poland as well, informal payments are common and socially acceptable.

Informal payments reduce access to services. They have been associated with delays in seeking care in Poland, declines in prenatal care in Tajikistan, and decreases in household assets in the Kyrgyz Republic (Lewis, 2000, pp. 25). McPake et al. (1999) associated informal payments with large reductions in use of services, due to financial inaccessibility of care. The burden of informal payments was shown to be regressive in Romania, with poor households paying twice as much as medium-income households, and medium-income households paying twice as much (proportionately) as high-income households (World Bank, 2001).

Box 4A. The Rise of Informal Payments in Russia

The Situation in 1990

Before the transition, the Russian government could expand the size/employment in the health care system to levels that are not sustainable in a market economy. Russia boasted more doctors per capita than most Western countries, and doctors could be paid low wages because many items were subsidized (housing, food) and few other consumer goods were available to buy. Government produced all pharmaceuticals and could subsidize production at the source. There were only a few drugs per therapeutic class, so essentially no distinction between brand name and generic existed. With prices subsidized, it was possible to charge affordable prices for outpatient drugs.

After 1991

The creation of a market economy meant that the Russian Government could no longer subsidize the factors of medical production at source. Health care personnel had to pay rising prices for necessities. The drug market was opened to international competition, and brand name drugs came on the market. The Government's weak tax collection systems could not sustain the level of total health expenditures seen under the Soviets. Salaries (if paid) to health personnel were inadequate to maintain their accustomed standard of living. At the same time, more consumer goods were available and more visible as private sector workers were able to purchase them. The Government refused to recognize that it could not support the health establishment it inherited; it would neither downsize, redefine the package of free services, nor institute formal fees that might be managed in such a way to reduce the impact on the sickest and poorest. Patients were forced to pay market prices for drugs now prescribed by brand name. Surveys show that drug costs are now particularly regressive, and many patients go without the prescribed drugs because of their inability to purchase. Under-the-table payments for medical services have soared as health providers try to assure themselves a living wage, and patients try to obtain the care they need.

Source: Communication with F. Feeley, Boston University School of Public Health (October 28, 2002)

Informal payments also reduce trust in government and in health workers, feeding feelings of hopelessness and alienation, particularly among the poor (World Bank, 2001a, p. 20). The text box describes the factors that led to the increase in the level of informal payments in Russia.[11]

Informal payments are a survival strategy for both underpaid professionals and patients, and may have root causes in inadequate overall rates of compensation for health workers, overstaffing in the public health work force, and provider payment systems with inadequate performance incentives. Some of the solutions being considered for dealing with informal payments include downsizing of the public system, changing payment systems for health care providers, legalizing cost sharing, and improving accountability through performance-based management and financing systems. In theory, downsizing government can allow increases in individual salaries without increasing total salary expense presumably resulting in a more livable wage, albeit for fewer personnel. In practice, there is little evidence of this occurring (Martinez and Martineau, 1998, pp. 345–358).

Another positive effect, in theory, is the gains in accountability that can result from moving doctors from salaried civil service status to a contractual relationship (either with payment per service or per capita, or other types of reimbursement contracting). These types of service arrangements acknowledge that providers often engage in both private and government service, whether this practice is legal or not. For example, in Bangladesh, an estimated 80 percent of government doctors engage (legally) in private practice as well, and most at least double their government salary this way (Gruen, 2002, pp. 267–279).

In practice, the effects of changes in provider payment mechanisms are mixed and depend on many things including how changes are communicated, values in society, and whether there is enough money in total being spent on reimbursing providers.[12] In Poland, the introduction of fee-for-service and capitation payment systems has not had much effect on the practice of informal payments; yet in Colombia similar changes in payment systems have been successful in decreasing the incidence of under-the-table payments. In the Czech Republic, informal payments have all but disappeared; however, in addition to changing provider reimbursement mechanisms the government has also greatly increased the total amount of spending in the health system and has communicated those changes in a systematic way.[13]

Moving from salaried civil service status to contractual relationships with key employees may increase accountability, but the state will still have a difficult role to play in regulating such a system. For example, in northern European countries such as Finland, Sweden, and Great Britain, health reforms have shifted health care provision from fixed-budget bureaucratic institutions to contract payments based on performance (Saltman, 2002, 1677–1684). While this has increased operating efficiency, it has also required the state to play a more sophisticated role in regulating services. The move from direct control of service provision to contracting actually increased regulatory action, rather than reducing the role of the state. Similar findings have been noted in the Czech Republic, Estonia, and Slovakia (Saltman, 2002, pp. 1677–2684). Government regulation is needed to avoid problems such as diverting of patients to private practice when they could have been treated in the public sector, conflicts of interest where physicians own government-contracted ancillary services, and supplier-induced demand (Gruen, 2002, pp. 267–279).

Table 4.5 summarizes anticorruption measures for dealing with informal payments and other human resources management issues. There is need for more research to determine the effects of these strategies in practice.

Table 4.5. Informal Payments and Personnel: Anticorruption Measures

Action	Likely Effects
Downsize government and pay workers higher wages	Improves incentives, though politically difficult
Promote government contracting for payment of private providers rather than civil service; encourage private alternatives	Increases accountability and improves incentives Competition from private providers increases clients' exit options (Gray-Molina, Perez de Rada, and Yanez, 1999)
Develop performance-based management systems and provider payment systems	Increases accountability and provides better incentives, since performance is rewarded
Legal cost sharing	Reduces opportunities for extorting payments
Increase role of community committees, local health board activism	Improves accountability by providing ways for users to voice approval and disapproval, increases chances corruption will be caught
Report cards for public services (Bures, 2002)[14]	Improves accountability and incentives
Analysis and dissemination of results of surveys and data collection (such as standards of living surveys, PETS, QSDS, and DHS) (Renikka and Svensson, 2002, p. 21)[15]	Improves transparency and accountability; helps detect gaps between what the service statistics say and what patients report

Health Reform and Global Funds

Health reform involves changing government institutions and policies in purposeful, fundamental and sustained ways (Berman and Bossert, 2000). Countries adopt health reforms in response to external and internal drivers for change, including economic crisis, inequitable resource distribution, gaps in quality, changing health needs and changing societal norms. Health reforms have taken different directions, but some important movements have included decentralization, privatization, health insurance and user fee systems, changes in provider payment systems, and restructuring of tertiary and secondary levels of care.

USAID has provided enormous support for countries undergoing health reform. Through multilateral projects such as Partners for Health Reform Plus (and its predecessors)[16] and through bilateral assistance projects such as the Russia Legal and Regulatory Health Reform Project,[17] USAID has collected data, conducted research, and informed policy decisions at many stages and levels. The relationships that have been developed through this process are a significant resource for the promotion of anticorruption strategies. As institutions and structures are changing, there are many opportunities to incorporate corruption prevention into new policies and designs or to highlight the anticorruption benefits in practices that are already being supported through health reform. For example, health insurance fund and hospital reform efforts in Kyrgyzstan and Romania, funded with USAID assistance, have included the design of new reimbursement methods that can improve accountability and reduce opportunities for corruption (Duncan, 2002). USAID's work in promoting National Health Accounts can also be used as a springboard for the construction of spending standards and comparison of expenditure patterns to improve accountability and transparency.[18]

Another recent development in international health has been the creation of public-private partnerships channeling financial assistance through global funds. These funds pose a huge opportunity and challenge for anticorruption strategy, especially due to the conscious structuring of global funds to circumvent national bureaucracies and speed the process of disbursement. The Global Alliance for Vaccines and Immunization (GAVI) has committed more than US$600 million for vaccines and vaccine program-related expenses, while the Global Fund to Fight AIDS, Tuberculosis and Malaria (GFATM, or Global Fund) plans to disburse US$600–$800 million in the year 2002 alone (Vian and Bates, 2002). The Global Fund has solicited proposals from Country Coordinating Mechanisms (committees of individuals from communities, churches, government and the private sector) who decide where the funds are to go. The Global Fund then intends to use accounting agencies as Local Fund Agents rather than channeling funds through slower bureaucracies such as national governments or international organizations like the World Bank, WHO, or United Nations Development Program (UNDP). One of the first proposals accepted was US$12 million for the Tanzanian National Malaria Control Program; however, the grant has been delayed due to accounting problems as described in a recent investigative report (Wilson, 2002). It seems that the government's accounting procedures allow grants to flow only through the Ministry of Finance. Questions about flows of funds have arisen in South Africa and Uganda as well (Wilson, 2002).

Because the Global Fund to Fight AIDS, Tuberculosis and Malaria is just beginning to release funds, the responsibilities of Local Fund Agents *vis-à-vis* the Country Coordinating Mechanisms used to develop the proposals are not yet clear, and this may create problems for accountability. In addition, approved proposals are not available to the public, signaling a lack of transparency in the process.

The real strategy being used to assure accountability for global funds (both GAVI and the GFATM) is performance-based grant mechanisms, which means that after the initial grants, countries will only be able to receive additional funding based on the achievement of performance benchmarks. Performance-based incentives have the potential to increase accountability, but the incentives for false reporting are also clear and costs of monitoring can be significant (Brugha, Starling, and Walt, 2002, pp. 435–438; Heaton and Keith, 2002). GAVI's measures for performance are targeted increases in vaccination coverage; the Global Fund's indicators for performance are yet to be decided.

If global funds are wasted or lost to corruption, this huge new source of international support for the needs of poor countries may be lost, as trust is broken and the public-private partners become disillusioned. The risk is real, as indicated by recent reports of diversion of donated anti-retroviral drugs from the public sector to the private sector, and from poor countries to developed country markets (Kibumba, 2002; Love, 2002). Additional costs are involved in extending models of performance-based financing throughout the health care management system in ways that are sustainable. USAID has had some experience in implementing performance-based grant systems in the Philippines and Haiti (Management Sciences for Health, 1993; Management Sciences for Health, 2001; Eichler, Auxila, and Pollock, 2002). More should be done to share the lessons learned from these programs.

Comprehensive Anticorruption Strategies: How Does Health Fit In?

An important element of strategy formulation is evaluating the external environment. For corruption and health, this means assessing what are the anticorruption strategies going on at the national level—or even international level—and how does health fit into these movements.

Because there will be many anticorruption strategies taking place outside the health sector, the health sector strategy must inform stakeholders at all levels of how health fits into overall anticorruption strategy and policies. Much of the corruption found in the health sector is a reflection of general problems of governance and public sector accountability. Thus, the strategy for preventing corruption in the health sector will need to include education of health professionals about overall government anticorruption measures such as civil service management reform, changes in public accounting practices, and anticorruption agencies, to promote better understanding of how these initiatives may benefit the health sector. It is also important to increase understanding of the costs of corruption in health and convey the sense that something *can* and *ought to* be done about it.

Donor coordination of approaches is also essential. Where improved financial management or inventory management systems are to be tested, donors should agree on a common approach and support it fully. A strategy of increasing the participation of civil society in oversight structures, for example, holds more chance of success if multiple donors support the initiative and share the costs of developing capacity and evaluating implementation.

Finally, any corruption prevention strategy must plan on conducting promotional activities to build commitment and support. To do this, donors must first show commitment to root out corruption and corrupting influences in their own agencies. For example, donors might want to address some issues directly, such as financial management and procurement corruption, potential dangers of nepotism from relying on local nationals as agents, and favoritism toward certain contractors. The World Bank, for example, has included self-analysis as one of the central tenets of its corruption prevention strategy. Other promotional strategies could include educational seminars and dissemination of research findings.

Conclusions

This chapter has suggested specific areas within the health sector that are most vulnerable to corruption. Priority areas of concern include procurement and distribution of drugs and equipment, and informal economic activities of health workers. These areas not only account for large losses in resources, but also have the most direct effects on health in terms of reductions in quality of care and access to services, especially for poor segments of the population. The chapter has also argued that corruption prevention strategies in the health sector should link with health reforms and initiatives in other sectors, and efforts must be made to convince health policy decision makers and frontline health workers that something can be done about corruption.

Finally, the chapter has revealed several areas where further research is needed.

- *Assessing Corruption in the Health Sector.* More research should be done to develop tools and methods to assess corruption in the health sector. For example, World Bank corruption surveys and other data sources could be mined for health-specific findings regarding the disproportionate impacts of corruption on the poor. The refined methods and tools could be used to document the extent and costs of corruption in accreditation systems, food and drug regulation, and other areas described in Table 4.1 (not covered in this chapter) and to broaden and deepen the analysis of the two areas included in this chapter (i.e., procurement and informal payments).

- *Corruption and User Fees.* Misappropriation of fee revenue was estimated to be 68 percent to 77 percent in Uganda. Is this range typical of what most user fee systems experience? What role do improved accounting systems and civic oversight structures play in reducing revenue loss? How scaleable are these types of solutions?

- *National Health Accounts and Other Data Sets as Anticorruption Tools.* How can National Health Accounts (NHA) data be used to improve accountability and transparency in health sector spending, identify problem areas or set standards? What other sets of data exist, and how have they been used to detect and draw attention to resource allocation/misallocation concerns? What are the technical and political issues that must be addressed before NHA or other data sets can be used as anticorruption tools?

- *Performance-based Financing Mechanisms.* The health sector seems to raise particular challenges in applying performance-based mechanisms. For example, there is a risk that performance-based financing for health results in health care needs not being met, or too much focus on easy-to-quantify indicators to the exclusion of important health activities that are harder to measure. How can performance-based financing mechanisms be structured to minimize negative health effects while retaining incentives for achievement? Can low-cost verification systems be made corruption-resistant? How have these challenges been managed in practice?

- *Global Funds and Corruption.* Global funds are already having a large impact on the budgets of the poorest countries and will need special vigilance. What are countries doing now to address the potential for corruption in these large-scale public-private partnerships? How are Country Coordination Mechanisms increasing transparency and accountability in practice, and how will they interact with Local Fund Agents? What measures should be used to evaluate the effectiveness of these different initiatives over time?

- *Targeting and Sequencing of Anticorruption Strategies.* What do we know about effective targeting and sequencing of strategies for preventing and curing corruption in the health sector? Should anticorruption strategies be targeted to the youth who may be more willing to change? What are the key factors that influence people's behavior *vis-à-vis* corruption and adopting anticorruption behaviors? Behavioral change models can be used to identify the extent to which people are influenced by personal beliefs, perceptions of what others are doing, and beliefs about personal control. This information can then inform the targeting and sequencing of anticorruption efforts.

Notes

1. The following people were interviewed and contributed to the development of the ideas in this chapter: Karen Cavanaugh and Anthony Boni, USAID; Richard Laing, Rich Feeley, and Kris Heggenhougen, Boston University School of Public Health; Ron O'Connor, Management Sciences for Health; Marc Mitchell and Peter Berman, Harvard School of Public Health. I am grateful to reviewers Mark Austin, Forest Duncan, Michael Johnston, Jerry O'Brien, Madalene O'Donnell, and Stephen Schwenke for helpful comments on earlier drafts of this chapter.

2. Johnston acknowledges that defining corruption is a complex issue, especially who gets to decide the meaning of "public," "private," "abuse," and "illegitimate."

3. See Azfar's chapter later in this book, where he summarizes evidence regarding the relationship between corruption and health outcomes. Although many methodological problems exist, Azfar reports that some studies have shown a significant negative impact of corruption on health indicators such as infant and child mortality, even after adjustments for income, female education, public health spending and urbanization.

4. This table is adapted from Vian (2002), with added components from interviews conducted for this paper. Klitgaard, Maclean-Abaroa, and Lindsey use a similar format to present issues of corruption in procurement at the municipal government level in their book *Corrupt Cities* (2000).

5. This topic is certainly of concern; however, it may be more an issue of ethics than corruption. For more on informed consent and research ethics issues, see: Angell (2000), Fitzgerald et al. (2002), and Niels Lynoe et al., (2001). For further discussion of the pharmaceutical industry's role in sponsored medical research, see Henry and Lexchin (2002) and Coyle (2002).

6. Diversion of budgets and resource-flow problems have been documented by Riitva Reinikka and Jakob Svensson in the World Bank-supported study "Assessing Frontline Service Delivery" (2002). Reinikka and Svensson use data from two types of surveys, the public expenditure tracking survey (PETS) and the quantitative service delivery survey (QSDS) to quantify resource leakage and other problems in Uganda, Tanzania, Ghana and Honduras. Findings include 41 percent leakage of the non-wage health budget in Tanzania as it passes from the central level down to the facility level; in Ghana the situation was even worse with only twenty percent of non-wage health spending reaching the frontline facilities where it was intended to be spent.

7. Peter Berman refers to these issues more broadly as "health care delivery rent seeking and pursuit of opportunities for private profit through or as part of public service" (personal interview, October 31, 2002).

8. Management Sciences for Health, *Managing Drug Supply* (1997). MSH discusses promotional activities of pharmaceutical companies as one factor influencing drug use (pp. 450–463). I have pulled out this topic as a separate function, due to the strong potential for undue influence and corruption.

9. Rose-Ackerman presents arguments by Steven Kelman, former director of the US Office of Federal Procurement Policy during the Clinton administration, who favored negotiated procurement with increased flexibility and outcome-based accountability for procurement officials. Although Rose-Ackerman believes that the US experience may have some lessons for developing countries, she notes that Kelman's reforms may not work in a climate of "grand" (high level) corruption. According to Rose-Ackerman, approaches that increase the competitiveness of the market, rather than the procurement process alone, might be more valuable for lower income countries (Rose-Ackerman, pp. 60–68).

10. Informal payments are considered separately from the theft or diversion and resale of drugs (mentioned in the previous section), though in practice it can sometimes be hard to distinguish these types of corruption.

11. The increase in informal payments in Russia is a problem that must be seen in the broad context of economic and health sector reform, including problems of oversupply of physicians, low wages, and very low levels of health spending. See Cashin and Feeley (2002) for more on this topic.

12. Peter Berman, personal communication, October 31, 2002.

13. Ibid.

14. Bures (2002). Available at: http://worldbank.org/poverty/empowerment/toolsprac/tools 16.pdf. Accessed November 24, 2002. Report cards have been used in Bangalore, India, Ukraine, and the Philippines, in addition to the United States and other Western countries.

15. PETS (public expenditure tracking survey), QSDS (quantitative service delivery survey), DHS (demographic and health survey). Reinikka and Svensson (2002, p. 21) note that when survey data from Uganda documenting leakages of funds became public knowledge, government officials implemented a number of reforms including the publishing of monthly transfers of public funds to the districts in the mass media and requiring facilities to post information on inflowing funds, thus increasing transparency and public accountability.

16. Web site: http://www.phrproject.com/.

17. Web site: http://dcc2.bumc.bu.edu/RussianLegalHealthReform. Accessed November 25, 2002.

18. Web site: http://www.phrproject.com/globali/nha.htm. Accessed November 25, 2002.

Chapter 5

Education

David W. Chapman

National education systems across the developing world are particularly vulnerable to pervasive corruption, largely for three reasons. First, as one of the few governmental units with high visibility representation all the way down to the community level, education is an attractive structure for patronage and manipulation of local sentiment. Second, decisions perceived to have significant consequences for people's lives are made by "gatekeepers" who control decisions at each of those levels (e.g., district education officers, headmasters, teachers). Third, a considerable amount of education funds is spent in small amounts, across many scattered sites, most of which have weak accounting and monitoring systems. Although there are ample examples of large-scale corruption within central education ministries, this chapter argues that the most serious consequences arise from the pervasive, petty corruption that permeates the day-to-day transactions at the classroom, school, and district levels. The real damage to a society occurs when entire generations of youth are miseducated—by example—to believe that personal success comes not through merit and hard work but through favoritism, bribery, and fraud. Widespread petty corruption breaks the link between personal effort and anticipation of reward. This, in turn, limits economic and social development well beyond the immediate corruption. Such lessons have the potential to undermine civil society well into the future.[1]

Vulnerabilities to Corruption in the Education Sector

How Is Corruption Manifested in the Education Sector?

One of the central problems in combating corruption is the difficulty in clearly defining the behaviors that constitute it. Five behaviors may be labeled, at different times, as corruption:

1. *Blatantly illegal acts of bribery or fraud.* There are many examples of blatant fraud and bribery, in which education officials at all levels demand some form of payoff for themselves, family or friends in return for their help in shaping the outcome of contracts, implementation efforts, distribution systems, and so forth. Although mechanisms may vary, there is wide agreement that these practices are corrupt.

2. *Actions taken to secure a modest income by people paid too little or too late.* When teachers sell grades or require students to pay for private tutoring in order to pass a course, most observers recognize it as corruption. Often, however, such behavior is judged less harshly in settings in which teachers' salaries are extremely low or salary payments are delayed for months. It tends to be tolerated because virtually all observers recognize that teachers have little choice if they are to survive. In some countries, such as Cambodia, these practices are tacitly condoned by government, which recognizes that it could not maintain a teaching force if teachers were unable to subsidize their salaries, even if they use practices that compromise the quality of education.

3. *Actions taken to get work done in difficult circumstances.* At times, what appears as corruption may be better understood as ministry

and project personnel cutting corners, ignoring rules, and bypassing procedures in order to move activities forward in ways important to the success of a project or ministry initiative. What appears as corruption to some people may be viewed as pragmatic project management by others. For instance, when project implementation requires government staff to work harder or longer hours than is their custom, a project manager may pay an unauthorized bonus as an incentive. Similarly, a project manager may pay government personnel to provide data that should be free. An unfortunate outgrowth of these practices is that it often teaches local staff that they can extort money by withholding services, and a pattern develops. Nonetheless, failure of the project manager to take these actions could undercut project success.

4. *Differences in cultural perspective (e.g., gift giving).* In some cultures, it is customary and expected that gifts are given even in return for small favors. Although token gifts of little monetary value often satisfy, the practice has sometimes mushroomed into widespread petty extortion. The practice of gift giving has often been exploited to mask a corrupt practice in the disguise of a cultural expectation. This is illustrated by the case of a Chinese student who, needing the signature of a local official in order to secure a passport to study abroad, offered a new television set to the official to thank him for his signature. In Russia, it is commonplace to provide small gifts—a box of candy, flowers (or a bottle of vodka)—to authorities as a token of respect, if not a request for special assistance.

5. *Behavior resulting from incompetence.* What appears to be corruption is sometimes merely the incompetence of key actors or the inadequacies of the infrastructure in which they work. When recordkeeping systems are weak or nonexistent, key personnel assign little importance to maintaining records. It is then often difficult to know whether education officials' inability to account for money or supplies reflects deception or poor management practices. For example, despite the expenditure of several million dollars of donor funds on textbook production and distribution in Laos and government receipts indicating the books had been delivered to the district education offices, international teams were unable to locate very many of the new books during site visits to the schools. It was never completely clear whether this was a case of poor recordkeeping or diversion of textbook funds (Asian Development Bank, 2000b).

The essential point is that thoughtful, reasonable people can disagree over what constitutes corruption. Even when observers agree that certain actions constitute corruption, they may differ in their tolerance of the offense (e.g., when the sale of grades is tolerated because teachers are underpaid). Moreover, those forms most widely condemned (e.g., contract kickbacks) tend to be the least visible; those forms that tend to be the most visible (e.g., forced private tutoring) tend to be the most widely tolerated. The annex presents a wide array of transactions in the education sector by which corruption is manifested.

What Are the Costs and Consequences of Corruption?

The most direct, and in some ways the most inconsequential, cost of corruption is the waste of the financial resources that get misdirected. The more serious costs are incurred when (a) children unable to afford bribes are denied access to schooling, (b) talent is misallocated due to promotion being awarded on the basis of bribery rather than merit, and (c) a generation of children come to believe that personal effort and merit do not count and that success comes through manipulation, favoritism and bribery. When corruption is so pervasive that it comes to be viewed as a basic mechanism of social and economic interaction, it instills a value that is highly destructive to the social and economic development of a country.

How Prevalent Is Corruption in the Education Sector?

Several organizations, like Transparency International, have developed corruption perception indices that purport to rank countries in terms of the extent of corruption. However, objective estimates of the prevalence of corruption specific to the education sector are hard to determine. Anecdotal evidence suggests that, while corruption is present in the education system of many countries, it is widespread in some countries of South and Southeast Asia and endemic in many countries of the former Soviet Union and Africa. Table 5.1 provides some insight into the pervasiveness of corruption. Across 17 countries, the percentage of citizens who believe corruption is widespread ranged from 1 percent to 53 percent, with about half the countries in the 20 percent to 40 percent range. The highest percentages of educators who report being asked for a bribe were in Southeast Asia (e.g., Bangladesh, Cambodia, Indonesia).

What Forms Does Corruption Take in the Education Sector?

Corruption can occur at any point in a system where decisions are made that have meaningful consequences for individuals. In the education sector that means it can happen at virtually every level, from the central ministry down to the school and classroom. It can happen any time educators operate as gatekeepers to real or assumed benefits. As education is widely viewed as access to life opportunity, higher lifetime earnings, and greater social mobility, even seemingly small decisions are often awarded great value.

Table 5.1. Perceptions of Pervasiveness of Corruption in Education (Selected Countries)

	% who perceive corruption is widespread among:			% who have been asked for bribe by:		
Country	University Professors	Teachers	Within the education sector in general	University Professors	Teachers	Education professionals in general
Albania	32	10		28	11	
Bangladesh						74
Bosnia	38	22	38	11	5	
Bulgaria	28	10		14	4	
Cambodia						41
Croatia	31	16		5	2	
Ghana						24
Honduras			2			
Indonesia			53			24
Latvia			1			
Macedonia	43	23		14	9	
Montenegro	32	21		10	6	
Peru	18					7
Romania	22	18		13	15	
Russia			20	16	6	
Serbia	42	33		27	20	
Slovakia			38			

Sources: Regional Corruption Monitoring (Vitosha Research, 2002); Diagnostic Surveys of Corruption in Bosnia and Herzegovina (World Bank, 2000); Corruption Indexes of Coalition 2000 (May 2002); Cambodia Governance and Corruption Diagnostic (World Bank, 2000); Corruption in Bangladesh Surveys (Transparency International Bangladesh, 2002); Ghana Governance and Corruption Survey (World Bank, 2000); Governance and Anti-Corruption in Honduras (World Bank Institute, 2002); Diagnostic Study of Corruption in Indonesia (Partnership for Governance Reform, 2002); Corruption in Latvia (World Bank, 1998); Voices of the Misgoverned and Misruled: Peru (World Bank, 2001) Diagnostic Survey of Corruption in Romania (World Bank, 2001); Corruption in Slovakia (World Bank, 2000); Corruption in Tomsk Oblast, Russia (Management Systems International, 2001).

Gatekeepers at different levels of the education system introduce corruption around the particular opportunities and benefits they control. Their motivation is often economic—to supplement their income—but may also be an effort to extend their status or power, create future career opportunities, or conform to expectations of those whose patronage they seek. Table 5.2 illustrates the types of corruption that can occur at different levels of the education system. At the central ministry levels, much of the corruption involves the diversion of funds associated with procurement, construction, and allocation to lower levels of the system. At intermediate levels of the education bureaucracy, the corruption tends

Table 5.2 Common Forms of Corruption in the Education Sector, by Level of the Education System

Level of Activity	Type of Behavior
Central Ministry	Kickback on construction and supply contracts
	Favoritism in hiring, appointments, and promotions decisions
	Diversion of funds from government accounts
	Diversion of funds from international assistance funds
	Ghost teachers and employees
	Requiring payment for services that should be provided free
	Withholding needed approvals and signatures to extort bribes (e.g., gifts, favors, outright payments)
	Directing the location of construction and services to locations that offer opportunities for gain by oneself, family, or friends
	Requiring the use of materials as a way of creating a market for items on which oneself, family or friends hold an import or production monopoly
Region/district	Overlooking school violations on inspector visits in return for bribes or favors
	Diversion of school supplies to private market
	Sales of recommendations for higher education entrance
	Favoritism in personnel appointments (e.g., headmasters, teachers)
School level	Ghost teachers
	Diversion of school fees
	Inflation of school enrollment data (in countries in which central ministry funds are allocated to school on basis of enrollment)
	Imposition of unauthorized fees
	Diversion of central Ministry of Education funds allocated to schools
	Diversion of monies in revolving textbook fund
	Diversion of community contributions
Classroom/teacher level	Siphoning of school supplies and textbooks to local market
	Selling test scores and course grades
	Selling change of grade
	Selling grade-to-grade promotion
	Selling admissions (especially to higher education)
	Creating the necessity for private tutoring
	Teachers' persistent absenteeism to accommodate other income producing work
International agencies	Payment of bribes
	Payment of excessive or unnecessary fees to obtain services
	Skimming from project funds
	Allocating (or acquiescing in the allocation of) project-related opportunities on the basis of candidates' connections rather than on merit

to center on procurement, diversion of money and supplies on their way to the schools, and bribes from educators lower in the system seeking to secure opportunity or avoid punishment. At the school level, corruption tends to center on bribes from parents to ensure student access, good grades, grade progression, and graduation. However, it also takes the form of teacher absenteeism—teachers collecting salaries but not providing the intended instruction.

Educators at the school level also can divert funds, school supplies, and sometimes food that the schools receive from community or government sources. Headmasters and teachers are also in a position to assess unauthorized fees for real or imaginary services (e.g., paper fees in order to take a exam), create the need for private tutoring, or take salaries for work not actually done.

Responses to Corruption in the Education Sector

Corruption is not inevitable and corruption is not a life sentence for a country or government. A key factor influencing differing corruption levels across countries and within the same country over time is the *quality of top leadership*. Leaders who respect the rule of law, emphasize transparency in the operation of the offices they oversee, take action against subordinates found violating rules, and exhibit integrity in their own transactions can make a difference. Honest leaders can be a powerful force in reducing corruption. Conversely, when top leadership is corrupt, they lack the moral platform to demand honesty in others.

Implementing honest practices can be tricky, possibly dangerous, even for highly committed leaders. In some cultures, it is widely understood that one of the benefits of public office is the opportunity to accrue personal wealth through manipulation of the system. Appointments to senior government positions are granted as rewards, a recognition that the appointee has earned a turn to loot. Just as incentives, when commonplace, loose their value, corrupt practices, when pervasive, become the norm. Those not participating may be considered naïve, odd, or stupid, even by those who suffer the negative consequences. Consequently, effective leadership that targets corruption often requires considerable personal courage. Leaders have to withstand criticism and overt opposition from colleagues who see their own self-interest threatened by the introduction of practices that emphasize transparency and accountability.

In some cases, senior officials fear retaliation by colleagues who are intent on protecting their income and influence. At lower levels of management, some fear they will lose their jobs if they do not participate in, or at least cover-up, the corrupt practices that may be going on around them. They confront a lead-or-bullets dilemma: they can participate and enjoy the fruits of their illicit gain or they can resist and risk professional and even personal injury. Nonetheless, the commitment of top leadership to the honest operation of the education system (e.g., greater transparency, introduction of a code of conduct) remains a central component in minimizing corrupt practices.

A second factor to consider in minimizing corruption is that educators and government officials need a *clear code of conduct*. This may originate in a country's administrative or criminal code or be introduced by professional associations or unions. For example, in the United States, every state has a teachers' code of conduct. Teachers who violate it can lose their teaching license. At the same time, professional organizations have codes of conduct that apply to the specific activities promoted by those organizations.

Educators need to know what behaviors might constitute corrupt practices, especially when proper professional conduct might run counter to social norms widely accepted outside of the education workplace. A code of conduct would, for example, clarify the propriety of and set limits on accepting gifts in return for professional actions, even though gift giving may be considered appropriate in other social settings. However, codes of conduct alone do little to reduce corruption unless there are effective means of communication, clear sanctions for violating the codes, consistent enforcement, and top-level support.

A third factor in minimizing corruption is the *creation or modification of organizational structures* and administrative procedures aimed at breaking the grip of entrenched practices.[2] A key element in this is a *clear and workable accountability system*. To be effective, an accountability system must clearly state the rules and procedures associated with managing the education system, provide a mechanism for monitoring compliance, specify the consequences for non-compliance, and be consistent in enforcement. Box 5A illustrates how the creation of a new organizational structure helped reduce corruption in higher education in Azerbaijan.

Box 5A. Successful practices in reducing corruption: Azerbaijan

Faced with rampant corruption in admissions to higher education, the Government of Azerbaijan took admissions authority away from universities and vested it with a newly created State Student Admissions Committee (Guluzadeh et al., 2002). This committee now oversees the development and administration of a national university entrance examination and subsequent selection of candidates for places in all public universities. Although broadly opposed by the universities, this committee is widely credited with significantly reducing corruption in university admissions.

Ironically, some accountability systems, intended to reduce corruption, sometimes fuel more corruption. Efforts to legislate corruption out of existence can backfire and inadvertently engender problems that are worse than those initially being addressed. This occurs when a government's response to corruption is to add rules aimed at eliminating particular undesirable practices or behaviors in a piecemeal manner. As the number of rules grow and multiply, the rules can interact in unanticipated ways, operate at cross-purposes, and ultimately stifle legitimate reform.

This was illustrated in pre-civil war Liberia. Given the complexity and corruption in the process of getting teachers hired to replace teachers who died or left teaching (new teachers needed twenty-nine official signatures to get on the payroll), headmasters were allowed to appoint temporary substitutes and let them cash the paychecks of the teachers they replaced. Principals quickly realized that they could cash these paychecks and keep the money, without bothering to appoint a replacement teacher. This eventually led to a high incidence of "ghost teachers" (USAID, 1988). When district and central officials realized what was happening, instead of trying to eliminate the practice, they demanded a cut of the proceeds. Moreover, when the World Bank introduced a new education management information system (EMIS) in an effort to help strengthen management capacity, education leaders feared that improved school level data would expose the fraud. Though initially successful, the EMIS died within two years as headmasters refused to provide accurate school level data in annual school surveys (Chapman, 1991, pp. 133–143). Despite these disheartening occurrences, there are examples of successful transparency programs from various developing and transitional countries (see Boxes 5B and 5C).

Box 5B. Successful practices in reducing corruption: Uganda

With World Bank support, the Uganda government conducted an audit of actual enrollments and funding flows in schools. Funds actually received by the schools were compared to the amounts disbursed by the central government plus the amounts collected from fees assessed at the local level. The audit discovered major leakages of money. For example, only 13 percent of funds allocated for nonsalary items like textbooks and supplies reached the schools. To promote transparency and fix the problem, all fund transfers to district education offices were published in the newspapers and broadcast on radio. Each primary school was required to post a public notice of all inflows of funds to the schools. Results were impressive. Within three years, 90 percent of nonsalary funds provided by the central government were reaching the schools (Siller, n.d.).

Box 5C. Successful practices in reducing corruption: Russia

In Russia, schools typically request money from parents each year supposedly to enhance educational programs, repair/maintain school buildings, and obtain equipment and supplies, and so forth. Technically, such requests are not legal. Parents typically comply, fearing retribution toward their children. There is little or no feedback to parents on how these out-of-budget funds are actually used or managed on a school-by-school basis. Under small grants to NGOs in Samara and Tomsk, Russia, in 2002, an activity was initiated to assess parental attitudes and to work with particular school districts to make the planning and expenditure of these budgets more transparent and generate more parent participation in the

---

Box 5C. (continued)

budgeting process. As a result of extensive lobbying with school administrations, the out-of-budget funds in several schools are now open and transparent, and parents are getting involved in how the monies should be spent (Management Systems International, 2003).

Accountability systems can only operate in the context of *laws promoting transparency.* These laws have an impact on reducing corruption only when two other conditions are met. The first is the operation of a *free press* that can utilize these laws to help expose questionable practices. Only as evidence of inappropriate practices is widely available can a critical mass of public concern be mobilized. The second condition is the engagement of citizens willing to push for honesty in the operation of the education system. Within the education system, citizen involvement can consist of parent-teacher associations organized around specific schools or community advisory groups organized by local NGOs. Box 5D presents an example of the impact of increased transparency on teacher deployment.

Box 5D. Successful practices in reducing corruption: Gambia

The introduction of an education management information system in Gambia helped reduce the role of favoritism in teacher assignments. The EMIS provided an objective means of tracking and ranking teachers by seniority, language abilities, subject specialization, and other factors that were supposed to be used in assigning teachers to schools. The availability of this information constrained the assignment of teachers on the basis of such factors as family connections, personal friendships, or other forms of personal influence (Department of State for Education of Gambia, 2001).

Although *community engagement* and collective community action can play an important role in fighting corruption, such action can be difficult to foster. Success depends on the perceived benefits of reducing corruption as opposed to the costs community members may incur for their efforts. However, for community engagement to be effective, it often needs to be supported *by community level training.* Citizens frequently lack experience in how to hold their local schools accountable for effective financial and personnel management. For example, a recent study of parent perceptions of effective schools in Ghana found that many parents considered a school to be effective if strict student discipline was maintained and no one complained about the school (Chapman et al., 2002, pp. 181–189). Community members had little knowledge of other dimensions on which they might judge their local school. Such training should be aimed at helping community members understand (a) the characteristics of an effective school, (b) what headmaster and teacher behaviors they should look for in assessing the effectiveness of those educators, (c) their own legal rights as parents and community members in addition to information about school budgets, expenditures, procedures, and operational decisions, and (d) the sanctions they as community members can bring to bear on under-performing schools. An example of where citizens have been able to work effectively in monitoring school practices is presented in Box 5E.

Box 5E. Successful practices in reducing corruption: Indonesia[4]

In some countries, the handling of community-generated funds for the local schools is highly susceptible to corruption. In Indonesia, however, these funds are often allocated with minimum corruption, due to the involvement of the parent association in deciding how these funds are to be used and in monitoring to ensure that the funds reach their intended destination. At the beginning of the school year, representatives of the parent association meet with school officials to establish a plan for how community-generated funds will be used. School officials provide detailed accounting of expenditures to the parent association during the year. The system works because (a) the use of these funds is highly structured, (b) expenditures are highly transparent, and (c) the community attaches considerable importance and pride to the success of this scheme.

In some countries, the operation of NGOs has been effective in helping to minimize corruption.[3] However, in some countries, a number of development-oriented NGOs sprang into existence solely as a means of capturing development funds, sometimes led by individuals more interested in money than development. As more funds have been routed through NGOs, there is growing evidence in some countries that NGOs can be just as corrupt as governments.

Where corruption is a symptom of a structural or operational flaw in the education system, governments and international agencies are unlikely to suppress it with more laws, at least until they have *addressed the underlying problems* that fuel the behavior. This may require efforts to *change the incentive systems* that fuel corruption. It is likely that corruption motivated by insatiable greed, arrogance, and blind self-interest may be influenced by some convergence of the strategies discussed above. However, it is also likely that the most insidious types of corruption in the education system—the petty corruption that shapes the day-to-day experience of students and their families—are driven by more complicated dynamics.

For example, as previously pointed out, corrupt practices are sometimes perpetrated by teachers who are severely underpaid or whose salaries have not been paid for months. Their corruption may be interpreted by some as a reasonable adaptive response to a difficult situation. At one level, it is easy to be sympathetic. However, it is this very type of petty corruption—and what it teaches students—that poses the greatest risk to the long-term fabric of a society. Regardless of one's sympathies for teachers' motivation in turning to corrupt practices, once started, these practices are difficult to eliminate. Although low salaries motivate teacher corruption, raising salaries does not necessarily reduce that corruption (Di Tella and Schargrodsky, 2002). Raising salaries is a necessary but not a sufficient intervention to reduce corruption, once entrenched.

Potential Donor Complicity in Corruption

International agencies that provide development assistance funds sometimes are not without culpability in the corruption evident in some education systems. Three forms of complicity are of particular concern:

1. Donors often overlook corruption in education when there were larger strategic political interests at stake. For example, when the United States is cultivating a country's defenses in the fight against terrorism or drugs or attempting to secure their participation in a coalition to support a regional peace plan or the rights to house a military base in the country, senior diplomats often do not want their efforts derailed by attention to corruption in what they may consider an area of marginal concern. Examples abound. American support was given to Barre in Somalia, Marcos in the Philippines, and Doe in Liberia even though US officials were aware of corrupt practices in the use of American development assistance funds. Few, if any diplomats questioned the prevalence of corruption at senior levels in those countries, but other, more strategic, considerations prevailed. Much can be done to reduce corruption in the use of development assistance in the developing world, but only if the donor state is willing to risk relationships and arrangements that may be crucial to other aspects of its agenda in these countries.

2. Money flow that exceeds absorptive capacity creates conditions that fuel corruption. When large amounts of money are infused into an education system that lacks sufficient numbers of trained personnel, clear procedures for handling the funds, or workable financial monitoring systems, both intentional and unintentional misallocation of funds is easy. One way to reduce corruption is to better align the flow of development assistance with capacity to effectively manage those funds and the project activities those funds buy.

3. International contractors seeking to minimize corruption in the projects they manage are caught in a conflict of interests. There are few incentives for contractors to fight corruption and there

can be very real costs if they try. Contractors who refuse to over-look or condone petty corruption of counterpart staff often encounter resistance and delays in implementation that reflect badly on their companies and on them personally. If these delays impede progress toward project objectives, home companies may incur financial penalties within donors' performance-based payment systems. At a personal level, they may be seen as inef-fective in managing their projects, a problem that can cost proj-ect managers their jobs. In short, those responsible for project implementation have few incentives and clear disincentives for resisting petty corruption.

As donor groups come to view corruption as a major impediment to sus-tainable progress in education development, they need to reconsider their own practices that overlook or tacitly condone it. They need to be willing to pay the price of enforcing rules aimed at minimizing corruption, even if this means withdrawing from important programs, risking important relationships, and jeopardizing the flow of assistance to innocent beneficiaries. Until international agencies are willing to incur these costs, they may continue to give a confused message that is not easy for aid recipients to ignore.

Annex. Corruption in education: What does it look like? How does it work?

Examples from the field:

- An underpaid teacher, to make ends meet, charges students a "paper fee" in order for them to take the end-of-year national examination for their grade. Students must pass this test in order to progress to the next grade.

- The director general of secondary education insists that transportation is a necessary condition for a donor-sponsored secondary education project to succeed. Once purchased, the Jeep was assigned by the min-istry to the personal use of the director general.

- A teacher training college was purchasing far more food than seemed necessary for the number of students enrolled. Staff were siphoning supplies for their personal use, justifying it because they had not been paid for four months.

- To be officially hired as a teacher, a person needed to secure signatures from seventeen different offices across four different ministries. The people whose signatures were needed each expected a gift in return for their signature.

- The director general for vocational education insists that the new technical training center be located in a particular town of his choice. Within that town, the local elders insist that the center be built in a specific location, even though the land was very expensive and not

---

Annex. (continued)

particularly convenient for the children. Later it becomes clear that the location was owned by the director general's brother-in-law.

- A district school inspector, while visiting a rural district, found the school seriously out of compliance with several ministry regulations. The headmaster was concerned that the inspector's report could seriously damage his career. That evening, the headmaster brought a goat to the inspector's guesthouse. After discussing the issue and exchanging the goat, the inspector decided that no report was necessary.

- An international adviser "borrows" money in a dollar-denominated project bank account, converts the money to local currency on the black market, then converts the money back to dollars using the official exchange rate. He returns the dollars to the project account and pockets the difference.

- The staff in the statistics office of the ministry insists that international consultants pay a fee for the enrollment and school data they need, even though the data is for a project sponsored by a different office in the same ministry. The consultant complains to the deputy minister. The deputy minister tells the statistics office to provide the data. The consultant receives the data, but it is incomplete and full of errors, even though the consultant knows the correct data are available.

Notes

1. This study benefited greatly by discussions with the following individuals: Tracy Atwood, Resident Representative, USAID, Almaty, Kazakhstan (personal conversation); Kimberly Bolyard, Office of Education, Bureau for Economic Growth, Agriculture and Trade, USAID (e-mail); Marc Cohen, Senior Education Specialist, Asian Development Bank, Manila, Philippines (personal conversation); Patrick Collins, USAID/W (phone conversation, e-mail); Todd Drummon Country Director, American Councils for International Education, Bishkek, Kyrgyz Republic (personal conversation); Ann Dykstra, WID Office, USAID/W (phone conversation, Email); Jon Gore, Deputy Director, British Council, Almaty, Kazakhstan (personal conversation); David Heesen, USAID (e-mail); Jane Hutton, Deputy Director, Education Support Program, Open Society Institute, Budapest, Hungary (personal conversation); Jessica Leonard, Education Specialist, USAID, Almaty, Kazakhstan (personal conversation); Malcolm Mercer, Education Consultant, Wales, UK (personal conversation); Michael Mertaugh, Lead Education Economist, Europe and Central Asia Region, World Bank. (personal conversation); Yolande Miller-Gradvaux, Education Advisor, USAID/Africa Bureau/SD/ED, AED/SARA (e-mail); Madelene O'Donnell, USAID/W (personal conversation); and Donald Siller, USAID/W (e-mail).

2. Decentralization is often advocated as a strategy for reducing corruption at central levels of government. However, this is a point of considerable controversy. Some argue that decentralization does little to reduce corruption and only serves to push it to lower levels of the education system. See Chapman (2000).

3. For good discussions of NGOs, see Edwards (1999); Bies, Moore, and DeJaeghere (2000); Bartlett, (2000); DeJaegher (2000); Sweetser (1997).

4. Personal communication with M. Mertaugh; World Bank, and World Bank (1990).

Chapter 6

Public Finance

Michael Schaeffer

Good governance and effective public finance are the two most important vehicles for establishing a country's economic and social priorities within the scarce resources that are available to government. Although good economic and financial management in the public sector stimulates the promotion of efficient institutions that are responsive to the public interest, as well as social and economic equity, corruption in public financial management can yield rapid deterioration of governance.

What is corruption as applied to public finance? There are many different definitions of this concept. The simplest, and broadest, definition of corruption is "the misuse of public or private position for direct or indirect personal gain" (OECD, 2001, p. 447). Various factors contribute to corruption (Tanzi, 1998). Some of these factors have a direct impact, whereas others only an indirect impact. The factors that have a direct impact include: regulations and authorizations; complex tax systems; government spending decisions; public provision of goods and services at below market prices[1]; and situations in which public employees have discretionary power over economic decisions (ADB, 1999, p. 6). Among the indirect causes of corruption must be included the professionalism of the civil service; the level of public wages; institutional controls; the transparency of rules, laws, and processes; and the severity of the penalty system if caught (ADB, 1999, p. 6). The following sections will discuss in some detail the relationship between public revenue and public expenditure in relation to governance in general and corruption in particular.

Corruption Impacts on Public Finance

The Fiscal Dimension

To perform the roles assigned to it by its citizens, the government (national and subnational) needs to collect resources from the economy in an efficient and appropriate manner, and allocate those resources responsively and efficiently. An important dimension in assessing the extent and efficiency of public finance is how the authority to tax and spend is distributed between the central (national) and local government. This raises a complicated set of issues because there are many different types of taxes, types of expenditures, and ways in which (economic) jurisdictions can be defined. In addition, tax expenditure assignments can be divided among different jurisdictions.

Particular types of governmental activities often create fertile ground for corruption. In this section, the fiscal aspects of governmental functioning are reviewed, specifically, incentive effects of fiscal decentralization, taxation, public expenditures, and the general provision of goods and services.

Incentive Effects of Fiscal Decentralization. The governance outcomes of decentralization efforts largely depend on the design of the fiscal transfers from the central government. These fiscal transfers take many forms, including block, conditional and matching grants and the assignment of shares of taxes collected by the central government (revenue sharing taxes). The variety of central government transfers and tax sharing schemes brings with it an equally wide array of incentive effects. Discretionary transfers frequently depend on the loyalty of lower level government officials. As a result, discretionary transfers may tend to strengthen the patronage networks of national political systems.

In many developing countries, grants and political mandates arise from centrally or nationally determined policy priorities. The centrally determined priorities may advance national priorities equally across the country. Sometimes these centrally driven priorities may deviate from, conflict with, or distort the political and fiscal initiatives that are being driven at the local level. Fiscal policy distortions between central and locally driven priorities usually create incentives for corruption.

Taxation. Good governance and public financial management requires taxes that are based on clearly written laws and do not require frequent contacts between taxpayers and tax administrators. The decentralization of fiscal responsibilities may create coordination problems with respect to tax rates and overlapping tax bases. One problem with overlapping tax bases is that the tax rate set by each layer of government creates vertical externalities by reducing the tax base of the other layer (Gordan, 1983, p. 321). Competition between the two layers may lead to tax rates that are too high. In this instance, the vertical externality may lead to increases in tax avoidance schemes.[2]

Tax Assignment: Revenue Sharing. It is generally recognized that assigning all or most taxation power to subnational governments with upward revenue sharing is not advisable, since such an arrangement does not allow the central government to perform its redistribution and macroeconomic roles. This arrangement however is carried out in a few countries, such as China. Upward revenue sharing is considered viable in loose confederations where stabilization and redistribution policies lie with the member states, as well as in countries where subnational jurisdictions have homogenous economic conditions and close tax policy coordination and harmonization (i.e., Germany).

On the other hand, assigning all taxation power to the central government and relying entirely on downward transfers to local governments is equally undesirable. The arrangement inhibits local governments from matching spending authority with revenue-raising power, hence reducing their fiscal accountability. Some countries completely separate the tax bases for each level of subnational governments, while others allow certain overlaps. Tiers of government in Australia and India have separate tax bases, while Canada and the United States have a certain degree of overlap.

Criteria for Tax Assignment. In decentralized tax systems, tax policies must be coordinated between jurisdictions to avoid distortion in the free movement of economic resources from one region to another. Such migration would cause jurisdictions to compete with one another through lower taxes or other inducements, and thus create an inefficient (possibly corrupt) fiscal system.

There should be rules for allocating tax revenues among jurisdictions to avoid double taxation or no taxation at all. Where tax bases are relatively mobile, decentralized tax assignment opens opportunities for tax avoidance and evasion. Taxes assigned to the central government should cover mobile tax bases, be sensitive to changes in income, and cover tax bases that are unevenly distributed across regions. Correspondingly, local taxes require a relatively immobile tax base, a stable and predictable tax yield, relatively easy administration, and an adequate tax yield to meet local needs and the buoyancy to grow at the same rate as expenditures.

Value Added Tax. Local administration of a value added tax is problematic, as each local government could set its own standard tax rates and methods of administration. There are also opportunities for local protectionism. Even if the value added tax (VAT) rate and base structure are determined by the central government, VAT proceeds should not be shared between levels of government; otherwise, some resource rich areas would benefit greatly, while others would collect little or no revenues. Nonetheless, the VAT is a subnational tax in Brazil (and in China), where the central and provincial governments share VAT proceeds on a derivation basis. Still, protectionist measures have been taken in some Chinese provinces (with the potential for increase in corruption). In Brazil, the decision to allow VAT as a subnational tax has lead to administrative problems and economic distortions. Overall, one useful way to funnel VAT proceeds to subnational governments is for the central government to administer and collect VAT and earmark a share of it for a distributable pool.

Corporate Income Tax. The corporate income tax must be levied by the central government since it fails all the tests of a good local tax; it imposes high compliance costs, generates incentives for tax avoidance and offers the opportunity to export the tax burden to other regions. Corporate income taxes are still levied at the subnational government level in many developing and transitional economies. Problems may not arise when businesses operate in a single province, but corruption issues will become more apparent once businesses begin to operate in more than one province.

Primary Areas of Tax Corruption. Taxes based on clear laws and not requiring direct contacts between taxpayers and tax inspectors are less likely to lead to acts of corruption (Tanzi, 1998, p. 567). Tanzi writes that corruption is likely to be a major problem in tax and customs administration, when laws are difficult to understand and can be interpreted differently so that taxpayers need assistance in complying with them. In addition, when the administrative procedures (e.g., the criteria for the selection of taxpayer audits) lack transparency and are not closely monitored within the tax or customs administrations, the potential for corruption is likely to increase. Most importantly, public sector corruption will be pervasive when acts of fraud on the part of the tax administrators are ignored, not easily discovered, or when discovered are penalized only mildly.

Tax and customs departments are often the locus of major fraud and corruption and thus are potential candidates for inclusion in national strategies to control corruption. Malfeasance in the tax and customs department can potentially be addressed by providing greater managerial freedom to the revenue agency (hiring and firing of personnel) and establishing decent pay levels for workers while at the same time subjecting the agency's performance to close scrutiny. By controlling theft, good financial management systems change the economics of bribery.[3]

Organizational restructuring of tax departments[4] and staff rotation can also help reduce the opportunities for corruption. Furthermore, supervisory oversight and control within the tax administration should be increased.[5] In other words, tax management supervisors should attest that they have scrutinized the work of their subordinates.

Computerization of Tax and Customs Administration. According to a World Bank technical note (2000c), computerization of tax and customs administration is an important element of capacity building and revenue administration. The most obvious benefit of computerization is more effective revenue collection due to better audit selection, easier detection of nonfilers, and faster payment and refund processing. Information technology can also increase the transparency of tax and customs administration, and thereby reduce corruption.

Tax computerization projects are effectively tax administration projects. Their timing depends on the status of legal and administrative reforms of the tax system. As a result, tax policy reforms during the installation of an information technology system can negatively affect the potential positive impacts of developing a computerized system. Ideally, tax computerization should follow and support tax policy reform.[6]

Tax Avoidance. The impact of corruption and tax evasion on tax collection is not new in the public finance literature. In a series of papers, Tanzi and Davoodi (1997) have provided evidence that countries with high levels of corruption tend to have lower collection of tax revenues in relation to gross domestic product (GDP). The implication is that some of the taxes paid by taxpayers are diverted (most likely to tax administrators). Tanzi (1999) argues that a distinction needs to be made between taxes collected by the tax administrators and taxes received by the treasury.

Low levels of taxation may lead to a high sub-optimal level of public spending (which may lead to higher fiscal deficits). In effect, tax corruption and tax avoidance may negatively impact economic growth through its effect on fiscal deficits (Tanzi, 1998, p. 16). Simplifying tax and tariff schedules and keeping rates at moderate levels thereby reduces the discretion of tax (and customs) staff and narrows the scope for corrupt payments.

Public Expenditures. Public expenditure management is instrumental to effective public service delivery and reducing public sector corruption. Access to information on the actions and performance of government expenditures is critical to achieving government accountability. Unless the public knows what goods and services are provided, how well they are provided, who the beneficiaries are, and how much they cost, it cannot demand (nor expect) effective government. To promote government accountability, government budgets and expenditure programs need to be disclosed to the public. However, many developing countries have weak or inadequate mechanisms for citizens to monitor actions of government.

Another mechanism that promotes transparency and accountability with respect to public finance is the periodic public sector audit. The public sector audit has proved to be effective in many developed countries (in the United States, Germany, and France, for example). Despite the effectiveness of this mechanism, many developing countries fail to utilize an independent public sector audit as a benchmark standard for enhancing public sector accountability.

A commonly used practice in many developing countries is a paper audit. In other words, there are no spot checks to verify the audit information and there may be blanket prohibitions imposed on releasing public sector audit information. As a result, audits in many developing countries become subject to bribes. The creation and existence in audit systems of physical audit requirements, sanctions for late submission or data manipulation, and making audit reports available to the public are critical pre-conditions for restraining corruption.[7]

Extrabudgetary accounts are common in many countries. Some of the extrabudgetary accounts have legitimate uses and are established for specific purposes such as pension or road funds. However, many extrabudgetary funds are established to reduce the political and administrative controls that are more likely to accompany spending that goes through a normal budget process.

Government contracting and procurement procedures play a significant role in public service provision, and also account for a significant share of resource leakage and corruption. The provision of goods and services to local communities poses special problems of information and monitoring. These challenges include, but are not limited to: bid-rigging and collusion; manipulation of engineering specifications; over-invoicing or undersupply of materials; and the wholesale diversion of funds. Administrative oversight and audit can help in restraining procurement corruption. However, sometimes the administrative oversight itself can be compromised.

Large capital investment projects have frequently lent themselves to acts of high-level corruption. Oftentimes, high-level public officials have a significant degree of discretion in influencing the scope and magnitude of public investment projects such that the type of public spending can become distorted. Public investment projects have frequently been developed to provide opportunities for some individuals or political groups to gain concessions. In general, this form of public finance corruption has resulted in projects and expenditures that may not have been justified by objective investment selection criteria.

Provision of Goods and Services. In many countries, the government (central and subnational) engages in the provision of goods and services, and resources at below market prices (Tanzi, 1998). In other words, various services such as electricity, water, public housing, health, and education may be subsidized. Substantial economic and financial analysis indicates that many goods and services are provided to the local citizens without consideration for cost recovery (including amortization/depreciation). Even access to some forms of pensions (i.e., disability) may fall into this category. In some countries, disability pensions have proven to be fertile ground for corruption.

Because many of these "subsidized" goods and services are provided at below market prices, supply may be limited. Rationing becomes unavoidable. In this instance, excess demand for those goods and services is created. Decisions have to be made to apportion the limited supply. These decisions to ration the supply are often made by public employees. In effect, the public employee may demand bribes in order to provide the citizen with the good or service.

Good Budget Formulation

In keeping with the three primary objectives of public expenditure management, the budget preparation process should aim at ensuring that the budget fits macroeconomic policies and resource constraints, allocating resources in conformity with government policies, and providing conditions for good operational management. In minimizing the corrosive influence of public financial management corruption, it is essential that these three items for effective budget preparation be improved.

The coverage of the budget should be comprehensive. The budget should include all revenues and expenditures of the government, whatever the arrangements may be for managing some particular programs. Operational efficiency requires taking into account the specific characteristics of different expenditure programs when designing budget management rules (e.g., rules concerning transfers of resources from one budget item to another). When there is a strong link between revenue and benefit, earmarking arrangements may be considered thereby enhancing performance in public service delivery.

Weaknesses in the budgeting process and vulnerabilities to corruption depend in large part on political factors and on the organization of the government (e.g., lack of coordination, unclear lines of accountability, and overlaps in the distribution of responsibility). Mechanisms for budgeting and policy formulation should be explicitly designed to reinforce coordination and cohesion in decision-making. Strengthening the budget preparation process requires improvements in the following directions:

- Decisions that have a fiscal impact should be scrutinized together with direct expenditure programs.
- Spending limits must be built into the start of the budget formulation process, consistent with policy priorities and resource availability.
- Operational efficiency requires line ministries to be held accountable for implementing their programs. However, they

can be held accountable only if they have participated in designing the programs and have authority for managing them. This requires countries to review and revise the distribution of responsibilities in budget preparation.

Is program-based budgeting or performance-based budgeting appropriate in developing countries? Injecting formal performance related elements into public management in developing countries requires extreme care because better performance orientation is critical for improving public administration and because there are many ineffective ways of pushing changes forward (and, only a few ways of doing it with minimal upheaval). The suitability of performance budgeting and the specific indicators themselves depend on the sector in question. The lessons from international experience include:

- Robust monitoring of performance should include swift and predictable consequences.
- Performance-based budgeting (and programs) should consider the probable impact of introducing performance indicators on individual behavior and take compensatory measures (if needed).
- In order to install performance-based systems, it is essential to understand the different limitations of input, output, outcome and process indictors of performance, and tailor the use of each to the specific sector in question.
- It is essential to build in provisions for the systematic assessment of performance of the performance system itself. In other words, the performance management system must be subject to a reality check.

Beyond the above caveats, it is important to constantly be on the lookout for any possibility to expand the service awareness of government administration, and raise the rewards and sanctions for good and poor performance, respectively.

Transparency and Accountability of Government Actions

Access to information on government performance is critical for promoting government accountability and minimizing corruption with respect to public finance. This section expressly reviews institutional controls and rules, laws and public sector accountability issues.

Institutional Controls. Corruption within the civil service bureaucracy can be minimized with the installation of institutional controls. This implies that there is honest and effective supervision, auditing oversight and control, and an awareness and internalization of the standards of ethical behavior. Supervisors and their civil servant employees should be held accountable for acts of corruption in their office.

Several countries and cities, including Singapore, Hong Kong, and Argentina, have created anticorruption or ethics offices. To be effective, these offices must be independent from the political establishment, have ample personnel and financial resources, and have high ethical standards. Ethics offices must also have the power to enforce penalties. However, if they lack true independence and report directly to the president (or prime minister), it may reduce their effectiveness and politicize the process thereby reducing overall effectiveness.

Transparency of Rules, Regulations, Laws and Processes. In many countries, the lack of transparency in rules, laws, and process creates favorable environments for corruption. Rules dealing with government procurement processes, financial management and accounting are often confusing. Even if an individual exercises some initiative and tries to understand the rules, the documents specifying these rules may not be publicly available. Furthermore, many organizational rules may be changed without public announcements to that effect.

In many instances, regulations and laws are written so that only trained lawyers can understand their true impact. Many laws are often conceptually opaque, thus leaving grounds for different interpretation. In the United States, the judiciary may be called in to discern the true nature of the law. In many developing countries, the judicial process is not as efficient. This may lead to additional corruption with respect to trying to obtain an effective interpretation of the regulation or law.

One of the ways to reduce the corruption inherent in opaque regulations and laws is to establish more efficient regulatory processes. The establishment of independent regulatory agencies, both at the national and local government level can be effective in promoting efficiency and limiting opportunities for corruption. These regulatory institutions however, must operate with transparency (hold public meetings), simplicity (rules-based principles), and accountability (election of regulators or term-based regulators).

The Audit Function. Management controls are the policies and procedures put in place by the managers of an entity, such as a government, to ensure its proper and effective operation. Developing an effective system of controls requires, first, a careful assessment of the risks confronting the organization. Policies and procedures can then be selected to control those risks effectively and at reasonable cost. No system of controls can provide an absolute guarantee against the occurrence of fraud, abuse, inefficiency, and human error. However, a well-designed system of controls can give reasonable assurance that significant irregularities can be detected. There are effectively two types of audit procedures, including:

- *Internal audit* as part of an organization's management control structure. The internal audit office on behalf of management audits lower level units. Among its most important functions, internal audits test the management controls themselves and assist senior management in assessing risks and in developing more cost-effective controls.

- *External audit* of government operations as typically performed by a supreme audit institution (SAI) or an independent external auditing firm. External auditors typically perform compliance/regulatory audits, financial assurance audits, and value-for-money (efficiency) audits.

To be effective, the external audit staff must have the professional skills required for the audits being performed. For an external auditor to move from ex-ante and regulatory audits to financial assurance and value-for-money (performance) audits, its staff will have to be extensively trained in the more complex audits. In order for the external audit function to be effective, especially when pursuing the strategic objective of improved management controls or undertaking more advanced types of audits, an effective means of communicating audit results and a sound approach for encouraging effective appropriate corrective action must also be developed.

Given the limited capacity to absorb change in most developing countries, anticorruption strategies need to focus on a few crucial elements rooted in the specific characteristics of each country. For example, Latvia's anticorruption strategy for revenue administration was part of a broader national strategy guided by a vigilance unit (World Bank, 1999). The organizational structure of the state revenue service was improved to integrate tax customs, social securities, and to create internal control and anticorruption functions. The vigilance unit operated independently of the financial police to monitor and educate staff on a code of ethics, conduct disciplinary hearings, develop incentives to foster integrity and good conduct, and monitor declarations of income and assets by public servants. The importance of citizen engagement and oversight is crucial to maintaining the integrity of public financial management.

Corruption and Investment

Public finance corruption may impact on investment in a number of ways including adversely affecting the total amount of investment, adversely impacting the amount of foreign direct investment; and adversely impacting the size and quality of public investment.

In several papers, Mauro (1997, 1998) has shown that corruption can have a significant negative impact on the ratio of total investment to GDP. Regressing the investment ratio in relation to the corruption index, GDP per capita income, secondary education, and population growth, Mauro shows that a reduction in corruption can significantly increase the investment/GDP ratio. On the other hand, a drop in the investment/GDP ratio as a result of corruption was shown to have an important effect on growth. Mauro (1997) estimated that a reduction in corruption equivalent to 2 points in the corruption index would raise the annual growth rate by about 0.5 percent through its positive effect on the investment/GDP ratio.

In a paper focusing on foreign direct investment (FDI), Wei (1997a) showed that an increase in a corruption index by a single point reduces the inflow of FDI by 11 percent. In a related work, Wei (1997b) showed that the unpredictability of corruption (as measured by the dispersion of individual ratings of corruption) has a further negative impact on FDI. Wei concluded that "the effect of uncertainty on FDI is negative, statistically significant and large."

Does corruption affect operation and maintenance expenditures? Despite substantial difficulties in obtaining good data, Tanzi and Davoodi (1998) have provided evidence that high levels of corruption are associated with low operation and maintenance expenditure and a generally poor quality of infrastructure. Tanzi and Davoodi show that in terms of statistical significance, the impact of corruption is strongest on the quality of roads and power outages.

In summary, Tanzi, Davoodi, Wei, and Mauro have shown empirically that corruption reduces total investment, distorts the composition of public sector investment, and generally reduces the quality of a country's infrastructure. The combined impact of these changes on economic growth is bound to be negative and substantial.

Policy Considerations

Reform Priorities for Public Financial Management

Improvements in the public financial management system are largely a function of creating the political will to develop reforms and make and sustain institutional change.[8] Budgeting and public financial management organizations can be improved, but economic, social and political behavior will not change unless the rules and procedures change, and are internalized, as well. The reverse is also true: rule modification is unlikely to produce results in an operationally meaningful time frame unless organizational improvements proceed apace (Schiavo-Campo and Tinnasi, 1999, p. 103). In other words, improving public expenditure management requires both institutional (regulatory and procedural) reform and organizational development.

Operational Approach. Reforming public sector management and public finance requires instilling meritocracy and adequate pay in public administration; clarifying government priorities, institutional goals and strategies, and institutional structures; enhancing transparency and accountability in fiscal management; and, stimulating policy reforms in service delivery.

A general review of governance and functional structures in ministries should be given high priority. Some governments have moved central government functions into quasi-private sector structures. These structures blur the lines of policy direction and accountability. In addition, these types of organizational structures create a large number of highly paid supervisory jobs that can serve to increase the potential for corruption and opportunities for payoffs. Off-budget agency funding also contributes to budget fragmentation and lack of transparency.

To improve transparency and accountability in fiscal management, it is necessary to ensure full budget control and coverage. Latvia, for example, diverts substantial resources into off-budget accounts. These accounts typically lack oversight and transparency. Off-budget transactions can take different forms, from extra budgetary funds to the lack of integration of investment planning. A further challenge is to eliminate (or reduce) contingent liabilities (off-balance sheet guarantees) stemming from non-transparent off-budget commitments. Argentina and Brazil are classic examples of the moral hazard that is created with these off-balance sheet liabilities.

In many developing countries, budget formulation is often flawed by the ambiguity between the executive and legislative branch of government, poor parliamentary processes, lack of policy coordination, and the inability to impose trade-offs at the executive level. In Bosnia, for example, expenditure projections lack a medium term perspective and revenue forecasts are often extremely unrealistic. The inability to develop realistic forecasts leads to non-transparent adjustments during budget execution. The potential for public sector finance mismanagement increases dramatically. In addition, unclear budget appropriations and unreliable disbursements leave budget managers unable to deliver reliable services.

Reforms to promote greater accountability and control over budgetary expenditures require strong accounting and auditing systems. In order to be effective, treasury systems must be strengthened. Investment in information technology, as seen in USAID-funded treasury, accounting, and audit systems in Russia, for example, needs to be grounded in broader institutional reforms. Furthermore, transparent competitive procurement is necessary to prevent corruption from inflating public expenditures.

The effectiveness of external and internal audit entities varies greatly by country. In Kazakhstan the external audit function is dominated by the executive branch of government, essentially limiting credibility of the process. To be effective in reducing public sector corruption, the external audit must be independent and equipped with strong auditing and diagnostic skills. In addition, an internal audit oversight must be strengthened with public dissemination of audit findings.

The Multipronged Approach. Standalone efforts to tackle administrative corruption in public administration and public finance are likely to have limited impact. Table 6.1 details some elements that can be applied to developing countries with respect to reducing corruption in public financial management.

Table 6.1. Reducing Corruption in Public Financial Management

Macroeconomic Stability	Efficiency Improvement	Technical Infrastructure	Accountability
Identification and assessment of the future implications of current policies.	Measurement and publicizing of the costs of important activities.	Establishment of an information system, which makes relevant operation data available to all policymakers and program managers.	Specific costs and expected performance, as an integrated part of the overall framework of accountability.
Recognition of the resource constraint	Factors or areas contributing to expenditure increase should be identified and addressed.	Focus on core tasks by central agencies responsible for financial management. These tasks include policies, costs, and specification of the desired performance levels.	Avenues for people to secure information on historical series such as government accounts.
Maintenance of an extensive database and profile of all agency expenditures.	Pursuit of alternative strategies for the delivery of services when costs tend to increase.	Managerial autonomy for spending agencies in the use of allotted resources.	Establish oversight bodies (where none may currently exist).
Maintain cost data where services funded by public agencies are provided by private and nongovernmental sector.		Selective conversion of accounting systems to an accrual basis particularly in agencies with large inventories.	Disseminate information.
		Eliminate patronage for public service appointment.	
		Eliminate off-budget/off-balance organizations/accounts. Independent audit functions and strong budget execution	

Each country however, must be diagnosed individually, and associated interventions must be country-specific. In addition, there is no simple formula for the proper sequencing of these anticorruption activities. Nevertheless, the sequencing of reforms should be designed to enhance the credibility of the leadership and the program to ensure early tangible results. This type of approach effectively strengthens the constituency for reform.

A Diagnostic Questionnaire: An Example. To improve the effectiveness and efficiency of programs, the first essential steps are to implement a sound budget process and effective management (internal and external) control systems. The Appendix presents a brief questionnaire that can serve as a diagnostic tool. It is faithful to the principles of public finance and government budget. It deals with comprehensiveness (the budget should include all revenue and expenditure); accuracy; authoritativeness (public funds should be spent as authorized by law); and transparency (the government should publish timely information). A program that implemented improvements based on the use of the questionnaire would have all the technical tools needed to improve its public financial management performance and enforce disciplined financial management.

Technical tools alone do not guarantee improvement in public financial management; the other key ingredients include well-trained and highly motivated staff and, above all, political will and strong focused leadership. This questionnaire is provided as only an example of the type and manner of diagnostic tools available. It is not exhaustive and can (and should) be expanded to include a broader range of diagnostic questions.

* * *

Our approach has been to review adverse impacts upon public financial management. The general conclusion is that programs to stem corruption with respect to public financial management need to consider carefully the country-specific context. Pragmatic anticorruption programs may deteriorate in their effectiveness if they are not guided by coherent and universal principles: strengthening governance (accountability, transparency, predictability, and participation); reinforcing the foundation of civil society; and engaging in improvements in public expenditure management programs to reduce opportunities for corruption.

Appendix

Example of a Diagnostic Questionnaire

Diagnostic Area	Question
A. Budget legislation	Provides a clear and comprehensive definition of public money? Establishes the following elements of intergovernmental fiscal relations?
	1. Basic principles of supervision, intervention, and audit responsibilities?
	2. Budget accounting classifications are coherent and common to all levels of government?
	Establishes the definition of budget deficit and surplus, which excludes borrowings from receipts and excludes repayments for principal from expenditure?
	Provides a legal basis for management (internal) control and internal audit?
	Defines the authorities and responsibilities for issuing and reporting on government guarantees?
B. Scope of the budget	Clearly defines appropriation and spending authority? All transactions of statutory extrabudgetary funds with the budget are defined? All fiscal transfers to subnational governments for general and special purposes are defined? Does the budget document include:
	1. Fiscal policy objectives?
	2. Complete information on past and projected spending?
	3. Complete information on financial plans and operations of statutory extrabudgetary funds?
	4. A statement of contingent liabilities?
C. Measuring and monitoring the government deficit and debt	1. Are there figures released for different fiscal balance definitions?
	2. Are the fiscal definitions calculated on a cash or accrual basis?
	3. Do government data allow a clear distinction to be made between domestic and external debt?
	4. Which ministry is responsible for contracting and managing debt?
	5. Is it the same ministry that is in charge of guarantee debt?

Diagnostic Area	Question

D. Budget execution and monitoring	Are there laws, regulations and procedures that:
	    1. Ensure that all public revenues are directly deposited?
	    2. If separate bank accounts are permitted, who is responsible for opening, monitoring the banking operations?
	The ministry of finance/treasury controls cash balances daily relative to borrowings?
	There are procedures to report and correct overspending?

E. Legal and policy framework	Are there laws, regulations, or policies that:
	    1. Limit and define the authorities at each level of the administration for transferring funds within the approved budget?
	    2. Prevent transfers between personnel costs and other sub-heads of the budget?
	    3. Specify how budget funds that are unspent at the end of the fiscal year should be treated?
	    4. Establish sanctions for overspending?
	    5. Bind all persons responsible for spending money to implement management control practices?

F. Performance monitoring	Does the government foster an environment that supports and demands improved performance by organizations and individuals? Is performance information on easily measured activities collected and used by spending units? by the Ministry of Finance? Are managers who are responsible for government programs and projects given clear short- and/or long-term operational goals and targets?
G. Evaluation	Is there an evaluation capacity sufficient to respond to the demands of the public sector/accountability?
H. Accounting and reporting	Is there a unified accounting and budgeting classification system regulated by the Ministry of Finance/Treasury? Are the final accounts produced, audited and tabled in parliament shortly after the end of the fiscal year? Does the system provide for recording commitments (obligations) as well as cash transactions?

I. Internal audits	Are internal audit units established in line ministries?
	Does the mandate for these units include:
	    1. Financial audit?
	    2. System audit?
	    3. Procurement audit process?
	    4. Review of management internal control arrangements?

Diagnostic Area	Question
J. External audit	Is there an external auditor established by law with independence from government?
	Does the external auditor have authority to audit/clear all public and statutory funds and resources?
K. Organization and capacity for reform	Is there a coherent written strategy for bringing public financial management systems into line with general accepted standards?
	Does this strategy have the support of the Ministry of Finance?
	Are there training programs to complement any reform process?

Source: Adapted from Schiavo-Campo and Tommasi (1999).

Notes

1. In addition, some state-protected monopolies may provide goods and services at exploitative prices. These protected state monopolies may provide shoddy or poor quality goods.

2. A simple remedy for reducing tax avoidance schemes in the instances where tax rates are considered to be too high (i.e., Russia in the mid-1990s, India) is to reduce overall tax levels (rates). Reducing tax rates has proved effective in increasing government tax revenues. However, steps to improve overall tax compliance by reducing tax rates should be undertaken in conjunction with increasing tax enforcement and compliance measures (penalties).

3. Businesses may no longer have the incentive to collude with corrupt officials to avoid taxes. The incentive may be changed, such that businesses may now have the incentive to report corruption.

4. For example, separating the tax assessment function from the collection function.

5. For a more detailed discussion of tax administration reform, see Meyer and Hester (2001).

6. The computerization of the tax and customs administration systems could allow for online filing of tax and customs forms in the most advanced countries. This would potentially eliminate many opportunities for corruption. Further, computerizing the tax system would enhance the adequacy of administrative procedures including compliance, tax audit, taxpayer services, sanctions and appeals, customs clearance procedures, preshipment inspection, and information sharing.

7. In addition, establishing an oversight board to ensure the integrity of independent auditors may also be warranted. Due to the perceived lack of independent auditing functions with respect to publicly held corporations in the United States, an oversight monitoring board is being established with the expressed intent to verify (validate) the integrity of the independent audit system.

8. For an exceptionally thorough discussion with respect to reform priorities for public financial management, see Schiavo-Campo and Tommasi (1999).

Chapter 7

Environment and Natural Resources

Svetlana Winbourne

This chapter examines public sector corruption in the environment and natural resources sector and suggests possible responses based on best practices. Corruption in this sector can divert funds allocated for environmental programs into private pockets through embezzlement and bribery. It can facilitate trafficking in wildlife and other natural resources. Corruption can deplete natural resources and pollute the environment as a result of bribery of environmental inspectors and permit processors. It can also contribute to the development of environmentally damaging policies and practices and to unfair allocation of resources that contribute to environmentally harmful practices.

Strategies to address corruption in the environmental and natural resources sector include enforcement, prevention, and awareness components. Recommended strategies include: better enforcement of the existing policies and laws, reforms to improve transparency and accountability, legislation to reduce loopholes and bureaucratic discretion, reasonable environmental standards and requirements, reduced bureaucratic red tape by simplifying and streamlining administrative processes, citizen participation and oversight through establishment of citizen watchdog groups and public-private dialogues, professional and responsible investigative reporting in the media, and comprehensive public awareness campaigns on the causes and costs of corruption to promote citizen intolerance of corruption.

Corruption in the Environmental and Natural Resources Sector

Corruption in the environmental and natural resources sector may occur across a number of transactions, starting from bribery and cronyism in developing national policy and embezzlement in implementing environmental programs to bribery in issuing permits and licenses and collecting "rents" while enforcing environmental regulations. It can be well organized from top to bottom and linked to organized crime (for example, in mineral, timber, and wildlife trafficking), and it can be widely represented through a number of governmental agencies and services. The areas most vulnerable to corruption include environmental and natural resources policy and regulatory development; environmental resources utilization; permitting and certification processes; and environmental enforcement (inspections and policing).

The environment can also be affected by corruption in other sectors, such as in agriculture, privatization, public procurement, customs, the judiciary, and others. For instance, privatization conducted through corrupt procedures may allow new owners to use privatized land or facilities in an environmentally damaging manner. As well, improper regulations and procedures established in customs may open opportunities for trafficking in wildlife.

The impact of corruption is very difficult to measure. Box 7A provides just a few documented examples of the impact of illegal activities in the environmental sector that can be attributed to corruption.

The causes of corruption in the environmental sector, broadly speaking, are similar to any other sector and include, among others, insufficient legislation, lack

---

Box 7A. Examples of illegal activities and corruption in the environmental sector

Trafficking in Wildlife

"The trafficking in threatened species, including cheetahs, chimpanzees, crocodiles, elephants and other species continues, earning smugglers profits of $8 billion to $12 billion annually. Among the most coveted black market items are tigers and other large cats, rhinos, reptiles, rare birds, and botanical specimens. Most illegally traded wildlife originates in developing countries, home to most of the world's biological diversity. Brazil alone supplies some 10 percent of the global black market, and its nonprofit wildlife-trade monitoring body, RENCTAS, estimates that poachers steal some 38 million animals a year from the country's Amazon forests, Pantanal wetlands, and other important habitats, generating annual revenues of $1 billion. Southeast Asian wildlife has also been plundered: the Gibbon Foundation reports that in a single recent year, traders smuggled out some 2,000 orangutans from Indonesia— at an average street price of $10,000 apiece" (Mastny, 2002).

Forest Sector

Loss of revenue to governments due to illegal logging is about US$5 billion annually, with a further US$10 billion lost to the economies of producing countries (Toyne, 2002).

Mineral Resources

About 20 percent of the total US$6.8 billion of global trade in rough diamonds is illicit (Renner, 2002).

---

of respect for the rule of law, weak democracy, wide authority given to public officials, minimal accountability and transparency, poor enforcement, low levels of professionalism, and perverse incentives. The weight of each component of this generic set of corruption causes varies from country to country and changes over time.

More specifically, though, the basis for corruption in the environmental and natural resources sector lies in a conflict between private interests concerning the commercial value of natural resources (mineral, water, land, forest, wildlife, for example) and reductions in production costs by using environmentally unfriendly technologies, on one side, and, public interests in a healthy habitat, on the other side. What makes the environmental sector distinctive from any other is that corruption here is triggered by large amounts of formal and informal revenues that can be gained from many natural products (such as minerals, timber, wildlife, and gems). For those countries that are rich in natural resources and whose economies are primarily based on them, resource distribution, extraction, and management become fertile grounds for corruption. Theoretical and empirical studies demonstrate how natural resource abundance creates opportunities for corruption and is an important factor in determining a country's level of corruption (Leite, 1999;

Renner, 2002). "Societies whose main income is derived from resource royalties instead of value added seem prone to develop a culture with widespread corruption. Resource royalties enable political leaders to maintain their stranglehold on power by funding a system of patronage that rewards followers and punishes opponents. And because such regimes rely less on revenues derived from a broad-based system of taxation, they also have less need for popular legitimacy and feel less pressure to be accountable" (Renner, 2002). Such countries as Indonesia, Nigeria, Sierra Leone, Colombia, and other developing countries with high levels of corruption and economies highly dependent upon natural resources could serve as demonstrative examples. As stated at a meeting of Transparency International in 2000 concerning corruption in natural resources industries, "...with income on the order of US$35billion/year for Mexico; US$30 billion for Venezuela; and US$22 billion for Nigeria, the potential for good and the temptation for abuse are immense" (Schloss, 2000).

Although abundance of natural resources can spark corruption, resource scarcity can be equally fertile ground for illicit systems to develop. Limited, but lucrative natural resources can have their value boosted in the black market and create temptation for public officials to fill their own pockets by granting illegally issued access to these resources. Thus, for example, corrupt officials may issue false permits or overlook illicit consignments of endangered wildlife species in return for bribes and kickbacks (Mastny, 2002).

Another reason why corruption often flourishes in the environmental sector relates to inadequate funding and, as a result, weak environmental institutions responsible for implementing environmental management and conservation programs, and conducting environmental control and policing.

Studies of corruption in the environmental sector are a relatively recent phenomenon. There is a scarcity of hard data to describe the problem, assess its magnitude, and point out the transactions most vulnerable to corruption in the environmental field. There are certainly no reliable statistics on prosecutions of environmental corruption cases or statistics on administrative sanctions for abuse of environmental regulations that are easily accessible.

The multicountry surveys on corruption that have been conducted by international organizations, such as the World Bank and Transparency International, do not specifically address the environmental sector or define it very narrowly, which results in information that is neither comprehensive or reliable on corruption in the sector. However, in the report accompanying the 2001 Environmental Sustainability Index developed by the World Economic Forum, researchers highlight, for the first time, the very high correlation between the level of corruption and environmental outcomes: the higher the level of corruption in a country, the lower the level of environmental sustainability (Levy, 2001). Some country-specific public opinion surveys conducted by these and a number of other organizations incorporate questions about corruption and the environment in a limited fashion; they provide some of the rare quantitative assessments of where corruption impacts the environmental field. Box 7B provides an overview of how corruption in the environment is represented in these surveys.

Box 7B. Surveys about corruption in the environment

As shown in the following examples from different country public opinion surveys, general questions about corruption in the environmental sector, when included, suggest that it is considered to be a moderately important problem. However, specific questions that would allow a more detailed understanding of the particular vulnerabilities of the environmental sector to corrupt practices are rarely incorporated in such surveys.

In the Diagnostic Survey of Corruption in Romania conducted in 2000, bribery in the environmental sector takes seventeenth place among eighteen listed sectors. About 3 percent of businesses admitted that they paid bribes frequently to obtain environmental licenses.

In a survey conducted in Bosnia and Herzegovina in 2000, the environmental sector is not even listed among those that are perceived as highly corrupted. However, when businesses were asked when they were extorted to pay bribes most frequently, they ranked the environmental sector as the highest, before twenty-two other sectors, including the traffic police, tax authorities, and customs.

In a survey conducted in Slovakia in 1999, the environmental sector again is not included in a list of twenty-six sectors, though 13 percent of enterprises admitted that they encountered bribery in environmental agencies, thus placing this sector in the middle of a list of twenty-one agencies where bribes were paid frequently. The average bribe is about 3,200 SK (about US$80), which is in the low-to-mid range among bribes paid to other agencies. Businesses admitted that in about 8 percent of their visits to environmental protection agencies, a bribe was suggested. In comparison, respondents said that they had to pay bribes in 24 percent of all visits to get construction permits.

In the Governance and Anti-Corruption survey conducted in Peru in 2001, about 8 percent of responding firm managers (3 percent, large; 10 percent, medium; and 12 percent, small enterprises) admitted to paying bribes frequently to get environmental licenses; this amounts to about 6 percent of the total amount paid in bribes to all public agencies. The average bribe amount was about 445 soles (about US$125).

According to the Honduras Governance and Anti-Corruption Survey of 2002, 4 percent of large enterprises reported paying bribes to obtain environmental licenses, though none of the small, medium or foreign firms admitted to any unofficial payments. Two percent of respondents said that they were made to feel that bribes were necessary to obtain environmental licenses. The average unofficial payment made in the environmental sector was 50,000 L (about US$2,980), which is the highest in comparison with other agencies.

The Bolivia Public Official Survey of 2001 calculated a Control of Corruption index for different public agencies and the Ministry of Sustainable Development is ranked at the sixty-fourth level with the best being the Presidential Ministry (in ninety-eighth place) and the worst being the Health Department and the police.

Box 7B. (continued)

The Indonesia Corruption Survey of 2002 put the Ministry of Forestry as among government agencies perceived to be the most corrupted (eleventh place among thirty-five other agencies); 20 percent of responding businesses consider this ministry among the four where corruption is most prevalent. It was reported that 56 percent of public officials in the Ministry of Forestry are perceived to be receiving unofficial payments on a regular basis.

There are a number of good reports on particular corruption-related cases and issues, produced by World Wildlife Fund (WWF), World Resources Institute (WRI), Resources for the Future, WorldWatch and others, as well as reports in the media. Several particular sectors have been studied more than others, including forestry (Callister, 1999; Contreras-Hermosilla, 2001), mining (Renner, 2002), fishery (Environmental Justice Foundation and Fisheries Action Coalition Team, 2000), and trafficking in biodiversity (Mastny, 2002).

It is typical in developing and transitional countries for their struggle with economic and social hardships to take higher priority than environmental issues, which are often pushed to the very bottom of the policy agenda. This results in limited systematic attention to the issue of corruption in the environment and a low priority given to this sector in the anticorruption agenda of both international organizations and countries themselves. Despite this, there are some good examples of countries implementing comprehensive environmental policies that are able to reduce opportunities for corruption and increase a wide range of benefits for their respective populations. Among them are Madagascar (where the government put environment at the top of its policy priorities and as a result was able to improve environmental governance and transparency significantly); and Namibia and Botswana (where both introduced effective diamond and gold resources management practices that resulted in reduction of corrupt practices and in a wide range of benefits for their respective populations).

Corruption is inherent in the environmental sector at both grand and petty levels, as well as at levels in between. Table 7.1 describes the nature of corruption vulnerabilities for each level of corruption.

Grand Corruption. Grand corruption occurs when high-level public officials engage in large illegal transactions. One type of grand corruption has been characterized as *state capture.* "State capture refers to the actions of individuals, groups, or firms both in the public and private sectors *to influence the formation* of laws, regulations, decrees, and other government policies to their own advantage as a result of the illicit and non-transparent provision of private benefits to public officials" (World Bank, 2000b). As mentioned earlier, the environmental sector usually takes a low priority in developing countries and countries in transition. Leaders in these countries are often tempted to sacrifice clean air and water, biodiversity and forests if they can turn them into profitable businesses or

Table 7.1. Levels of Corruption and Vulnerabilities in the Environmental Sector

Level of Corruption	Typical Areas Vulnerable to Corruption
Grand corruption	• Environmental and natural resources policy and regulations development.
Midlevel corruption	• Distribution and designation of environmental/natural resources and territories for particular utilization (including public procurement). • Permitting and certifications: issuing permits and certificates for use of territories and natural resources, and operating industrial sites including permits for emissions, discharges, and solid wastes. • Environmental assessments (including Environmental Impact Assessments (EIA)).
Petty corruption	• Enforcement (inspections and policing): inspections by environmental protection agencies and other related agencies to assess whether established environmental standards are being met, and policing of violations such as poaching, illegal logging, resource trafficking, excessive emissions, and so forth.

they support short-term political agendas or medium-term economic benefits. As a result, corruption can become invasive and systemic. Although decisions to adopt such environmentally unfriendly policies or laws can be made on the basis of inadequate appreciation of environmental consequences, the potential for private influence over environmental decision makers—state capture—is great.

Gibson (1999) demonstrates, using evidence from Zambia, Kenya, and Zimbabwe, how political and private institutions influence politicians and bureaucrats to construct wildlife policies that further their own interests. Different configurations of electoral laws, legislatures, party structures, interest groups, and traditional authorities in each country can shape the choices of policymakers—many of which are not consistent with conservation. In addition, due to shortages in national or local budgets, governments often underfund their programs and allow governmental agencies to supplement resources through engagement in commercial activities (logging, banking, construction, etc.). In so doing, they open their doors for financial abuses and corruption.

Among the major reasons for grand corruption in the environmental sector are a lack of transparency and accountability in decision making process, disproportionate influence of wealthy external interests, insufficient laws including those on financial disclosure and lobbying, and broad authority given to public officials that is not coupled to accountability and oversight.

There are a few documented examples that can be used to demonstrate the effects of state capture in the environmental sector. One of them relates to biodiversity loss on the Philippines' Negros Island that began when large tracts of forested land in the second-half of the nineteenth century were converted to sugar plantations. This situation worsened after independence when the national political system was dominated by sugar oligarchs, who constituted a powerful lobby known as the "sugar bloc" and who "successfully twisted economic and foreign policy to serve their short-term ends" (World Wildlife Fund, n.d.). Another example can be found in widespread patronage in the Philippines during Joseph Estrada's presidency when construction on the San Roque Dam in Pangasinan commenced despite warnings coming from environmental experts (Pabico, 2000). In Indonesia under President Suharto, licenses for mining, logging, and use of lands—with no environmental considerations—were awarded to domestic and foreign businesses that were closely linked to or broadly supportive of the regime; this ultimately resulted in depletion of resources and deforestation (Renner, 2002).

Midlevel Corruption. Midlevel corruption is more frequent and, as a result, those who work in the environment and natural resources sector can provide numerous examples. This type of corruption is defined as midlevel because either comparatively large amounts of money are at stake or the corrupt activity is widespread. It usually involves midlevel officials either at the national or local levels. This corruption is manifested in many ways: as bribes, gifts, influence peddling, favoritism, nepotism, speed money, kickbacks, and embezzlement.

Examples abound in the forestry sector where significant amounts of money are often paid to obtain timber concessions or such concessions are handed out as political patronage to key supporters (Callister, 1999). Such concessions are not constrained only to the timber industry; other resources, such as minerals, petroleum and water, are also vulnerable. An example in the Philippines focuses on a congressman who was quietly issued an environmental license for his rubber processing plant by a regional official whom he had promoted less than two weeks before (Severino, 1998).

Another example that demonstrates widespread corruption in the environmental sector and that involves both grand and midlevel corruption took place in Mexico. In his speech at the National Accord for Transparency and Combating Corruption in 2001, Mexican President Vicente Fox described corruption as deeply rooted in the environmental sector in Mexico under the previous administration. According to the President, "the nation's public property was invaded and used for private interests; beach areas and ecological reserves illegally exploited by former and current public servants as well as businessmen and foreigners; environmental impact certificates and forest, fishing, and hunting permits granted on a discretionary basis; preferential treatment given to companies responsible for polluting; distribution of water for political purposes; an punitive actions not carried out." Interviewed by the world press, Mexican Environment Secretary Víctor Lichtinger described this as a system of agreements and privileges: there were semi-official companies and political leaders engaged in this activity who could not be touched, who were beyond the reach of the law. To illustrate this, José Ignacio Campillo García, the head of Mexico's Environmental Protection Agency, pinpointed licenses granted to private individuals for use of beach areas that resulted in underpayment of about US$88 million in fees and taxes and construction of residential and tourist facilities within protected natural areas in the sea coast zone, licenses for exporting wildlife that allowed an individual to export 50,000 birds, and licenses for extensive logging. The Fox administration is facing the monumental challenge now of reviewing actions taken by the previous administration to develop new policies and practices to prevent irregularities and corruption in the future (Monge and Ortiz, 2002).

Petty Corruption. Many public officials who are grossly underpaid or depend on small payments from the public to feed their families, practice petty or "survival" corruption (TI Source Book, 2002). Petty corruption in the environmental sector occurs mostly during environmental inspections and the policing of illegal acts such as poaching, illegal logging, discharges, emissions, and the like. In this kind of corruption, insignificant amounts of money and low-level officials are usually involved, unless it is part of a vertically organized scheme that can reach into higher levels of government. The most common forms of corruption at this level are bribery, influence peddling and nepotism. The major support mechanisms include inspection regulations that are open to overly broad interpretation, insufficient inspection procedures, lack of accountability, low salaries for inspectors, and unattainable environmental standards that are established without consideration of the resources and technologies needed for businesses to meet these standards.

The vulnerability to corruption of particular environmental sectors can be deconstructed into their component elements. Box 7C presents an extensive list of corrupt practices in the forestry sector developed by Callister (1999). Such lists can help to suggest the most appropriate and efficient tools and strategies to address corruption in particular sub-sectors.

All levels of corruption can coexist in a country or province with or without explicit linkages. Frequently, petty corruption "is simply a downwards projection of much more damaging forms of corruption at higher levels" (TI Source Book, 2000).

Experience Addressing Corruption in the Environmental and Natural Resources Sector

Solving problems of potential corruption is not the typical focus of environmental programs, though a number of current programs recognize the impact that corruption has on the environmental sector. They seek to address it by including activities to promote transparency and accountability in environment and natural resources management and enhance community participation in governmental decision making processes with regards to natural resource allocation and

---

Box 7C. Examples of corruption in the forestry sector

Grand Corruption

- Companies providing support to political parties or bribing politicians, senior government officials, or military officers to:
    - obtain a timber concession;
    - obtain extensions to existing concessions;
    - obtain approval for a timber processing venture;
    - avoid prosecution for transgressions;
    - avoid payment of fines or other fees; and
    - negotiate favorable concession/investment agreements, including tax holidays and other investment incentives.
- Politicians, high-ranking military and government officers using their status to effect the same outcomes as above, for their own companies or those of relatives or political allies.
- Companies bribing communities to agree to grant them timber harvesting rights.

Petty Corruption

- Companies bribing military personnel or junior and local government officials to:
    - falsify declarations of volume or species harvested;
    - avoid reporting harvesting of prohibited species or diameters;
    - falsify export documentation or ignore document irregularities;
    - avoid reporting and prosecution for noncompliance with forest management regulations established in the concession contract;
    - permit illegal movement of timber;
    - ignore logging in protected areas and outside concession boundaries;
    - allow timber processing without the necessary approvals; and
    - ignore infringements of timber processing regulations, including pollution controls.

Source: Adapted from Callister (1999)

---

management (e.g., in Nepal, the Philippines, and Indonesia). When corruption is not taken into account and no anticorruption measures are incorporated, the risk that the project can fail to achieve its objectives increases due to possible diversion of funds through corrupt activities or obstacles created by corrupt practices. Several cases of corruption in environment-related activities can help illustrate these points.

Case 1. Russian Far East Forest

World Wildlife Fund estimates that the Russian budget loses over US$1 billion in taxes, fees, and other payments annually due to illegal wood harvesting, processing, and trade, while legal revenue constitutes approximately US$6 billion per year. Illegal logging flourishes in all the primary wood-producing areas of the country; it is estimated by different sources at 20 to 50 percent of total harvested timber, varying from area to area. Among 6,383 forest-related illegal action cases investigated in Russia in 1999, 3,113 cases were brought to court and in only 907 of these cases have any parties been found guilty and received sentences (Kotlobay, 2002).

The Russian Far East region differs from other regions of Russia in terms of its specific climate, distinctive landscape, and unique plants and animals. However, the region suffers from significant loss in biodiversity, rapid loss of its most valuable forests, and change in microclimate and hydrological regime due to forest mismanagement, illegal logging, and other illicit activities. WWF has been implementing the Forest Program in Russia since 1994. It has witnessed frequent cases of illegal logging and forest crime. To address this problem, in 1998 WWF initiated a monitoring force, the CEDAR Mobile Group, within the Tiger State Inspectorate of the Department of Natural Resources of Primorskiy Krai. It has the authority to conduct inspections of any wood processing enterprise. During inspections, the CEDAR Mobile Group revealed more than twenty-four cases of illegal logging, for which fourteen criminal investigations have been initiated. Penalties of over 1 million rubles (about US$34,000) have been imposed, and about 3,000 cubic meters of wood, along with tractors, chainsaws, and other equipment used by illegal loggers were confiscated. The CEDAR Mobile Group cooperates effectively with local police in the region. To improve the professionalism of the inspectors, WWF conducted two training sessions with forty forest inspectors on current legislation related to the forestry sector and legal aspects of forest harvesting crimes. The experience of WWF and other NGOs has attracted the interest of the Ministry of Natural Resources of the Russian Federation, which as a result has conducted a large-scale inspection of forest areas to pinpoint logging infringements.

To approach the problem of illegal logging and forest crime in a more systematic way, WWF commissioned in 2001 several studies in the Primorskiy Krai to identify vulnerabilities and assess the magnitude and impact of forest crime. These studies revealed that illegal logging in Primorskiy Krai constitutes from 30 percent to 50 percent of the total amount of harvested timber, that up to 80 percent of the timber in storage is of illegal origin, and that several hundred thousand cubic meters of illegally cut and subsequently legalized timber is exported from the Primorskiy Krai every year. The studies showed that practically each stage and level of forest management and use is vulnerable to crime and misdeeds that involve bribery, favoritism, nepotism, embezzlement, and other kinds of corruption. They also mapped out some particular processes to pinpoint exactly where and how such crimes are committed. The studies concluded that current enforcement measures are not strong enough to fight forest crime and called for the design of comprehensive strategies that include both preventive *and* enforcement measures (Kotlobay, 2002; Kotlobay and Ptichnikov, 2002).

Lessons Learned. This particular case demonstrates how within a traditional environmental program, WWF initiated several activities targeted at corruption and other kinds of forest crime. Starting from small but aggressive activity focused on the consequences of illegal activity, WWF concluded that a more comprehensive strategy was needed. A lesson that can be learned from this example is that in order to secure resources and ensure effective results at the program design or implementation stage, it is necessary to assess the potential risks due to corruption and, if necessary, embed safeguard activities and strategies to prevent it. It may require a single but powerful institution to address the major threats caused by corruption (such as the CEDAR Mobile Group). In other cases, it might be more effective to look at the problem of corruption in a systematic way and develop a multidimensional strategy that includes preventive, educational and public awareness measures that would have long-lasting effects.

Case 2. Lesotho Highlands Water Project

The estimated US$8 billion Lesotho Highlands Water Project was designed to divert water from the Orange River to the urban and industrial Gauteng region in South Africa through a series of dams and tunnels blasted through the mountains. The first dam in this multidam scheme, called Katse, was completed in 1995. The second, called Mohale, is currently under way, despite the fact that critical social and environmental problems affecting thousands of people remain unresolved. Widespread corruption in this project is thought to be one reason that the social fund intended to help affected communities has not reached its recipients (International Rivers Network, IRN's Lesotho Campaign, n.d.).

In April 1999, a major corruption scandal was exposed involving the chief executive of the Lesotho Highlands Water Project and twelve of the biggest dam-building companies in the world. The companies were accused of paying bribes to win lucrative dam building and engineering contracts. In November 1999, the CEO was convicted of thirteen counts of bribery and sentenced to eighteen years in prison for taking more than US$2 million in bribes over a ten-year period from intermediaries representing the twelve construction firms, including ABB (Swedish/Swiss), Acres International (Canadian), Impregilo (Italian), Lahmeyer (German), and Sogreah (French). In September 2002, Acres International was convicted of two counts of bribery for paying more than US$260,000 to the CEO through an agent in order to secure contracts in the dam building scheme. Though no Acres staff or officers will receive jail sentences, the company expects to be fined (Probe International Press Advisory, 2002).

In this particular example, the corruption revealed by Lesotho authorities was manifested in the public procurement process. It appears that there were no effective control mechanisms in place to prevent corrupt activities that had been occurring for a period of ten years and ultimately led to damaging environmental consequences that adversely affected thousands of people.

The groups concerned with the environmental impact of the Lesotho Highlands Water Project mobilized a strong lobbying campaign to bring the attention of the public and decision makers to the environmental problems associated with dam construction. However, they did not attend to the corruption problems plaguing the project. Given the large amounts of money involved in the project, one might speculate that the profit interests of construction firms and some public officials influenced project decisions more than environmental concerns.

Lessons Learned. This example demonstrates that in order to advocate for their traditional interests, environmental groups might also serve a useful public oversight and monitoring function to assess whether environmental projects are vulnerable to corrupt practices—from planning to procurement to implementation. Also, this example demonstrates how corruption in other sectors (in this case, procurement) can become damaging to the environment. A lesson that can be learned from this example is that it is necessary to assess and address corruption risks imposed by sectors outside of environment programs.

Tools and Strategies to Address Corruption in the Environmental and Natural Resources Sector

There have been several attempts to identify particular anticorruption strategies that relate directly to environmental sector vulnerabilities. For example, at the Workshop on Corruption and the Environment at the 9th International Anti-Corruption Conference, the director general of the World Conservation Union (IUCN) identified the following measures that need to be taken to minimize the scope of corruption related to the environmental sector (Steiner, 2000):

- "Clearly articulate and define the values corruption accords to the environment and natural resources. This can be done through **legislation** (protected areas, pollution standards etc), **policies** (environmental management), and **conventions** (World Heritage Sites; Ramsar; Biodiversity; Climate Change etc).

- Establish an effective **monitoring system** that relies on public, private and civil society input. Only by **pooling resources, information and exposing corrupt practices** through joint initiatives can we close the loopholes. The environment—perhaps more than any other sector—lends itself to such a collaborative effort as NGOs and business have extensive networks, resources and knowledge they can deploy in the absence of adequate public sector funding.

- Develop an effective system of **incentives and sanctions** to reward compliance. The price of corruption must increase dramatically but at the same time the rewards for clean business transactions must also be raised. Simply banning a corporation from all future tenders for one case of corruption may not be as powerful an incentive as a one year ban after which it can regain access to a market if it has put in place checks and balances to avoid future corruption."

These strategies reflect some of the very basic measures towards preventing corruption that can be embedded directly into most environmental programs.

Sector-specific strategies have been developed for the forestry sector. Both Callister (1999) and Kotlobay and Ptichnikov (2002) suggest particular activities targeted at transactions that are prone to corruption. Box 7D presents very specific activities suggested in the WWF report to address illegal logging and forest crime in the Russian Far East.

BOX 7D. WWF suggested strategies to tackle illegal logging and other forest crime (Kotlobay and Ptichnikov, 2002)

Taking urgent measures to counter illegal forest turnover and degradation:
- Banning or considerably reducing the procurement of hardwoods for two to three years.
- Conducting effective forest management (forest cadastre) and determining the remaining stocks of hardwoods and valuable coniferous trees.
- At least doubling the payment for the use of forests, especially hardwood trees.
- Creating a regional center to coordinate activities and train personnel of all state structures that control the distribution, procurement and sale of biological resources.

Making accounting for forest resources more transparent and effective:
- Tightening control over the accuracy of statistics provided by lumbering enterprises in their annual reports.
- Introducing mandatory sale of standing timber to commercial timber procuring organizations through auctions, and reducing considerably the non-competitive use of timber by issuing appropriate instructions by the heads of administrations at all levels.
- Ensuring the publication of information in the mass media about the allotment of sites, introducing open registration of applications for use of forests, holding contests and giving leasing rights with investment requirements for reforestation and non-commercial intermediate wood cutting.
- Stopping short-term lease of forest sites. Promoting long-term lease of forest sites and rejecting short-term lease.

BOX 7D. (continued)

Tightening control over logging:
- Separating the controlling functions of leshozes (local public forest management agency) from economic ones.
- Ensuring that all leshozes are financed from the budget (by 2005).
- Making the work of the State Protection Services more effective by improving its financing from the budget and revising and expanding the powers of its staff, including rewarding its employees through the use of funds obtained in the form of penalties and compensations paid for violations of forest use rules.
- Developing a document at the federal level that regulates the confiscation of technical and transport means used for illegal logging and transportation of timber.
- Establishing a ceiling for damage that may be caused by breaches in forest utilization rules beyond which a lease-holders company will be stripped of his lease and logging license.

Control over timber transportation and storage:
- Proposing that regulations on transport certificates for the transportation of unprocessed timber be worked out and enacted at the federal level.
- Tightening control over mandatory registration of all warehouses and exchanges of unprocessed timber by appropriate administrative and tax authorities.
- Raising penalties for the transportation of timber without proper documents.

Control over the sale of timber:
- Introducing customs codes for Korean and Siberian Pine.
- Developing and enacting regulations on the mandatory sale of unprocessed timber to foreign countries through auctions.
- Raising export duties for unprocessed timber and lowering them for processed timber in order to encourage timber processing inside the country.

In developing an anticorruption strategy, the first and the most logical step should be to conduct a sectoral diagnostic assessment of corruption. This process should include both a multidisciplinary assessment, involving targeted audience surveys and focus groups, and assessments of existing legal frameworks, institutions and programs. The focus of the assessment should be to identify and analyze existing programs and activities conducted by different institutions and stakeholder groups, to pinpoint particular transactions in the environmental sector that are the most vulnerable to different kinds of corruption, to identify openings for anticorruption interventions, and, finally, to develop priorities for anticorruption strategies. Such an overview can provide clear direction to develop practical programs that target the most vulnerable and harmful impacts of corruption. Development and implementation of the strategy should be based on best practices and lessons learned from anticorruption activities implemented in the environmental sector and any other sector when it is appropriate.

It has been proven in practice that the most effective anticorruption strategies are those that combine enforcement, prevention and awareness elements. For sustainability, anticorruption efforts need to emphasize the preventive reforms and public awareness components because these ultimately reduce the opportunities for corruption to occur in the first place.

Table 7.2 presents the areas vulnerable to corruption and anticorruption tools that are likely to be appropriate and effective in addressing these vulnerabilities.

To address corruption on the level of policy development, anticorruption programs should be focused on reforming the decision-making process to be more transparent, opening draft documents to public discussions, conducting negotiated rule-making, implementing control mechanisms to ensure public official accountability, and introducing clear and open procedures for lobbying. Anticorruption strategies on a policy development level can be viewed as inherently cross-sectoral. To achieve better results, interested civil society groups representing different sectors can develop coalitions or alliances around common interests and goals, and together lobby government for reforms.

To prevent corruption and pursue particular environmental interests on the level of policy development, additional activities can be considered. Citizen watchdog groups, for example, have proved to be very effective in monitoring the government. Such watchdog groups usually consist of professionals in environment and policy development who design and implement a system of monitoring of government activities including, for example, establishing policy priorities and decision making processes, and reporting and publicizing any discovered wrongdoings. Another tool that can be effective is establishing an institutionalized dialogue among stakeholder groups and the government to address and resolve potential corruption problems in environmental programs early through developing policies and laws. This can be accomplished by establishing joint working groups or councils, or implementing negotiated rule-making procedures. The mass media can also play an important role, working along with the watchdog groups, to conduct investigations into alleged corruption and publicizing their reports. Public awareness is a very essential element in developing public understanding and getting public support for reforms.

To address corruption in the *distribution of environmental resources,* and in *permitting and certification,* anticorruption strategies should be focused on several areas: bylaws and regulations, process reengineering, and effective oversight. It is essential to ensure that bylaws and regulations are clear and do not leave too much room for subjective interpretation and bureaucratic discretion. Existing and draft laws and regulations should be assessed to increase the risk for committing corrupt transactions. Laws and regulations should be written in plain language to reduce the opportunity for subjective interpretations.

Table 7.2. Vulnerabilities and Possible Responses

Level of Corruption	Areas Vulnerable to Corruption	Anticorruption Tools
Grand corruption	• Environmental and natural resources policy and regulations development	• Lobbying for reforms: transparency, accountability, citizen empowerment • Watchdog groups • Public oversight • Public-private dialogues • Investigative reporting • Public awareness campaigns
Midlevel corruption	• Distribution and designation of environmental/natural resources and territories for particular use (including through public procurement) • Permitting and certifications: issuing permits and certificates for use of territories and natural resources, and operating industrial sites including permits for emissions, discharges, and solid wastes • Environmental assessments (including EIA)	• Process reengineering (streamlined procedures: "one-stop-shops," transparency with embedded control mechanisms) • Straightforward regulations to minimize discretion and enhance transparency and accountability • Justified reasonable standards and requirements • Watchdog groups • Investigative reporting • Stakeholder awareness and education
Petty corruption	• Enforcement (inspections and policing): (1) inspections by environmental protection agencies and other related agencies to assess whether established environmental standards are being met, and (2) policing of violations such as poaching, illegal logging, emissions, and so forth	• Process reengineering (streamlined and transparent procedures with embedded control mechanisms) • Strengthened and more efficient enforcement • Incentive/reward system • Stakeholder awareness and education • Independent inspection groups (like WWF CEDAR groups in Russian Far East)

Streamlining is an important element in preventing corruption in any process related to the distribution of resources or issuing permits. Streamlining or simplifying makes procedures clear and straightforward, reduces the number of direct interactions with officials, and reduces bureaucratic red tape to enhance process transparency and embed internal and external controls.

Enhancing transparency in bureaucratic procedures and decision making processes is essential to reduce opportunities for bureaucrats to manipulate rules and regulations for their personal interests. Laws and regulations should be publicly available so that operators can know and understand the rules. This would reduce opportunities for official extortion due to the legal ignorance of citizens. Watchdog groups can also be very effective in dealing with this kind of corruption by monitoring decisions made by government and keeping officials accountable for their actions.

Corruption that occurs in enforcement practices (inspections and policing) requires a similar type of response with regard to process streamlining and establishing clear regulations. At this level, direct interactions between citizens, businesses and representatives of environmental enforcement agencies are most frequent. Officials who conduct inspections are usually underpaid and are not given incentives for conducting fair inspections. Incentive-based systems that envision rewards for professional, honest inspections should be introduced along with stringent control and oversight mechanisms.

Conclusions

The environmental and natural resources sector is vulnerable to different kinds and levels of corruption. Some environmental programs and projects address corruption by improving transparency and accountability in governance practices, for example, increasing public awareness, introducing better management practices, conducting training, and improving the legal and regulatory system. But often, environmental programs underestimate the damaging impact of corruption on their environmental objectives and do not include direct anticorruption activities into their scope of work. Those programs that address corruption often do it in a nonsystematic way or as a single activity and thus are not very successful in achieving significant results.

If environmental and natural resource programs assess the potential risk of corruption and develop an adequate strategy to address it, they will be off to a good start. Anticorruption activities can either be embedded into environmental programs or anticorruption programs can be extended to the environmental sector. By encouraging partnerships between experts with both environmental and anticorruption specialties, development programs can be made more professional and effective, and the destructiveness of corruption on the environment can be checked.

Chapter 8

Energy

Matthias Ruth

Energy is central to most socioeconomic activities. It powers machines in all sectors of the economy—from agriculture and households to manufacturing and transportation. Those individuals and institutions that control access to the sources, transformation, and distribution of energy hold significant influence. Among the various sources of energy, the fossil-based fuels—coal, natural gas and oil—dominate world energy production (79.8 percent), followed by nuclear energy (11.1 percent) and alternative sources (9.1 percent) (U.S. Department of Energy, 2000).

Extraction of fossil fuels and radioactive materials for nuclear power generation and transformation of these extracted materials into usable forms of energy are typically carried out in large scale at a few locations. Similarly, locations with ample river flow for hydroelectricity, sufficient solar influx for photovoltaic conversion into electricity, geothermal vents for district heating or electricity generation, and significant amounts of biomass for energy conversion are limited. Because of the growing need for energy and limited sources of supply, governments have both natural monopolies in the energy sector and significant interests in protecting their energy supply from disruption. The supply chain from energy extraction to transformation and use typically involves complex infrastructure systems, many institutions and jurisdictions, and, potentially, a large number of end users. Within this energy scenario, ample opportunities exist for high profits and resource rents (Mauro, 1996; 2002), and for individuals to engage in corrupt practices to gain access to, or use, the power associated with access to energy.

Corruption in the Energy Sector

Corruption has been defined by Klitgaard (1988) as "the abuse of office for personal gain." Corruption takes many forms, ranging from grand corruption (the capture of high government office by elites and the use of these offices for private gain) to petty corruption (the use of bribes or other "facilitating payments" to provide services, and bend or break laws) (Azfar, 2002). The ways in which either form of corruption expresses itself is in part a function of the political and economic features of a country (Johnston, 1996, p. 71). Countries with strong private interests and political and economic competition (e.g., the United States and many Western European countries) are susceptible to *interest group bidding* that is largely nonsystematic and carried out on an individual basis. This may thus include bribes to gain assess to markets. In contrast, countries with limited political competition and an *elite hegemony* (e.g., countries of the former Soviet Union and several Asian countries) may be susceptible to individuals and groups selling political access to enrich themselves at the cost of the state.

The key role that the energy sector plays in society and the economy make it vulnerable to corruption. Individuals in the public sector may find opportunities for personal gain due to the influence they hold over access to, and transformation and distribution of energy, including procurement for the development, operation and maintenance of energy system components. In cases where energy systems are being privatized, new opportunities may arise from differences in availability of, and access to information by the public and private sector. For the same reason, individuals in the private sector may have economic and personal motivations to offer bribes to gain access to energy sources, build and maintain transformation and distribution systems, or influence outcomes of privatization efforts. Where energy systems or system components are already privatized, private sector decision makers may have considerable power over regional or even national socioeconomic growth and development, and thus opportunities to abuse that power for personal gain. Lack of budget transparency and oversight—in public and private energy sector components—provide opportunities to hide corrupt activities.

Since the mid-1990s, Transparency International has produced various annual corruption rankings of countries, and since 1999 has provided information on both the "demand side" and "supply side" of corruption. The Corruption Perceptions Index (CPI) combines information from at least three different sources to gauge the level to which individual countries are perceived to be corrupt. Conversely, the Bribe Payers Index (BPI) is a survey-based index intended to reflect a country's presumed propensity to pay bribes.

The CPI takes on a maximum score of 10 for countries considered not corrupt. Of the thirty-two leading mining countries—where, among others, extraction of coal, oil, natural gas, and uranium take place—only nine have a score above 5.0 and the remaining twenty-three have scores of 4.8 or below (Transparency International, 2002). The most recent BPI contains sector-specific as well as country-specific information (Transparency International, 2002). It indicates that many of the sectors associated with energy systems (such as mining, oil and gas, power generation, transmission, public works, and construction) are perceived to be vulnerable to corruption.

A special mention must be made of Botswana—a country rich in mineral resources—which has taken measures to reduce corruption through the enactment in 1994 of the Corruption and Economic Crime Act, which created new categories of offenses associated with corruption, including being in control of disproportionate assets or maintaining an unexplained high standard of living. To deal with these offenses, a Directorate on Corruption and Economic Crime was instituted and given special powers of investigation, arrest, search, and seizure (International Anti-corruption Newsletter, 2000). To increase the chances of success, the creation of the new directorate was accompanied by a public education campaign.

Corruption and Anticorruption Efforts in the Energy Extraction Sector

Causes of Corruption

Mining and drilling operations are significantly dependent on government approval to extract mineral deposits (Schloss, 2000). They involve large lump sum capital investments; long time lags between prospecting and ultimate extraction; supplemental infrastructure development (roads, ports, pipelines, transmission lines); procurements for operation and maintenance of mines and wells; potential negative impacts on local communities, health, and environment; volatility of energy markets; uncertain returns on their investment over long periods of time; underpaid bureaucrats who control access to energy resources, have oversight over infrastructure development and procurement, or assess social, health and environmental impacts (Marshall, 2001); and perceptions that energy sources are part of a "national treasure chest" that rightfully belong to the people and should be exploited for *their* benefit, thus making it easier for individuals to justify their corrupt behavior (Marshall, 2001).

Forms and Extent of Corruption

Because extraction of minerals and fuels is a highly time-sensitive operation and typically requires significant paperwork, bribes or other forms of "facilitating payments"[1] may be made to prompt timely delivery of goods and services, such as permits and licenses for exploration, development of wells and mines, and extraction of minerals and fuels. Though in many cases such bribes amount to petty corruption, the sum total of such payments can be considerable. For instance, approximately one half of total system losses (amounting to an estimated US$100 million) of the Bangladesh Power Development Board (BPDB) and the Dhaka Electricity Supply Authority (DESA) are accounted for by mismanagement and falsified meter reading (Lovei and Alastain, 2000).

Because the extraction of minerals and fuels often involves large physical quantities that may be difficult to track with sufficient detail, opportunities exist to misreport quantities and use the difference for personal gain. For example, anecdotal evidence from the coal industry in Russia and Ukraine suggests that unrecorded coal production illegally sold for the benefit of individual mine managers is a widespread phenomenon, involving local industrial customers, the rail transport system, and port authorities (Lovei and Alastain, 2000).

Corrupt practices may also involve non-cash transactions. For example, because of its strategic importance and significant political influence, Russia's coal mining sector has received considerable subsidies, amounting in 1994 to almost US$2.8 billion, or more than 1 percent of its GDP. Until late 1997, control of these subsidies was the prerogative of RosUgol, the national coal monopoly. Allocation, distribution, and use of these budget funds were highly nontransparent, with no effective monitoring arrangements. Audits of 1996–1997 coal subsidies ordered by the first deputy prime minister and the Duma found that significant sums of money had either been disbursed to the wrong recipients or used for the wrong purposes (Lovei and Alastain, 2000).

Opportunities and Constraints to Address Causes of Corruption

Increasing transparency of transactions and budgets, as well as increasing accountability of institutions and decision makers can help reduce corruption. For example, the Russian government tackled corruption in the coal sector (Lovei and Alastain, 2000) by dissolving RosUgol, transferring all subsidy management functions to the appropriate agencies, establishing earmarked federal treasury accounts for all subsidy categories and recipients, and putting in place mechanisms that ensure that individual entitlements go directly to individuals, and not through coal companies.

In cases that involve international companies, introducing codes of conduct, monitoring foreign partners and their collaborators, training employees and establishing organizational structures to monitor and enforce codes of conduct, may reduce corruption.[2] These may include establishing internal audit departments or other codes of conduct that represent corporate values in a consistent manner.

Anticorruption strategies may be stifled by the fact that those individuals who are most influential in bringing about change (e.g., political elites, bureaucrats, chief executives) are often also the ones who may lose the most if corruption is curtailed. This is reinforced by the lack of transparency in economic and political decision making. Additionally, companies engaging in corruption may gain market access and power, and thus out-compete *non-corrupt* firms.

Corruption and Anticorruption Efforts in the Energy Transformation and Distribution Sector

Causes of Corruption

Transportation of primary energy sources (e.g., coal, oil, gas), their transformation into more useful forms (e.g., in refineries or power plants), and their distribution to end users (e.g., with pipelines or power lines) all typically involve large capital investments and movement of large physical quantities. Movement of coal, oil, gas, and electricity may occur within districts and/or across countries and thus involve a range of firms, institutions and jurisdictions.

If transportation and distribution of energy occurs across national boundaries—and especially if transactions occur on spot markets or are arranged through short-term deals—opportunities exist for off-budget transactions that are difficult to trace. Such off-budget transactions may provide (potentially sizeable) opportunities for appropriations by, or payments to the decision makers involved. To the extent that distribution of energy from producers to consumers involves large numbers of people who individually account for small shares of final consumption and revenues, corruption in this part of the energy sector is typically small-scale, involving petty bribes and theft. For example, lack of adequate supply, cumbersome paperwork, noncomputerized databases, and large backlog make petty corruption more prevalent in developing countries that are overwhelmed with demand and are relatively less regulated. The consumer's willingness to pay for convenience (getting new connections quickly, avoiding time-consuming paper work, etc.) has created a supply side pressure that serves to perpetuate this form of corruption.

Forms and Extent of Corruption

The main areas of corruption in the distribution of energy—and electricity in particular—include, among others, nontechnical system loss (e.g., falsified meter readings, altered invoices and illegal purchases); interference in the flow of funds/barter/offsets within the system and to fuel suppliers; manipulation of the flows of electricity to favored customers; and opaque uneconomic import arrangements. For example, surveys sponsored by the World Bank, as part of load management and agricultural electricity studies in India, have shown that 20 percent to 30 percent of electricity attributed to unmetered agricultural consumption is in fact appropriated by high-income households, industry and large commercial establishments, such as shopping malls (Lovei and McKechnie, 2000). Such "appropriations" constitute corrupt behavior if those entities that receive electricity for free or at reduced prices provide in return financial or political support to individuals who are in charge of collection of payments.

Preliminary estimates for the electricity sectors of Ukraine, Moldova, Georgia, Armenia, Kazakhstan, Bulgaria, Romania, and Kyrgyzstan suggest that theft and other corruption amount to 15 percent to 30 percent of total electricity sales. The lack of revenue from electricity generation and distribution may jeopardize financial stability of the power sector—insufficient funds may be available to purchase input fuels or maintain generators or distribution networks—and as a result consumers may experience loss of service and/or individuals and institutions in the electricity sector may be enticed to engage in corrupt practices to ensure that electricity can be generated and distributed. In such cases, corrupt practices may ripple through the electricity sector and from it through the sectors that extract energy or help develop, operate, and maintain energy infrastructures.[3]

Other corrupt practices may involve accounts receivable collections and procurement, including corruption in the acquisition of capital goods, operating materials, and retaining consultants (Munshi, 2000). For instance, bidding on a project may be closed and re-opened repeatedly until a certain vendor wins the contract. The bribery mechanisms that are typically used in these cases include accessing inside information, influencing specifications and purchasing recommendations, and may range from small fees paid to clerical staff to large-scale bribes to senior officials. Political influence is usually applied at the highest levels and then allowed to work its way down the chain of command (Munshi, 2000).

Corruption at the consumer level in the power sector is endemic to developing and transitional economies because lack of weak judicial and regulatory systems make it difficult for investors to take parties that have violated contracts to court. The existence of a political culture that overlooks corruption acts as an incentive for corruption. Some perceive such attitudes as part of a traditional culture predating, for instance, the Communist period wherein officialdom traditionally viewed public property as belonging to no one. The breakdown of order because of the dissolving former Soviet Union and a subsequent failure to create a new system may have furthered opportunities for corruption to take place. Opportunities for corruption are further increased when civil servants are underpaid (Kramer, 1999).

Opportunities and Constraints to Address Causes of Corruption

Anticorruption measures in the transformation and distribution segment of an energy system may include establishment of a legal framework and an autonomous, transparent regulatory body with sufficient authority to oversee energy transformation and distribution. Clear guidelines must exist for accounting practices; budgets need to be transparent and accessible; and auditing systems must be developed to ensure that existing guidelines and rules are followed. Other strategies that could reduce corruption include unbundling of the power system into separate energy transformation, transmission, and distribution entities; establishment of decentralized, competitive electricity markets; and decentralization of payments between distribution and generation companies.

Privatization of a utility monopoly such as a power distribution company poses special regulatory challenges. In a bribery economy, deregulation may spawn new corruption opportunities. Whenever a portion of the enterprise is privatized, the privatized portion must carry on business transactions with the public portion that are subject to corruption. For example, if accounts receivable collections are out-sourced then a vendor may be able to underreport collections and if power generation is privatized, power vendors may be able to overreport sales. Again, accounting guidelines, budgetary transparency and auditing can help identify corrupt behaviors.

Potential industry architecture changes would minimize the role of the public sector without creating a private sector monopoly. It is anticipated that as microgeneration of power (e.g., with combine-heat and power systems or from alternative energy sources) becomes popular, many large industrial and commercial consumers will generate their own power. This new technology may encourage proliferation of small-scale utility cooperatives that could create a new kind of power distribution architecture with little scope for the government to become involved.

Other approaches may include formation of *integrity pacts* (IPs) to help governments, businesses and civil society establish mutual contractual rights and obligations. IPs are typically developed for contracts between state-owned enterprises and private entities interested in obtaining such contracts. Integrity Pacts thus aim at enabling the bidders, or the contractor implementing the contract, to abstain from bribing. Whenever possible, IPs should cover all the activities related to the contract from the pre-selection of bidders, the bidding and contracting proper, through the implementation, to the completion and operation of business (Transparency International, 2001).

Conclusions

The time-sensitive nature of energy resources, combined with the possibilities of generating considerable economic rents from energy extraction, transformation and use, the need for large capital investments and procurements, as well as a central role of government agencies to oversee virtually all aspects of the energy sector—whether privatized or not—make the energy sector a prime target for and source of corruption. Corruption occurs in many different forms, depending on features of the supply chain of each specific energy source, the significance of that specific energy source in the local and national economy, the sociopolitical and institutional context within which extraction, transformation and use occur, the number of individuals participating in decision making and the cultural environment within which decisions are made, and the transparency of those decisions and accounting methods, as well as a lack of effectiveness of legal systems to sanction abuse of power by decision makers. Efforts to reduce corruption need to consider simultaneously these issues in order to be effective. However, empirical and anecdotal evidence suggest a set of general recommendations that may be followed:

Privatization and Development of Markets. To the extent that privatization exposes producers to the incentives and disciplines of the market, it serves as a natural counterbalance to corruption among company managers, who may be, for the first time, answerable to private owners with an interest in protecting and increasing the value of their assets (Lovei and McKechnie, 2000). However, privatizing the power sector is not a panacea, and benefits of markets may only be realized if they are supported by the appropriate institutions. Such institutions may include independent energy regulatory bodies that help increase accountability and transparency. Similarly, international management contracts may help improve governance. It is thus a cooperative process between the government, the private sector and nongovernment organizations (Asian Development Bank, 2000a, p. 28) that can help make privatization and market-orientation a successful anticorruption strategy.

The developments of markets (such as sophisticated national and international markets for energy sources and energy-system infrastructure for transformation and distribution) need social peace and the enactment of enforceable laws. Corruption is more likely to retard than augment commerce and contribute to the very existence of poor laws and weak legal systems.

In cultures used to public sector corruption, corruption seems to continue to thrive when an organization moves to the private sector. Although the private sector may not have a formal monopoly, given time and quality constraints on the purchaser, the seller's employees may still be in a position to extract monetary "inducements" from the situation. The lack of accountability in newly privatized firms without adequate financial controls allows employees to take personal advantage of their corporate position in much the same way that lack of account-ability in the public sector enables civil servants to abuse their public sector positions for personal gain. This is often exacerbated by the fact that public officials are intricately involved in the process of privatization and often hold personal and financial stakes (e.g. in the form of shares, board memberships and voting rights).

Decentralization of Political Decision-making. It has been argued that decentralization improves governance and public service delivery by increasing "allocative efficiency" by better matching public services to local preferences and "productive efficiency" through increased accountability of local governments to citizens, fewer levels of bureaucracy, and better knowledge of local costs. The allocative efficiency argument presumes that citizens are able to "vote with their feet" (e.g., citizens are free to find alternatives to centralized power supply), and the productive efficiency argument assumes that decentralization occurs within an institutional environment that provides political, administrative, and financial authority to local governments, along with effective channels of local accountability and central oversight (Kahkonen and Lanyi, 2001).

Empirical evidence on the links between decentralization of power and corruption are mixed. Fisman and Gatti (2000) find that countries where subnational governments control a large share of expenditures are less corrupt but acknowledge that this could be driven by reverse causality, as the central governments in highly corrupt countries are unlikely to devolve expenditure authority to local governments.

Development of Alternative Energy Sources. A key obstacle to many anticorruption efforts lies in the highly centralized nature of the energy sector, which requires large capital investments, large (public and private sector) bureaucracies, and has high stakes associated with decisions. In contrast, a decentralized energy system may rely more heavily on local energy sources to meet local needs—solar collectors on rooftops, combined heat and power plants for small residential neighborhoods or businesses, windmills for local energy generation, or local biomass-to-energy conversion facilities. Decentralization of the energy system may provide more local control over energy supply and thus help reduce opportunities for corruption by complementing privatization of the energy sector, development of energy markets, and decentralization of the political decision making process.

Strengthening Legal Systems. For legal systems to be effective in fighting corruption, laws prohibiting corrupt activities must be in place, the police force and prosecutors must be effective in investigating corruption and bringing charges against offenders, and the judiciary system must act in a fair and impartial manner. A strengthened legal system may involve establishment of an inspector general or an anticorruption commission with powers to investigate corruption and bring charges.

Transparency and Development of Civil Society. Because granting authority without accountability can lead to corruption and lower productive efficiency, decentralization of the political decision-making process and privatization of the energy sector need to be accompanied by reforms that increase the transparency and accountability of local government and business decision-makers. Providing citizens with information about government and business activities and an opportunity to have their voices heard is key to transparency and development of a strong civil society. It requires the media to play a crucial role in information dissemination and education (Kahknonen and Lanyi, 2001) and freedom of information (FOI) legislation to support the information collection and dissemination activities of the media and citizens.

Development of Codes of Conduct. Globally active energy companies may temporarily gain market share and raise profits by engaging in corrupt practices, but when such practices are exposed, their reputation may be affected and their ability to engage in contracts in the future may be severely hampered. To ensure consistent, ethical behavior of company employees will require establishment of codes of conduct, training of employees to abide by these codes, and monitoring and sanctioning of employee behavior. To administer codes of conduct in energy companies that often have employees from different countries that hold their citizens to different legal standards of corruption, will require high corporate standards. Companies have tried to incorporate anticorruption measures in the company policy. For instance, in case a corrupt practice is observed, it is investigated and employees involved are dismissed and, if possible, prosecuted.[4]

Collective Action. Energy sector businesses that implement and abide by high, internationally recognized standards may together with government representatives and NGOs advise countries on possible reform of their legislation to reduce corruption. Such collective efforts may directly contribute to legislative reform and indirectly strengthen industry–government–citizen relationships, overall improve the political and economic environment within which energy-sector-related decisions are made, and thus improve economic efficiency and welfare. The formation of the Petroleum Advisory Group (PAG) in Georgia is an illustration of this sort of initiative. The PAG consists of industry representatives, international energy consultants, USAID representatives, and government officials who look into causes of corruption within industry and offer solutions to address corruption. Not only is the PAG involved in developing recommendations for the government, it is also involved in implementing them.[5]

Many of the strategies to address corruption can make good economic and political sense in their own right. In order to avoid offending local decision-makers and thus undermining their effectiveness, anticorruption strategies may pursue these strategies without explicit reference to corruption-related issues. For these strategies to be fully effective, however, will likely require pursuing several (if not all) of them at once.

Notes

1. "Facilitating payments may include "signature bonuses" by oil companies to gain access to rights to oil resources. See *The Economist* (2002, p. 59).

2. Several energy companies have developed codes of conduct, training programs and mechanisms for sanctioning individuals who do not abide by these codes. See, for example, http://www2.shell.com/home/media-en/downloads/dealing_with_bribery_and_corruption _primer.pdf.

3. USAID's India Mission has recently decided to focus their reform efforts on energy distribution, in part because the generation and transmission subsectors will not be able to pay their bills until the service that the distribution sector provides is moved from a political to an economic good, based on market-driven principles, and with availability/reliability/quality issues resolved such that people will be willing to pay for the service.

4. See, e.g., http://www2.shell.com/home/.

5. B. Shenoy, personal communication, October 23, 2002.

Chapter 9

Private Sector

Russ Webster

Let's imagine for a moment two people each running a different business. The first is a small shop owner who makes and sells pastries, cakes, and other delectable treats to many satisfied customers, from local townsfolk to the many tourists that visit from spring to fall each year. He has been in business for five years, but he is starting to worry about the future. He has noticed the health inspector is making more visits, unannounced, and asking the usual questions that lead up to the inevitable, subtle, and unspoken cash transaction, followed by a smile and topped off with a *gratis* espresso and slice of his renowned chocolate torte. Other officials were on the move too for some reason. The tax inspector had already made twice as many visits this year than last. And, just the other day, the director from the local business licensing office unexpectedly stopped by. After small talk, complimentary cakes and ice cream, he mentioned that, "oh, by the way," our shop-owner-friend should stop by the licensing office soon to discuss some "irregularities" in the licensing papers he had filed this year. This, of course, could mean only one thing: yet another payment to keep his business "legal." His *unofficial payments* to government officials this year would certainly double at this rate.

Our second businessman manages a large holding company with several subsidiary interests in trade, telecommunications, print media, and light manufacturing exports. Right now he is on his way to a cocktail reception where he hopes he will meet the deputy minister for public works and communications. He has already had two meetings with the deputy to discuss the government's plan to privatize the largest TV broadcasting network in the country. The deputy knows of his company's interest in winning the bid, but our business manager is becoming less certain of success. He recently learned their major competitor was lining up a foreign joint-venture partner with the promise of additional financing and access to new technologies that could sweeten their position and give them an unbeatable edge. Unfortunately, his company had not been able to line up such partners. He was hoping that tonight the deputy would agree to have dinner with him next week. He would, for sure, have to offer a substantial gift to win the deputy's favor, particularly in light of his competitor's growing advantage.

The involvement of a foreign investor did add another wrinkle that he might be able to work to his advantage, however. Several parliamentarians recently had introduced a draft bill to prohibit foreign investors from operating in certain "strategic sectors." Broadcasting was on that list, but he had heard from his friends in parliament that certain private interests were lobbying heavily to get it removed. Tomorrow, he would call his cousin who works in the prime minister's office to find out which members of parliament were wavering on this issue, and then try to go meet with them. It could prove to be an expensive year for doing business, but he would give it his best shot.

Many factors affect corruption between the public and private sector.[1] In the case of our baker, he must pay bribes out of necessity. If he did not pay, he would face several dangers. The paperwork might slow down to the point he has to spend more and more time chasing bureaucrats and less time running his business. Or, even worse, the corrupt officials could deny him a license and force him to shut down. Taxes present him with another problem. If, as in many early stage open-market economies, his taxes are high and the tax code frequently changes, then it is probably cheaper (and quicker) to pay off the tax inspector than it is to put the time and money into following the letter of the tax laws, even though this is a short-run solution with dubious and unpredictable risks attached.

So, like a good business manager, our baker weighs his options, and chooses the most economical means of staying in business. But, what appears to be a quicker way to get the job done now (paying the bribe) can become an expensive proposition over time with uncertain outcomes. The costs and risks of corruption are economically *inefficient* and thereby distort growth potential. The bribes he must pay are nothing but uneconomical transaction costs: they are rent payments that add nothing to his business. If he could instead invest those monies, he could grow his business and create more jobs, produce more and better goods for his customers, generate higher incomes for himself and his employees, and generally contribute to a better standard of living for his community. Because so many businesses face the same problem, the negative impacts on the local economy can be significant.

We might try to argue that the bribes are simply another form of taxing our baker, and if his bribery payments are less than what he would pay in taxes, then he is, in fact, better off. Well, yes...and no: yes, the *costs may* be less, but the *returns certainly* are less. In a developed economy, tax payments go towards the public good: infrastructure that businesses need (water, electricity, roads), education that builds human skill and knowledge, health services for employees, a central banking system that stabilizes financial markets, a police force that protects citizens, a judicial system that upholds the law, and the like. With an adequate and reliable tax system, governments can pay a living wage to bureaucrats and inspectors so that they are under less pressure to engage in bribery and corruption.

But this brings us to yet more issues that shape the mindset of our baker. Public services may not be improving. In some former communist countries, they may even be worse than before. He certainly is not convinced that the government uses its budget wisely. So why should he pay his taxes? The streets are in shambles. Telephone service is erratic. Health costs are skyrocketing. He is being told that soon the cost of electricity will almost double. He has little police protection, if any; the police certainly are not protecting him from the local mafia thugs that he *also* has to pay for "protection." So, in his cynical view bribery and corruption are a necessary evil, a fact of life and the reality of running a business. He sees no alternative. There is no one to complain to that will set things right.

The case of our large business manager is a bit different. He is trying to "buy" decision outcomes that will favor his enterprise and create a better growth opportunity. As we can see from the example, this significantly distorts the marketplace by eliminating competition that would produce greater value for consumers; when pressured out, the more efficient international investor will take his business and go somewhere else. In the short run, buying influence may produce growth opportunities for his business, but these are uneconomical and unsustainable in the medium to long term. Having paid once, he will likely have to pay again and again to secure his noncompetitive position. Herein is a strong similarity to our baker: the money spent on bribes is money taken away from productive invest-ment. Capital productivity declines, markets distort, and the economy suffers.

A number of studies over the past decade seek to explain the dynamics or underlying causes of corruption as well as the economic impacts. Although researchers debate the methodological rigor and statistical validity of specific stud-ies, evidence is emerging of a definite relationship between corruption and eco-nomic growth. The causal relationship may not be clear, but we know that economies with less corruption perform better. Most experts accept that there is a cyclical nature to corruption and poverty, where each feeds on and contributes to the other. However, until recently many scholars regarded corruption as a rel-atively low transaction cost compared to the benefits from increased employment and income in, for example, less-developed countries. Using mainly macroeco-nomic variables, these studies argued that bribery was an efficient means to secure productive capital investments that contribute to economic growth; in other words, the bribe simply helped to "grease the wheels" for the immediate transac-tion. This macro view was based mainly in Coasian theory, which states that if market transactions are costless, a rearrangement of rights will always take place if it leads to an increase in production value.[2] Another way of stating this is to say that if nothing obstructs efficient bargaining, then the parties to the negotiation will reach the most efficient agreement, commonly called a state of Pareto effi-ciency.[3] The problem with this model is that the Coasian world of costless bar-gaining, perfect information, and efficient markets is far different than the real world, where affected parties are kept out of negotiations, information is restricted, and wealth accumulates to a few who control access to markets and to the levers of decision-making that establish un-economic rules of the marketplace.

New evidence, however, better illuminates the negative affects of corruption. The World Bank and other donors have supported research that looks at a broad range of institutional and legal variables affecting (a) the competitive position of enterprises and in turn (b) the comparative strengths of the economy. For exam-ple, Mauro (1995, pp. 681-712) argues that corruption has a negative impact on the ratio of investments to GDP. There is also a strong correlation between GDP and rankings on corruption indexes. In their work on economic growth and gov-ernance, Kaufmann and Kraay (2002) analyze the strong positive correlation between governance and per capita incomes, for example. Among the more inter-esting current debates is the question of "causality," that is, does corruption result in low GDP or does low GDP cause corruption? Many scholars have been uncon-vinced by the evidence, concluding that this is a "vicious cycle" of one affecting the other, and that the focus should be on "breaking this cycle" through economic growth and governance improvements.[4] The Kaufmann/Kraay study, however, suggests that there is more likely a flow of causality from good governance to increased incomes, rather than the reverse flow, which in fact may be somewhat negative. How then would we explain the phenomenon of China's economic growth without democratic reforms? Kaufmann et al may explain this by looking at the negative reverse relationship between growth and governance. Recent studies of China have looked closely at the tenuous nature of its growth, which is being held together through unsustainable state intervention and dubious fiscal management, and an alarming level of corruption. In fact, it appears that areas of China that successfully institute good governance reforms are out-performing other areas still plagued by corruption (Kynge 2002).[5]

Where Corruption Occurs

Some level of corruption is common in most of the world. (See Tables 9.1 and 9.2 for comparative regional data on corruption.) Most international companies have long accepted bribery as necessary for doing business in less developed economies where public officials had substantial control over contracts, licenses, and foreign investment decisions. Until recently, most Western countries even allowed bribery payments to foreign countries as legitimate business expenses.[6]

Times are changing, however, and the anticorruption movement is growing in the business world. This movement has some roots in the Foreign Corrupt Practices Act passed in the United States in 1977 and similar laws passed in other countries with global business interests. Today there is a host of organizations promoting the benefits-social, political, and economic-of ethical business practices. And, their credibility has been strengthened by recent studies showing not only the negative economic impacts of corruption, but also the positive effects on markets and economic growth that a stable investment climate and rule of law can have. Businesses are starting to listen and adopt "good governance" or "ethical business" programs for several reasons. Many global enterprises have prominent places in the market; they also know that a good public image and good public relations will help secure this position. And, aside from their sense of social responsibility, some enlightened business managers have a longer-term vision and know that corruption hinders social and economic development. By doing their part to foster growth of under-developed economies, they are creating new markets and wealthier consumers.

Some basic concepts will help us understand the impacts of corruption. How does corruption harm private sector development? How does it harm the economy? If an under-paid government worker can make a little on the side to better feed his or her family, why should we be concerned? The fundamental issue is about short-term gain to a few versus long-term harm to many. As we saw from the two examples above, although the business (and the corrupt official) may gain in the short run, the bribe payment shifts money away from potentially productive investments in the business. These noneconomic transaction costs keep the level of enterprise development low relative to those enterprises that are able to invest in growing their business.

Table 9.1. Comparisons of Bribery Payments by Region and by Firm Size

Category	Percentage of firms that responded they had to make "irregular payments" to get things done always, mostly, or frequently.
By Region	
South Asia	65%
Developing East Asia	62%
Africa	52%
Middle East and North Africa	36%
Central and Eastern Europe	33%
Commonwealth of Independent States	29%
Latin America and Caribbean	28%
Organization for Economic Cooperation and Development countries	12%
Developed East Asia	11%
By Firm Size, All Regions	
Small	40%
Medium	34%
Large	31%

Source: Bata, Kaufmann, and Stone (2002).

Table 9.2. Percentage of Revenues Paid in Unofficial Payments to Public Officials, by Region

Region	Percentage of revenues paid	Percentage of firms responding "0% paid"
Africa	Not asked	Not asked
Middle East and North Africa	Not asked	Not asked
Central and Eastern Europe	5.5%	0.9%
South Asia	5.0%	18.8%
Developing East Asia	4.6%	22.7%
Commonwealth of Independent States	3.4%	3.4%
Latin America and Caribbean	2.0%	58.0%
East Asia (not including China)	0.6%	86.3%
Organization for Economic Cooperation and Development countries	0.6%	83.0%
Average	3.0%	38.7%

Source: Bata, Kaufmann, and Stone (2002).

To generate growth, businesses must use their capital resources productively. When capital is drawn away into non-economic transactions, this negatively affects enterprise growth as well as the marketplace in general. Corruption distorts growth incentives also by forcing out potentially better producers of goods or services. As we can see in the second example, bribes to policy decision-makers give one firm an edge over the competition; it is, however, an uncertain edge that may be good only for the time being, for this one transaction, for the parties to the negotiation and *not* for the market. This "edge" too is not based on market factors; it is a non-economic advantage granted through rent payments to the state. That is, one firm wins the contract or pushes out the competition not because of the value they bring to the market, but because they can distort market-effects by controlling political decisions and their outcomes. The competition-who is prepared to bring new communication technologies and other sources of financing to the deal-loses the deal and their competitive advantage is kept out of the marketplace. Who loses? Workers who could have received a better wage working for a more competitive enterprise; consumers who could have gotten better quality goods or services at a better price; ultimately, the economy, which could have generated a better standard of living for all citizens.

This is a basic description of how corruption affects enterprise growth and economic development. But where do these corrupt transactions typically take place? Before we look at this range of "vulnerabilities" where corruption between business and government occurs, let's turn back to our two examples because they illustrate two broad categories of corruption that are useful to our understanding. Our baker faces the problem of *administrative corruption* or what is sometimes called "petty corruption" (although this term, I believe, understates the impact of a single corrupt act that is typically repeated numerous times and collectively produces significant harm by keeping poor people poor and holding back those who could move ahead). He must pay bribes to public officials to keep his business running. These could be in the form of "processing fees" to get documents, or what we might call "blinder fees" to keep an inspector's head turned in the other direction. These payments do not "grease the wheels" of the plodding bureaucracy like some would think; they establish rules (albeit unpredictable) for the game that create *incentives* for public officials to fabricate more and more delays.

The second example illustrates another form of corruption called *state capture*. This is the payment of bribes and use of influence to shape the policy and legal environment to the captor firm's advantage. A *capture economy* is one where such payments and influence are common variables in the state's decision-making procedures. The negative impacts of state capture are not insignificant, even over a short period of time. A recent study by the World Bank showed that the overall growth rate of enterprises in a *capture economy* is about ten percentage points lower than a non-capture economy over a three-year period (Hellman, Jones, and Kaufmann, 2000).

The dynamics of state capture can involve active solicitation from the public sector side as well. In our example, the businessman is buying a decision from a policy maker. In reality, decision makers frequently abuse their position and offer up their influence to solicit support from business in the form of cash or gifts. It would be misleading to portray public officials as passive players that can be "engaged" or "captured" for the right price. Public officials also seek to sell their influence and power to the highest bidder. Public sector corruption also perpetuates a kind of illicit hierarchy where lower level jobs are sold off and these in turn create informal systems of kickbacks and patronage that perpetuate corrupt practices, inefficiencies, and barriers to meaningful public sector reform. In this way, the higher levels of corruption that we have characterized as state capture are linked down through the bureaucracy to administrative corruption that occurs at lower, seemingly less harmful, levels. The point here is that public sector corruption creates a murky culture of abusive alliances where power and influence flow in many directions among players in government as well as business.

Table 9.3 describes the situations where corruption can most commonly occur in the relationships between public officials and private businesses. Notice that most of the situations described fall into the category of *state capture.*

We can readily see that there is wide opportunity for corruption between business and government in an environment where rules and regulations are ambiguous and where oversight is weak. It is a natural tendency for businesses to

Table 9.3. Vulnerabilities: Instances Where Corruption Can Take Place

- Where a government agent is responsible for issuing of licenses, permits, customs clearance and border-crossing documents, banking licenses, and so forth.
- Where government regulators decide about price controls or taxes on commodities (e.g., to keep prices high on locally produced commodities that have an inelastic demand; or to assign high duties on imported goods that compete with domestic producers).
- Where policies are set that could block new firms and investors from entering the marketplace, and thereby allow a monopoly position of another firm.
- In the awarding of contracts for publicly procured goods or services.
- In making policy decisions or enacting laws that would grant to certain classes of enterprises subsidies, soft credits, or tax exemptions.
- Where government inspectors monitor tax compliance or evasion.
- In the setting of and administration of foreign exchange control mechanisms.
- In allocating real estate/privatizing state properties.
- Where government agencies could "selectively" enforce socially desirable regulations (e.g., location of certain types of businesses, enforcement of equal employment regulations, etc.)
- Where monitoring mechanisms are weak and allow government officials to maintain obscure or secret budgetary accounts.

Source: Kaufmann (1999), p. 94.

seek advantage over their competitors, and it is not surprising that public officials would take advantage of weak institutional frameworks to peddle their influence for personal gain. Weak institutions, an uncertain rule of law, insecure property rights and the like encourage the kind of short term focus on day-to-day business survival that makes corruption appear more beneficial than it in fact is. The correlation between the rule of law and the "marketplace for corruption" is an inverse one. A strong rule of law would be characterized by:

- A rational set of laws governing the operations of private business, the protection of property rights, and the enforcement of contracts.
- Antimonopoly policies and procedures to enforce them.
- A reasonable rate of taxation on private business.
- An efficient system of patents and protection for intellectual property.
- An efficient and stable set of regulations governing licensing, inspections and audits on business.
- An efficient judiciary (and alternative dispute resolution mechanisms) for sorting out contract disputes.
- Administrative procedures that guarantee public access to government decision makers and to their deliberations that shape policies and laws.
- Laws and administrative procedures that protect "whistle blowers" from reprisal.
- Laws and enforcement mechanisms that ensure accountability of private firms to their shareholders and capital markets.
- Disclosure laws that compel those in public office to disclose private financial interests.

In addition to public laws and governmental institutions, the private sector can also play a role in supporting the rule of law by promoting, for example, efficient capital market systems and institutions; practice of good corporate governance and business ethics (this is a role for associations, for example), and quality standards for goods and services in the marketplace. There is also an obvious role for education and training institutions that target entrepreneurs and business managers.

Aside from the negative impacts of corruption on private enterprise development and economic growth, why is a strong rule of law important to individual businesses? A major problem facing all businesses is risk. From the early stages of developing a business plan, to the point of running a successful operation, business managers are constantly dealing with risk. Risk is a natural force shaping the behavior of enterprises and the character of the marketplace in any economy. But, a strong rule of law helps to reduce risk or at least make it easier to estimate accurately by creating institutions and laws that are predictably-not idiosyncratically-enforced. Risks therefore are higher in an economy characterized by administrative corruption, rent-seeking officials, or a plethora of firms seeking to capture the state. If risk can be lowered through a rule of law that successfully mitigates corruption, investors are more likely to enter the market in greater numbers and dollars.

Up to this point we have highlighted the public sector side of corruption by focusing on the rule of law and how the absence of transparent, accountable public institutions and regulations creates the opportunity (and the incentive) for corrupt transactions. Within this view, we are naturally led to look towards "fixing the public sector" as a solution to the problem of corruption. No doubt the public sector has a major role to play, and indeed much of the literature to date is focused on the role of government, and on how ineffective public institutions and legal frameworks breed corruption. However, recent debates and studies are focusing more on how *corruption breeds inefficient and unaccountable governments*. (The popular cliché is "corruption is a two-way street.") This is a more complete picture because it highlights the role that business plays in perpetuating corruption, and leads us to explore strategies that involve changing the behavior of business, not just of government. In this regard there have been several conferences, papers, and workshops of late that explore the linkages between good *corporate governance* and corruption.

Corporate governance describes the relationship between the managers of a company and other stakeholders. How does this relate to corruption? Basically, if a company is accountable about its use of capital resources, then bribery payments should be disclosed. The threat of "exposure" is a disincentive to corruption. But, beyond simple accounting, ethical business practices are regarded more and more as important aspects of corporate governance. In 1999, twenty-nine member countries of the OECD adopted the principles of corporate governance appearing in Table 9.4. In 2000, these principles were included among the 12 core "standards for global financial stability" which are recognized as important benchmarks by international financial institutions. According to the OECD,

"A good corporate governance regime helps to assure that corporations use their capital efficiently. Good corporate governance helps, too, to ensure that corporations take into account the interests of a wide range of constituencies, as well as of the communities within which they operate, and that their boards are accountable to the company and the shareholders. This, in turn, helps to assure that corporations operate for the benefit of society as a whole. It helps to maintain the confidence of investors—both foreign and domestic—and to attract more 'patient,' long-term capital." (OECD Principles of Corporate Governance, 1999, p. 7)

Table 9.4. OECD Principles of Corporate Governance [7]

The Corporate Governance framework should:

1. Protect shareholders' rights.
2. Ensure the equitable treatment of all shareholders, including minority and foreign share-holders. All shareholders should have the opportunity to obtain effective redress for violation of their rights.
3. Recognize the rights of stakeholders as established by law and encourage active co-operation between corporations and stakeholders in creating wealth, jobs, and the sustainability of financially sound enterprises.
4. Ensure that timely and accurate disclosure is made on all material matters regarding the corporation, including the financial situation, performance, ownership, and governance of the company.
5. Ensure the strategic guidance of the company, the effective monitoring of management by the board, and the board's accountability to the company and the shareholders.

We can see from this how lax corporate governance and the lack of corporate accountability facilitate corruption "vulnerabilities" between business and the public sector. If managers are not answerable to shareholders and other stakeholders about how they use corporate funds and negotiate agreements, then there is less risk of getting caught. In fact, the incentives to be corrupt and the likelihood of succeeding at it become greater as oversight structures become weaker. Hellman et al. discovered that in capture economies (characterized by a high degree of state capture corruption), captor firms grew four times as fast as other firms in the capture economy, and also had substantially greater levels of investment. But, let's not be misled by these growth rates. In spite of these gains to a few, the losses are greater to the private sector as a whole when compared with non-capture economies: the average growth rate of sales for all firms in high capture countries is only 11.1 percent, compared to 21.4 percent in low capture countries (Hellman, Jones, and Kaufmann, 2000, p. 18). The long-term wealth of "gainer firms" in a capture economy is questionable too. Their "gains" are only relative in comparison to those firms they have been able to push out of the marketplace. The fact that they substitute corruption for productive investments and sound business practices undermines their long-term viability and global competitiveness.

Responses to Corruption in the Dealings Between Business and Government

Mitigating corruption that takes place between the public sector and business is a huge challenge. People in developing and transitioning economies have long accepted corruption as common practice. They do not like it when it directly affects them, but they see no alternative to getting business done. Effective anticorruption programs also require resources, so although politicians denounce corruption, they may lack the funds to finance the institutional, legal, and human resource changes that are necessary to get positive results.

Faced with serious budget constraints, government leaders find it very difficult to accomplish two things necessary to mitigate corruption. The first is to shift the incentives so that public officials are not tempted by bribes. This means increasing government salaries and benefits, and putting in place performance incentives with monetary rewards. The second area has to do with establishing a rule of law and the means to enforce it. This means implementing new laws, strengthening public agencies, building an effective and efficient judiciary, and creating reasonable yet effective oversight agencies that can identify and punish offenders, both from government as well as business. Although these measures are costly, the negative impacts on enterprise development, global competitiveness, and economic growth are worse.

What needs to be done to support anticorruption efforts in the public sector? The list is long but necessary if governments want to pursue a serious anticorruption program:

- Immediate adoption of laws that require public hearing periods for proposed laws and amendments, and implementation of public sector reforms that open the policy process to broad civic participation.
- Setting of harsh criminal penalties for extortion by public officials.
- Adopting laws on political financing and asset declaration.
- Adopting laws and regulations on lobbying.
- Adopting laws and creating effective regulatory agencies that protect markets from monopolization and enforce antitrust.
- Enacting "sunshine" laws that enable public access to government hearings, legislative debates, and require publicly available minutes.
- Adopting "freedom of information" legislation that allows public access to all official documents, and mandatory disclosure of individual votes in parliament/legislature.
- Creation of a "corruption impact" agency to monitor and analyze potential vulnerabilities in government operations and new legislation.
- Requiring publication of court decisions and case schedules.
- Working with the media to inform and educate the public.

In addition to these legal and institutional reform efforts, governments must set a high priority for basic training and capacity building efforts for elected officials and all public agencies (including the judiciary) that interact with the private sector. The best way to raise awareness is through public education and open dialogue about corruption and how it affects the community and the economy.

Some recent innovations seem to hold particular promise in mitigating administrative corruption. One is "one-stop-shopping" for business licenses and other operating permits. Naturally, the greater the number of official stamps or signatures that a business needs to operate, the greater the number of vulnerabilities or opportunities there are for bribery. Local governments are beginning to realize that they will attract more investment if they simplify these procedures and assign one office to interact with local businesses on all official matters. This approach has been piloted successfully in a number of transitioning economies of the former Soviet bloc. E-government is a variant of this approach, using information technology to de-personalize and simplify the transaction between citizen and government official.

Another innovation builds on the theory that government ultimately is a service organization, and it should gauge its success on the basis of citizen (i.e., "customer") satisfaction.[8] One simple monitoring tool for tracking customer satisfaction is a "point-of-service evaluation survey" or POSE. These are short surveys that are given to customers (e.g., a truck driver passing through border customs) that "score" the quality of government service provided to them. They can then be dropped into a collection box or returned by post (pre-stamped) anonymously. The advantage is that they are short, they provide ongoing feedback to senior public sector managers, and they can tell citizens whom to contact if they have complaints about the services. The other advantage is that they promote positive attitudes about the proper role of government services. Such a system can be implemented anywhere that government is responsible for a transaction that affects an individual or a business. And, it could be tied to an awards system or certification of excellence program based on customer satisfaction (Hellman, 2002).

What can be done with the business community to encourage good corporate governance practices? At the international level, there already are several conventions and "codes of conduct" in place that are designed to level the playing field in trade and foreign investment. Transparency International (Pope, 2000)-a leading NGO in this field-has cited numerous examples of best practices in the private sector to mitigate corruption and promote ethical businesses practices in the corporate workplace. There are also many examples of businesses collaborating with civic groups to speak out on issues of corruption, promote public education, and advocate for market-led policy reforms and economic development. Many global companies have adopted their own standards of ethical conduct in an effort to "self-regulate." A number of institutes, associations, and other NGOs offer services to large companies in how to design, implement, monitor, and provide training to staff on managing a corporate ethics program.

Can these "self-regulation" practices be successfully transferred to enterprises working primarily in domestic markets in underdeveloped or transitioning economies? How can they be motivated? It is safe to say that global companies are motivated by their high profile and broad market base to maintain a good public image, and to adopt standards of conduct that will protect that image and those markets. This is particularly important in today's "information age." If a company is accused of corruption in one country, it is only a matter of minutes before that news can be broadcast around the globe.

But what motivates companies operating in much smaller domestic markets to practice good corporate governance, let alone set up mechanisms to monitor and enforce a code of ethics? Here, the size and ownership structure of a company may be a factor. Smaller, privately owned companies deal mainly with the day-to-day problems of administrative corruption; they truly are at the mercy of the government. Their problems are affecting them and their employees, not a broader group of shareholders, board members, or venture capitalists. They are only accountable to themselves. Plus, they probably cannot afford the cost (or the risk) of liquidating their business and moving to another location. For them the best course of action would be to organize themselves and pressure the government to stop bribery and extortion. By teaming with other local interests-business associations, NGOs, and civic groups-micro, small- and medium-sized enterprises will speak with greater force and authority. And, by teaming with the media, they can educate the public about how corruption negatively affects consumers, discourages investors, and stifles employment and income growth in the community. In addition, businesses can propose that the government create a public-private partnership or task force to monitor anticorruption efforts. Organization, political pressure, and public awareness are key strategies to fight administrative corruption at the local level.

Larger businesses that are traded on the local stock exchange, however, can have an impact on state capture and administrative corruption by adopting corporate governance principles, instituting a code of ethics, and engaging in open dialogue with their peers, the government, and the media about the problems of corruption. Their public commitment to stopping corruption can help shift expectations, redefine business norms or standards of practice, restore public confidence, and spur government to make legal and institutional reforms that promote competition.

But let's not be too enthusiastic or naïve. There is a problem inherent in this approach. Some, maybe even many, of these larger businesses have already been party to corruption, and very well may be in the future. Why would they promote a practice that they do not subscribe to? The same argument was certainly made a few decades ago about global companies. A few "enlightened" ones, however, found a connection between their corporate interests and the interests of the society at large in denouncing unethical business practices. Although there is no empirical evidence at hand, there should be a few leaders from this class of enterprises-those that are larger, publicly traded, and prominent in the local economy-willing to be partners in promoting good corporate governance and ethical business practices. Local businesses with foreign interests may be good candidates; the foreign partner may be more familiar with the importance of good governance, and, in addition, may welcome this opportunity to improve their image in the local society.

Program Strategies

Even considering the possible range of programmatic interventions, effectively reducing corruption and promoting real competition among enterprises in developing economies are enormous tasks. Success will be determined mainly by the will and commitment of political and business leaders. They must be convinced that corruption is holding back their entry into new markets and stifling economic growth. Leaders must be found in both the public and private sectors that understand and advocate the "level playing field" argument, that is, that open markets will best serve social and economic objectives as well as private business interests over the long term. Program strategies include the following:

- Promoting decentralization and fiscal accountability.
- Creating systems and institutions that promote public participation in policy dialogue and policy implementation.
- Creating more responsive and transparent public service mechanisms at the local level.
- Strengthening business associations as advocates for market reform.
- Promoting trade liberalization policies and competitiveness strategies.
- Improving accountability and efficiency of capital markets.
- Promoting and implementing transparent and efficient programs to procure state services from the private sector.
- Helping businesses in a "cluster" or subsector to enhance their competitiveness in global markets.
- Opening up and improving legislative processes.
- Developing independent media that is educated about corruption and its affects on the economy.

- Creating public-private partnerships of businesses, civic groups, and local government to fight corruption and monitor results.
- Educating the public on the social and economic costs of corruption.
- Improving public communications capabilities of government officials.
- Strengthening the role and participation of independent "think tanks" to analyze political and economic issues.
- Legislating public disclosure of corporate interests held by elected officials.

Each of these objectives will affect corruption by helping to reduce vulnerabilities between government and business. At the same time they are strengthening institutions and relationships among stakeholder groups that are necessary for successful enterprise growth and economic development. In addition, stakeholders should promote innovation in areas that directly address vulnerabilities. For example:

- Helping local governments institute "one-stop-shops" for enterprises to conduct official business and give business owners and citizens a place to provide customer feedback on services, and so forth.
- Helping business associations or think tanks conduct, analyze and publicize corruption surveys.
- Introducing a corruption curriculum (focused on the costs to enterprise growth and economic development) into public administration training programs and workshops.
- Instituting point-of-service-evaluations wherever businesses and government agencies interact.
- Supporting public education programs.
- Encouraging larger businesses to adopt governance standards and corporate codes of conduct.

The most promising new area for cost-effective impact may be the development and implementation of monitoring tools that expose corruption, mainly administrative corruption. But this alone is not enough. Changing the higher stakes, higher return culture of state capture may be more daunting, but it is nonetheless more important to achieving fundamental and sustainable change. In government, as in business, standards and expectations start at the top. For these reasons, international donors must continue pushing for policy change and institutional reforms at all levels of government wherever possible, while at the same time researching, testing, and promoting best practices that mitigate, or at a minimum expose, corruption where vulnerabilities are highest.

Notes

1. Although not the subject of this study, there are forms of business corruption, racketeering, and extortion that exist outside the sphere of public sector involvement. Many small businesses, for example, are extorted for "security" or "protection payments" by mafia thugs. Mafia groups sometimes will pressure successful enterprises to buy from certain suppliers or retail through certain outlets. In other cases that do not involve organized crime, loan officers may demand kickbacks in return for the business applicant's credit approval. Whatever the source, corruption takes capital away from productive investments that will help grow an enterprise and make it more competitive, which is a principal argument presented here. Because this chapter focuses on public sector corruption, these other areas are not explored here.

2. Ronald Coase introduced this proposition, now known as the Coase theorem, in his 1960 article "The Problem of Social Costs." Coase's ideas have since had a profound impact on economic and legal discussions.

3. A "Pareto-efficient state" is where no one in the economy can be better off without someone else being worse off. In other words, this occurs when the economy is making optimum use of available resources for the greatest possible number of beneficiaries. Later the team of N. Kaldor and J.R. Hicks elaborated Pareto's work to formulate a test for comparing proposed changes (Economic Journal, 1939). Simply stated, the Kaldor-Hicks test compares the net benefits of two options: if the net benefit (aggregate benefits minus aggregate costs) of option A outweighs the net benefit of option B, then A is the better choice.

4. For a summary discussion of the economic impact debate, see Andvig, et al. (2000).

5. See the *Financial Times* five-part series on "China's Future" by Kynge (2002).

6. The US government stopped allowing tax deductibility of foreign bribes in 1958.

7. For the complete document, go to http://www.oecd.org/pdf/M00008000/M00008 299.pdf.

8. The World Bank, for example, is developing a series of "governance monitoring tools" that include a range of instruments and procedures to evaluate governmental service performance and measure improvements over time. These include surveys, scorecards, feedback forms, and hotlines.

Chapter 10

Agriculture

Rodney J. Fink

Agriculture in developing countries employs a large percentage of the population and, for the most part, a very impoverished segment at that. Farms in these countries tend to be small: in Africa, for example, more than 90 percent of the farms are in the hands of small landholders. In transitioning economies, by contrast, the agriculture sector employs less than a third of the labor force, and the average farm size is large. For both groups of countries, corruption issues affect land title and use, credit availability, quality of supplies, water allocation, product standards and certification, marketing, and the development of agribusinesses. In transitioning economies, however, the governments are typically more intimately involved in supply, production, and marketing so there are relatively more opportunities for corruption. Yet, societies depending on survival agriculture are affected proportionally more by corruption as the bribes farmers pay impact a higher percentage of their already low income. This chapter describes the various manifestations of corruption in the agricultural sector, its key points of vulnerability, examples of anticorruption strategies that have been applied, and recommendations for future initiatives.[1]

Corruption Vulnerabilities

Land Title and Use

Problems with land ownership, registration, tenure, and sales impede agricultural development in many countries. Multiple titles exist on many parcels and the rights of family members, especially women and children, are not well defined in some societies. Moreover, registration of title is often a slow, complex, and costly process, which is vulnerable to bribes offered or demanded for service. Informal properties, that is, parcels with no official documentation as to "who owns" or "occupies" the land, are common. According to Barnes, the absence of property adjudication and land market institutions is a major institutional weakness in the sector (Barnes, 2000). This problem is particularly pronounced in transitioning economies, where properties rights were not recognized in the former socialist systems. The development of an active land market for buying, selling, leasing, mortgaging and inheriting the land is a major objective of privatization, but bribes and payoffs abound in the system.

Credit Availability

Credit must be available for the agriculture sector to flourish in developing and transitional countries. Yet corruption occurs in the allocation of government-subsidized credit. Most typically, unnecessary fees and percentage payments are ways that government officials garner funds when granting credit.

Supplies

Corruption in government contracts or licenses for agricultural supplies is common. Poor quality, undelivered goods, and high prices are typical outcomes of collusion between government officials and private sector firms. An example is a government agency buying fertilizer from a private sector company at an elevated price and receiving a share of the profit. This increases the cost of agricultural production and eliminates competition in the fertilizer industry as other firms have little chance of getting the government contract. Along these lines, the Egyptian chairman of the Agricultural Development Bank and Minister of Agriculture was recently arrested on charges of taking bribes from a company to whom he gave rights for importing pesticides (Arabic News Weekly Edition, 8/26/2002). In another example, the Philippine Center for Investigative Journalism has documented that farmers receive low quality planting materials, unhealthy farm animals and undelivered farm equipment from the state (Sarimiento, 2000).

Water Allocation

Irrigated agriculture is a favorite of bureaucratic and centralized governments and promotes "rent seeking" (Renger and Wolff, 2000). Rent seeking is described as lobbying superior regulatory bodies to garner financial income not matched by labor or investment. Rent seekers use political soliciting, including bribery, as a means to get water or facilities to regions favoring them. The allocation of water and irrigation facilities, thus, often turns on connections and corruption rather than on economic and development policy. Renger summarizes some steps important for addressing irrigation problems (Renger and Wolff, 2000). These include the importance of involving farmers in regulating and monitoring financial responsibility so that resources are used for their original purpose.

Product Standards and Certification

Product standards and certification constitute another source of corruption, as individual producers attempt to bribe produce inspectors to get the desired certification. The development of quality improvement centers in rural communities has helped support objective grading of products by pooling produce for inspection and eliminating the opportunity for individual producers to offer bribes.

Marketing

The government's role in product pricing and the sale and purchase of produce create significant opportunities for corruption. In a speech to the U.S.-Russia Business Council's Agriculture Committee, for example, the president and CEO of Dow Agro Sciences spoke of the role of local governments that try to control agricultural production and pricing (Fischer, 2000). Either they get directly involved in buying and selling produce or they place quotas on inter-regional exports. In either case, this breeds corruption and graft. Many underpaid civil servants compromise their integrity and solicit bribes in return for favors, which may involve purchasing inputs or selling agricultural produce. Similarly, agriculture marketing boards create opportunities for corruption in the developing world. These parastatal boards provide a marketing avenue for producers, but often deliver smaller profits to farmers than a competitive market would provide because of embezzlement or because the boards hold down food costs to consumers. The ability to set price independent of market forces creates a further source of potential pay-offs. Finally, the sale of PL-480 commodities, by public officials, out of the country for personal gain provides another example of corruption in agriculture marketing.[2]

Agribusiness

Private sector agribusinesses are necessary for supplying inputs, processing food, transporting and marketing of agricultural products, yet corruption also impedes agribusiness development. The licensing and permits for transportation, storage, processing and business startup are vulnerable to corruption, which impedes the development of competitive agribusiness.

Risks of Corruption in Private Sector Groups

Carrying out agricultural programs with private sector groups can avoid the bureaucratic corruption pitfalls that may exist in government, but runs the risk of similar problems arising in these groups. Agricultural projects may use NGOs, private voluntary organizations (PVOs), and private farmer organizations to deliver services and thereby bypass government, but these groups can also devolve into corrupt relationships with farmers, suppliers, and purchasers. Members of private sector organizations are sometimes aligned with the government and can use their connections for self-serving deals.

The Middle East Regional Cooperation Program (MERC) is an unfortunate example of this phenomenon. The project aimed to introduce modern plant propagation methods, initiate a pot-plant nursery, improve open-field production of tomatoes and ornamentals, train specialists, and expand the agribusiness industries in Morocco. An American firm managed the contract, and Israeli and Moroccan partners ran the project. As it turns out, the Moroccan company was unwilling and unable to account for its use of funds. Table 10.1 outlines some of the problems with the project.

Transparency was absent as the books were not available, and only the company president knew what happened to the money. Accountability was absent as the company did not formally report to stakeholders, the government or the donor for its actions and use of resources. Moreover, nepotism was likely as at least one family member was on the payroll. There should have been greater awareness by the committees and the US contractor about the nature, extent, and consequences of mismanagement and corruption at an early stage. They could have taken a position of terminating or redirecting the project. Preventive actions to avert or contain corruption were absent as the operation was a closed system and access to the books closely guarded. Designing and implementing a positive and open plan would have been the most effective way to prevent corruption. Enforcement of the objectives was not forthcoming because control rested with one person. Guidelines for implementing and enforcing the project should have been in place from the beginning to see that the company was accountable.

Table 10.1. Problems in the MERC Program

Action Taken	How It Was Done	Outcome
1. Project set up with private sector company	Little background work done on the company selected.	The president of the company, on subsequent background check, had past problems.
2. Management assistance by nine-member technical and steering committees	The two committees often disagreed on major items. Technical committee was to advise. Steering committee did not follow suggestions.	The organization structure was large and unmanageable. Each committee had members from three countries including Morocco.
3. Conflicts between company and US contractor, steering committee, and technical committee.	The company wanted a tissue culture laboratory but the technical committee said no. Steering committee said yes.	President of company declared a budget crisis because money promised had not come. Audits could not account for funds.
4. Technical advisor had conflict with company president.	Income not returned to the business. Income not regenerated.	Advisor abandoned project over conflict with work and questions of company integrity.
5. Involvement with country scientists	Project was to involve local scientists but few were ever involved.	Minimal local interaction or accountability.

MERC was a high profile project gone wrong, though some phases (transplant nursery, for example) were successful from a technical perspective.

Lessons for Fighting Corruption

One lesson from the MERC case is that placing a large amount of responsibility on one person can make a project vulnerable to corruption. Few checks and balances were written into the project and being a private sector operation meant there was no oversight of the company. Chances for success might have been better working with a producers' group, which would have provided a built-in oversight from the many members of the group. Involvement of local scientists and producers in the planning and execution of the project could have provided a better threshold for success.

The procedure used by a small cooperative in Swaziland (Khutsala Poultry Cooperative) serves as a guide for consideration. This poultry cooperative was owned, managed, and operated by women and consisted of a central production and service unit that provided genetic stock, veterinary supplies, feed, and marketing.[3] Each member had a share in the cooperative and shared in the profits of the central unit. Some of their corruption prevention procedures are described in Table 10.2.

This project required minimal inputs but carried out many of the steps that must be taken if corruption is to be reduced in donor-funded projects. The project had one technical assistant, some donor funds and was self sustaining after two years of operation. There was trust among those involved in the project, and there was transparency in that open participation, access, and information were provided. In this case, transparency was instituted in both the public and private sector. Accountability was an integral part of the process for the players, the manager, and the donor. When it was time to expand the central unit, all members had their say and eventual vote. Awareness of what was happening was one ingredient of the success of this project. The project had standards that were understood and totally open. Prevention was built into the design of the project. The

Table 10.2. Corruption Prevention Measures at the Khutsula Poultry Cooperative Project

Initial Action	How Accomplished	Evaluation
1. Donor identified players.	Initial meetings were conducted and the program described.	Those women who had an interest signed on.
2. The operating document for the coop was prepared.	Meetings were held (under a big tree) with the 100-plus women who became cooperative members.	Members were enthusiastic and wanted to participate.
3. Seed money was identified and payback set.	Donor agency presented their financing potential and a business plan was adopted.	All coop members knew their responsibilities and accepted the conditions.
4. Accounting of central business.	A simple accounting system was designed and was available.	There were no secrets in the accounting process.
5. Individual accountability.	Each member maintained books and provided a monthly report.	Children of illiterate parents did books.
6. Cooperative meetings.	Held on a regular basis (under the same tree).	Well received by all. Good participation.
7. Government involvement.	Yes, the ministry of agriculture was informed and helped.	Ministry representative gave technical support.
8. Did it work?	Yes. Major effort to provide a quality product and keep viable markets open. Good communication and involvement.	Successful project and good organizational and working procedures were followed.

entire strategy of the project was to decrease the tolerance for corruption by reducing and eliminating the chances for individual gain through corruption. Enforcement of this project was automatic as the rules of conduct had been established which kept everyone informed of what was to take place. When a member did not live up to agreed standards, action was taken to ensure accountability. In the event the egg market soured, the same approach could have been used to establish another business. As a matter of fact, members of the group were planning a new cooperative for growing vegetables to sell in local markets and South Africa.

Another obstacle facing agricultural entrepreneurs is certification, an issue that is constantly present in Africa.[4] For example, a US company working in West Africa dominated the baby food market with a good product and a successful marketing approach. They advertised the safety of their standards and quality, suggesting that local products could not match them. Goods produced in these countries were often sold only if the marketers were willing to pay a bribe. Buyers confirmed that the local products were of poor quality. In response to this shoddy and potentially harmful system, local people, led by women's organizations, put in place a certification system to determine if locally produced baby food met product quality and safety standards. By bonding together, they were able to have enough voice to be heard. The local government, marketers and producers were involved and assisted with the project. This intervention helped producers, improved food quality, lowered food cost, reduced corruption, and helped businesses succeed.

The time to ensure that a project maximizes its potential is in the planning stages, before funds have been committed. Whenever possible, projects should involve all players in a nonconfrontational manner to set up positive, descriptive, and clear guidelines. Full disclosure and knowledge of what is to take place will help bring about project success.

Recommendations

Efforts to fight corruption in the agricultural sector should emphasize transparency, public awareness, accountability, prevention, and enforcement. Within this framework, the following strategies have been proven useful.

- Evaluate corruption in a country's agriculture sector by starting at the market and working backwards to production (warehousing, transportation, licenses, grading, etc.). Join private and government sources to remove impediments such as road inspection points and replace them with effective "non-rent-seeking" methods. Build the case for the government to monitor problem areas while privatizing as many of the steps as possible. Shorten the commodity chain from the producer to the market by introducing contract arrangements between the cocoa farmers (for example) and the ultimate processor of the product.

- Where commodity chains are shortened, explore the possibility for the processor granting credit to the farmer. Develop creative approaches for solving the credit problem and the supply chain simultaneously.

- Promote development of a land market by eliminating corruption in the registration and titling process. Facilitate simple and inexpensive procedures for transferring land title. Enhance involvement of the private sector in land survey, titling, and real estate sales. Remove the legal and regulatory restraints to private ownership.

- Where marketing boards fail to be effective, encourage their entry into competition with emerging private sector businesses.

- Promote quality improvement centers (especially in Africa). Work with private and public groups to facilitate standards, grading and certification.

- Develop projects with producers' groups and involve stakeholders. Develop a broad base of cooperating host workers.

- Promote oversight of private sector groups.

- Avoid projects that allow rent seeking via hidden subsidies.

Corruption in agriculture can be reduced by careful project selection and good procedures in project implementation. The key is to develop programs that have a wide range of support, which, if properly implemented, can improve the quality of life and reduce corruption. Full disclosure between the public and private sector players (especially the farmers) can do a great deal to facilitate this cause.

Notes

1. Conferences with USAID employees and contract employees were used to gain insight into corruption issues facing the agriculture sector. Discussions included a look at corruption problems in a variety of countries and approaches to the problems. Contacts included USAID employees Madalene O'Donnell (telephone), Raymond Morton, David Soroko, Jim Dunn, and Mark Winters and contract (or previous USAID) employees John Mullenax and Lance Jepson.

2. PL-480 provides for U.S. government financing of U.S. agricultural commodities to developing countries and private entities on concessional credit terms.

3. The project was a joint USAID/Israel program implemented by the Israeli Embassy to Swaziland.

4. Telephone conversation with Jeff Hill, USAID.

Chapter 11

Sectoral Synthesis

Stephen Schwenke

The presence and character of public sector corruption varies significantly from sector to sector. On one hand, much of the corruption encountered in the developing and transitional world is petty in nature and scale and causes little public outcry. In the education, health, and justice sectors, it is common to find school teachers, health care providers, and police charging extra for services, seeking small favors, or using public facilities and materials for their own marginal personal gain. Such activities are often accepted by the public as a needed corrective to systems that fail to provide a living wage. The impact may be less benign, however, as these activities set a precedent that makes it difficult to draw clear boundaries between right and wrong.

In sharp contrast, public sector corruption in other sectors can be large in scale, hidden from view, and controlled by a small number of powerful individuals or groups. In energy, environment, the private sector, and in some situations in the justice and political sectors, deals are made that result in enormous distortions to the economy to the benefit of the few, at the cost of the many. These can revolve around major public procurements, massive infrastructure projects or large humanitarian assistance efforts induced by crises or disasters, for example.

In the middle ground between hidden but large-scale corruption and common but petty corruption, a wide variety of corruption forms exist that often start small but grow into enormous drains on the economy. In the energy sector, massive misuse of meter payment systems resulting in the dramatic loss of sales from energy production (e.g., in Bangladesh one half of the electricity supplied by the Power Development Board ends up as system losses through mismanagement and falsified meter readings) is echoed in the political party system, as vote buying undermines the democratic process. All sectors have examples in this middle ground.

The elites pursue their interests in this middle ground of corruption, where they benefit from advantageous treatment and favored access to scarce resources. For example in agriculture, only the well connected are able to offer inducements to government officials to get access to the best land, irrigation infrastructure, and preferential credit terms. The elites organize special arrangements to shelter themselves from taxes, avoid legal sanctions, and obtain desirable positions within government institutions.

Corrupt government officials also find ample opportunities in the middle ground, where corruption is far from petty. Officials in all public sectors use their positions to extract a wide range of payments, gifts and favors from the public, from inducements to grading crop quality at a higher level, claiming salaries for "ghost teachers," charging business people "fees" for permits and business licenses, receiving payments to influence the decisions of judges and magistrates, charging "handling fees" at customs offices, and a multitude of other examples in all public sector activities where officials come into regular and unsupervised contact with the general public.

Corruption can be manifested in the pervasive evidence of severe waste, damage, or deterioration—all with no identifiable accountable party. Massive environmental pollution and habitat destruction from energy extraction is all too common, as is the wasteful loss of human potential and time through the intentional imposition of bureaucratic impediments and red tape.

Perhaps the greatest manifestation of corruption is underdevelopment itself, and the inhibition of states to embrace transparency in their operations—across all sectors—or to decentralize decision-making to local governments. Economies do not flourish, nor does democracy grow strong, in situations where corruption is embedded and pervasive, and where decision making is controlled tightly at the top and the use of public resources hidden from public oversight. In such conditions, government legitimacy remains weak, quality of life erodes, formal sector employment opportunities decline, and underdevelopment becomes persistent.

Corruption Vulnerabilities

Although the terminology may vary, most analyses of corruption draw attention to the combination of monopoly power, unfettered discretion, and minimal or no accountability as the optimal conditions of vulnerability to corruption (Klitgaard, 1991, p. 75). This perspective was common to the nine preceding sector chapters too, but other conditions of vulnerability—some sector-specific—were also noted.

The role of the state, and specifically the central government, often was cited as giving rise to conditions of tight control by a self-interested few, with little or no transparency. For example, in the agricultural sector in many developing countries, the central government enjoys a preeminent position of power and decision-making in nearly every aspect of commercial agriculture throughout the commodities chain, from actual production to grading, pricing, storage to distribution.

Those in powerful positions within the central government also often face great incentives to corrupt behavior in the handling of major public infrastructure projects, where large sums of money become the subject of nontransparent deal making, vulnerable to arrangements favoring illicit kickbacks and influence buying. Major infrastructure projects are common within the energy sector (and, though not a sector of this analyses, the transportation sector), and significant public infrastructure investments also occur in the health, education, agriculture, and private sectors. The public finance sector is vulnerable in a related manner, in that this sector provides the institutional mechanisms for monetary transactions associated with public infrastructure.

A different but related vulnerability occurs when the central government fails to monitor the integrity of lower, decentralized echelons on government, or fails to establish transparent linkages between the tiers of government. Although decentralization generally does shorten the accountability linkages between government and public user, it can also favor the interests of powerful local elites who find new opportunities to seek illicit gain through pressuring local government officials with less fear of powerful central government oversight. Public finance is vulnerable to distortions in the character of the financial flows between central and local government, for example.

There are also other similar vulnerabilities. Corruption can easily flourish when public services cover the majority of the population, such as in education and health, or where the massive scale of services and the large number of individual transactions make central government monitoring ineffectual. Vulnerabilities to corruption arise any time that multiple sources of government control exist at different levels of government, disbursing a very large quantity of resources in numerous small transactions. Political patronage schemes often find inviting vulnerabilities within these large decentralized systems.

The difficulty of government to monitor the integrity of public officials also owes much to a low level of public awareness of the nature and real costs of corruption, and to a high level of tolerance (or resigned acceptance) of corruption. The environmental sector perhaps best exemplifies this vulnerability, but the problem of public tolerance also invites generally low level but embedded corruption within the health, education, and justice sectors, with political parties, and with public sector interactions with the private sector. The justice sector has a distinctive vulnerability, in that it is highly susceptible to external (and often inappropriate) government pressure from a variety of powerful sources.

One step removed from direct or official government control, both political parties and the private sector generally shelter behind few requirements for public transparency and accountability, making them particularly vulnerable to corruption. The activities of political parties are difficult to monitor (unless it is in their interests to monitor each other), and vulnerabilities occur with biased or manipulated selection of candidates, buying of votes, political party fundraising and financing of candidates and issues, political party manipulation of decisions by elected officials, or party co-optation by special interests.

The Enabling Environment for Corruption

Corruption in the public sector finds root and can easily become embedded in many less developed and transitional countries where political leaders fail to display concern for the public interest or fail to set examples of integrity, where social and political institutions are relatively weak, and where civil servants—often underpaid and held in low public esteem—have self-interested incentives to engage in corrupt alternatives to formal rules and procedures. Adherence to the formal rules of society's institutions may lack motivational weight if those empowered with authority perceive these rules to be weak, unfair, inappropriate, or punitive, or where the distinctions between public and private are blurred. This superficiality of personal investment in such rules is further stretched by a sense of impunity—either the lack of meaningful sanctions, or the high probability of not being punished for engaging in corruption even if severe sanctions exist. For those who may be unwilling participants on the receiving end of corrupt transactions, as may be common in the justice, education, health, public finance (particularly tax and customs), energy, and environmental sectors, there may be few or no alternatives to accomplish a necessary task or avoid an unpleasant consequence but to comply, or it may be perceived as expected or convenient to do so.

In the justice sector, and to a lesser extent in the environment, energy, and private sectors, weak judicial and regulatory systems also make it difficult for injured parties to seek redress in the courts for contract violations. Complexity of laws, government regulations, and procedures provide fertile ground for arbitrary discretion by self-interested officials. Institutional complexity also exacerbates corruption vulnerabilities, where overlapping or unclear management responsibilities allow for poor levels of oversight and inadequate accountability—a common situation in public finance, education, health, and public finance sectors.

The lack of political competition, the dominance of monopoly interests, political parties that are either too strong or too weak, and the weakness or absence of watchdog institutions also contributes to a situation prone to the growth of corruption.

In the environment and energy sectors, the problems of poor governance and diffuse public ownership (i.e., no one "owns" energy, so its misuse is not well monitored) create conditions favorable to corruption. Globalization plays an important role in these two sectors, since one of its goals is to seek the lowest cost for resources without regard to how or where they are obtained. The character of global capitalism is often to focus on short-term profits over long-term sustainability, which also can lead to corruption influencing decisions that lead to consequences counter to the public interest.

It is in the interest of many to resist change. Those individuals best placed to effect the necessary reforms in public policy, public attitudes, and public behavior, as well as their counterparts in the private and civil society sectors, are often also the ones who stand to lose the most from significant curtailment of a corrupt status quo.

Stakeholders and Actors in Corruption

Corruption takes two. Consumers are often willing to pay bribes for the sake of "convenience" (avoiding burdensome and lengthy bureaucratic steps, for instance)—a willingness that stimulates a supply-side pressure to perpetuate associated forms of corruption. In some cases, both parties to the corrupt act appear to gain, at the expense of the general public (and specifically the poor). In other cases, there is a vulnerable victim and someone who exploits that victim—a loser and a winner. The multiple permutations of corruption reflect the complexity of human and institutional interactions, making the analysis of distinct stakeholders and roleplayers a challenging undertaking. In some cases the stakeholder group may not even yet exist: for example, in the environment and energy sectors, future generations cannot argue their claims for the judicious use of nonrenewable resources.

Those who have power to exercise and who enjoy minimal accountability—such as senior public officials, judges, police, political party bosses, or trade union leaders—are the commonly cited perpetrators of corruption, preying upon those in need who generally are powerless to resist such approaches. In some extreme cases of deeply embedded corruption, entire institutions become the perpetrators, such as corrupt central government ministries or government controlled marketing boards and parastatal organizations. Private sector actors, both domestic and international, can corrupt public officials. For example, international consumers of natural resources may provide a strong stimulus to corruption by choosing to accept local corruption as a cost of doing business.

In every sectoral analysis in this book, the important role of the public, and the attitude of the public, was noted. Corruption flourishes when the public is poorly informed, apathetic, cynical, tolerant, or so politically weak as to be unable to protest. The most vulnerable individuals in society are the poor, and they often encounter petty corruption on a daily or regular basis: for example, poor patients who must pay fees for "free" government health services. The poor also bear the heaviest burden from the larger economic and societal impacts of corruption: the slowing of development, the dissipation and wastage of public resources, the erosion of formal sector employment, the decline in investment, and the loss of government legitimacy through poor governance.

Several of the authors of the sectoral analyses called attention to two particular role players in the problem of, and solutions to, corruption that are largely overlooked: civil society and the donor community. Civil society has played a positive role in limiting corruption by means of its activities in education, oversight, and facilitating access to public services, yet not all NGOs perform satisfactorily in this regard. Some NGOs are more "in the money than in development."

Donors and development assistance organizations have often chosen to ignore corruption when formulating and implementing their programs and projects, so that other strategic aims can be focused on. Examples include members of the donor community who may be aware of corruption in education systems, for example, but who pursue an agenda that stresses strategic donor self-interests, ignoring this set of corruption problems. This form of selective vision warrants reevaluation, as it provides a potent example of an intentional and strategic tolerance for corruption that almost certainly has significant negative impacts in the longer term.

Interventions to Prevent and Combat Corruption

Preventing corruption, or curbing corruption when already present, can be approached from both the general and the particular. Each of the nine sectors called for interventions that are directly aimed at attacking the enabling environment for corruption. Chief among these are improving the example of leadership that models integrity, raising public awareness of the cost and character of corruption, and seeking an economic and social solution to underpaid civil servants who additionally suffer from low public esteem.

Other systemic recommendations include: improved public access to information on decision making and resource allocation and public participation in these processes; a more active, free, and professional press; strengthening the rule of law; minimizing unsupervised contact between private individuals (or businesses) and tax or customs officials, and more aggressive enforcement of laws against corrupt practices. In education, for example, it is argued that training the community and enlisting community support in the fight against corruption offered real prospects for effectiveness, making parents effective agents of change in their local schools.

Technical approaches also have their place. In the education, energy, agriculture, and health sectors, and in public finance, it is argued that the better use of information technology to monitor accounts, and the use of outside independent auditors to provide oversight of the conduct of government agencies and institutions would reduce opportunities for corrupt transactions.

Certain anticorruption interventions have particular relevance to specific sectors. In the energy sector, for example, the use of an autonomous, transparent regulatory body is an effective means to oversee energy transformation and distribution. Similarly, decentralization and privatization of some government functions can constrain corruption; for example, a move toward decentralized, competitive electricity markets. In the environmental sector, improvements might result from generating better environmental data and from the regular monitoring both of environmental resources and environmental quality standards. In the health sector, downsizing public health care system and/or charging cost-sharing user fees to achieve better pay and improved status for health sector workers are possibilities, but such interventions are often very difficult to implement, and may adversely affect the poorest. Decentralizing government health care services and privatizing some services may be more realistic intervention options. In the justice sector, the analyst argues for increasing autonomy while raising transparency, and allowing the justice sector to have control over its own budget and administration. With respect to political parties, they might be restructured so that internal institutional processes are transparent and accountable, and that effective campaign finance legislation be enacted and enforced.

Throughout public service institutions, a strong case is argued for appointments and promotions to be transparently made on basis of merit, combined with periodic disclosure of assets by senior public sector officials.

Sectoral Interventions

There are several common threads across the sectoral recommendations for action:

- There is a wide range of anticorruption approaches that are common across sectors.

• Although many development sectors share basic anticorruption approaches, these remedies need to be implemented in a customized way, within the particular context of each sector, to be effective.

Many of the authors observe that sector-specific anticorruption strategies are of limited efficacy if not carried out in conjunction with broader, integrated anticorruption initiatives systemically applied across many sectors. While fully accepting the need for such a broad approach, the scope of this current analysis does not lend itself to the identification of a comprehensive set of integrated, systemic recommendations; clearly there is a need for further research in this context. In all cases, it is recommended that a donor should carry out a diagnostic appraisal of the source and opportunities for corruption, so that any subsequent interventions will be formulated with reference to a specific country and sector context.

Shared Anticorruption Remedies

Addressing Governing Competence and Capacity. Lack of competence and capacity including insufficient educated and skilled staff; understaffing; lack of adequate equipment, research materials and data; and poor working conditions all combine to create the enabling environment for corruption. The prevailing conclusion to date has been that a significant reallocation of public revenues in a developing country to fund a higher standard of government service is prohibitively expensive, politically sensitive, and therefore unrealistic as a policy option. Institutional weakness however surfaces again and again as a fundamental contributor to embedded corruption and a resulting low level of legitimacy for the government. Without strong government legitimacy, all development aspirations are hindered, and the resources allocated to development assistance are of questionable efficacy.

The clear conclusion of this summary analysis is that this situation of pervasive institutional weakness, high incentives for corruption, and poor levels of government service to the public needs to be confronted. A strategic assessment of the opportunity costs and actual wastage in loss of productivity, increasing levels of corruption, declining economic growth, and misuse of government resources due to an underfinanced civil service are likely to far exceed the actual costs of providing adequate salaries and working conditions. This should be established empirically through a comprehensive analysis in a given country, and, assuming the results support this expectation, the data should be used by appropriately placed stakeholders to advocate for a dramatic change in policy to improve the performance standards, integrity, prestige, and benefits for civil service employees.

Dramatic, sweeping changes to civil service institutions may not always be possible or warranted. In such cases, targeted interventions to improve selected aspects of government performance and to limit the spread and damage of corruption may be chosen. These are described below; it is noteworthy that the more comprehensive restructuring to achieve a better paid, more professional (and almost certainly smaller) civil service would incorporate all of these recommendations.

Specific recommendations include:

- Professionalism should be encouraged and fostered through training and continuing education for all public officials who must exercise sophisticated skills, discerning judgment, and comprehensive subject-matter expertise (e.g., judges).

- The budget process should be improved so that it is accurate and comprehensive, including all revenue and expenditure.

- Attract and retain competent staff within the public sector by improving salaries, working conditions, and prestige.

- Set standards for competent and professional performance, and enforce these standards through formal monitoring, regular personnel evaluations (and, in some cases, examinations), through incentives for meeting and exceeding standards (rewards, merit-based promotions, public honors) and through disincentives for failing to meet standards (warnings, sanctions, demotions, dismissals, prosecution).

- Privatize those government functions that demand levels of competence that the private sector can more readily generate and sustain.

Addressing Tolerance of Corruption. There can be little incentive for government to arrest the spread and limit the damage of corruption when citizens simply do not care about this scourge. In many societies, the public assigns a low priority to preventing and combating corruption. This complacent attitude springs from a sense that corruption is inevitable and that nothing can be done to address it. In such societies, the public may consider it a futile exercise to express outrage when their political (and private and/or civil society sector) leaders behave unethically and ignore the broader public interest in favor of narrower group or self-interest. Despite this apparent complacency, significant majorities in all countries find corruption to be shameful and undesirable (Noonan, 1984, pp. 702–703), and this pervasive dislike speaks of a strong set of moral values that can be the catalyst for positive change.

Among the most common of all recommendations within the sectoral papers is that concrete steps should be taken to raise public awareness about the negative impacts and costs of corruption, to foster the qualities of integrity in leadership, to give voice to public outrage when the public interest is forsaken, and to punish those in authority who flout the laws for their own ends.

Specific recommendations include:

- Government, as well as both the private sector and civil society, should take steps to actively encourage, publicize, and reward integrity in leadership. Changing public attitudes and expectations to become less tolerant of corruption and more demanding of a corruption-free society depend on the sustained example of integrity by senior public sector, private sector, and civil society sector leaders.

- Government, the private sector, and civil society should collaborate on the provision of training in ethical discernment and ethics-based judgment. Although codes of conduct can provide valuable guidance to stakeholders in many sectors as to how to recognize, prevent, report, and limit the damage caused by corruption, such codes must have comprehensive buy-in from those who most stand in need of their guidance. Codes of conduct do not directly translate into the ability of people to perceive ethical dilemmas and modify behavior to become consistently ethical; codes of ethics must be internalized and supported through training, deliberative dialogue, and enforcement if they are to be effective.

- Employ "integrity pacts" as appropriate to help governments, businesses and civil society to establish mutual contractual obligations and rights, among which are mutual agreements to refrain from bribery from bidding through to implementation and operation of the business or public service.

Addressing Independent and Autonomous Bodies. Government is the exercise of power, and in many successful and mature democracies it is clear that power must be balanced by consistently and rigorously enforced checks and controls, so that the public interest may best be served. In some cases, such as in the appointment of judges, there should be an institutional solution that optimizes independence from subjective political influences and encourages objective, merit-based decision-making.

Specific recommendations include:

- Establish a suitable legal framework and autonomous and transparent regulatory bodies with "teeth" to enforce compliance for those sectors where public goods are exploited or distributed (water, energy, environment) or where critical

democratic activities are undertaken (political party operations and elections)—provided that these regulatory bodies
do not become yet another fulcrum to leverage illegal returns.

- Depending on the specific country context, the appointment
  and promotion of highly qualified and competent judges and
  magistrates would be strengthened if such appointments
  and promotions were made—or at least closely monitored—
  by an apolitical and independent institution.

- Depending on the specific country context, the justice sector
  should control its own budget and the administration of the
  courts.

- The justice sector—the integrity and competence of which
  are fundamental to the effective and just rule of law—should
  not be subject to direct control and manipulation by other
  government institutions or officials in certain key aspects
  (determined with specific reference to local context).

- In most cases, it is advantageous to encourage a system of life
  term appointments for judges, selected from candidates with
  demonstrated competence and integrity. In so doing, judges
  have improved job security and are able to make their judicial
  decisions without fear of loss of their jobs by disgruntled senior government officials.

Addressing the Donors' Role. As the embodied voice of the international community, donors and international financial institutions bear a special responsibility for moral leadership by example. Ignoring corruption so as to attend to other
"strategic development objectives" telegraphs a powerful message that corruption
is tolerated. In the past, international development assistance sent a similar message or complacency about environmental degradation and gender inequality, but
no longer does this apply. Corruption should be added to the list of situations of
which the international community will no longer "look the other way."
Specific recommendations include:

- Incorporate specific corruption-prevention measures in all
  development interventions.

- Donors should record and make public the degree to which
  they are aware of corruption existing in recipient countries,
  and the extent to which their bilateral (or multilateral) programs take due cognizance of this problem in their design and
  in the establishment of priorities and procedures.

Addressing Political and Institutional Reforms. The practices, procedures, traditions and values that combine to characterize any given public institution, and the legal context in which it exists, directly influence the behavior of that institution, and its vulnerability to corruption. The frequency and manner in which the officials of that institution interact with the public, the level of discretion exercised by officials, the degree of oversight and management throughout all levels of that institution, and the accountability of individual officials to the public and to the laws of the land all are significant in diagnosing contributory factors for corrupt behavior. So too are the prestige enjoyed by government officials within any given society, the value of their remuneration relative to the attainment of a reasonably secure and comfortable standard of living, their job security and work environment, and their institution's commitment to their own professional development. Ultimately, the broader professionalism and ethical standards of the entire institution, and that institution's awareness of and compliance with the law, together shape that institution's effectiveness, responsiveness to the ideals of public service, and integrity.

Specific recommendations include:

- Limit the authority of monopoly political parties and support—through increased civil liberties—the toleration of opposition parties, thereby encouraging a competitive liberal democratic regime.

- Prepare and implement monitoring and evaluation methods to improve effectiveness, detect and reduce corruption, and promote results-based attribution of cause and effect for various reforms to institutions.

- In situations where political parties are weak, support legislation that defines the scope of activities for and authority of political parties, allows for transparent public funding of party activities, provides reasonable controls and limits for campaign spending, and generally fosters a "level playing field" for political competition.

Addressing Administrative Streamlining and Eliminating Administrative Barriers. Complexity may often be unavoidable as government functions become more diverse and sophisticated, but in a great many instances the plethora of bureaucratic procedures is unnecessary and counter-productive to the objectives of providing public services of a high standard of quality and efficiency. In many instances, complexity is artificially imposed to create a demand for corruption, so that corrupt officials can offer "short-cuts" for a fee.

Specific recommendations include:

- Simplify and expedite the land registry and title process, and remove legal and procedural constraints to private ownership. Private ownership and the formalization of private capital drive economic growth, and should be a high priority of government.

- Review all bureaucratic procedures at the interface between public and government officials, to evaluate the potential for streamlining and to reduce opportunities for illicit shortcuts.

- Reform tax laws so that private ownership of land and capital is not unfairly or inappropriately taxed.

Addressing Transparency and Accountability. Corruption does not flourish is an environment open to public scrutiny and in which the law and administrative procedures clearly define the obligations of public officials to be accountable for their stewardship of public resources.

Specific recommendations include:

- Evaluate and diagnose corruption in appropriate sectors by following commodity chains starting at the market and working backwards towards production (warehousing, transportation, licensing, etc.) to identify corrupt links in the chain.

- Reform systems and institutions that allow for evidence of corruption to be easily hidden, for example by requiring periodic disclosure of assets by senior government officials (and their families).

- Make appropriate judgments of the courts public.

- Implement effective and professional accounting and audit practices to prevent and constrain corruption.

- Make public budgets accessible, completely accounted for (no off-book accounts), and transparent. Government has an obligation to regularly publish accurate, accessible, and complete information on the allocation and distribution of public revenue.

- Provide for independent monitoring of expenditures by political parties.

- Require political parties to formulate and implement transparent procedures for candidate selection and nomination.

- Exploit the ability of privatization to improve accountability. To the extent that privatization of government assets and operations exposes suppliers and producers to the discipline of the market and to market-based incentives, it can serve as a useful counterbalance to corruption among company managers, who become directly accountable to private owners who have a direct interest in protecting and increasing the value of their assets.

- Institutions should restructure their operations to provide better quality and more thorough oversight of staff by management, the minimization of private (unsupervised) contact between staff and the public, and the periodic rotation of staff so that illicit personal arrangements can be constrained.

- Public funds should be spent only as authorized by law.

Addressing Information Technology. New IT applications offer significant potential to not only make government function more efficiently and openly, but also to remove many government operations from inappropriate manipulation by self-interested officials.

Specific recommendations include:

- Make appropriate use of IT solutions, coupled with demonstrated high level political support, to support institutional reform and facilitate sustainable corruption prevention (e.g., the World Bank's education management information system, EMIS, successfully applied in the Gambia; the use of computerized applications in tax and customs administration; and the computerization of court records).

Sector-Specific Anticorruption Remedies

To date, the traditional emphasis of many bilateral and international donors has been to concentrate anticorruption interventions in such sectors as public administration, public finance, judiciary and legal reform, political parties, and governance generally. The analyses of these sectoral chapters make a strong argument for broadening the range of donor interventions so that anticorruption measures are integral to interventions in such sectors as agriculture, education, energy, environment, health, the private sector (including microenterprise and entrepreneurship initiatives) and civil society. The major recommendations in both the traditional sectors of anticorruption intervention, and these less traditional sectors are summarized below.

Most of these remedies are not unique to the sector; they include such generic anticorruption approaches as raising public awareness, increasing government transparency, and improving control mechanisms. However, these remedies are framed in the sectoral context – to be implemented within particular institutions and processes, with particular stakeholders, and using appropriate legal structures and standards. A conclusion that can be drawn is that these sector-specific remedies are best implemented taking into account the sensitivities and peculiarities of the sector. As indicated earlier, they are considered to be most effective when initiated as part of an overall anticorruption program that includes general, non-sectoral activities as well.

Agriculture

- Raise public awareness of corruption in agriculture, and educate people on their right of access to critical information on how decisions are made and financial resources utilized in pursuit of the public interest in this sector. Provide more consistent and aggressive enforcement of laws against corrupt practices in agricultural production, distribution, and marketing.
- Design development programs and projects so that beneficiaries are able to participate more effectively in targeted corruption-prevention decision-making in all aspects of agricultural production, marketing, transportation of products, access to extension agents, setting of fair prices, and determination of product quality (and hence price). Publicize examples of successful interventions.

Education

- Ensure that teachers earn a living wage, linked with clearly articulated standards of professional performance, so that incentives for corrupt activities are dramatically lessened and the sense of corruption being "justified" is no longer supportable.
- Following a broad-based public awareness campaign to bring to public attention the high costs and damaging impacts of corruption, and to reinforce a sense that corruption can be tackled effectively, enlist local community engagement in the fight against corruption. Begin with community training, so that parents become effective agents of change as demanding and discerning consumers of the public service provided by

public schools. Teach parents how to assess the effectiveness of their local schools, what their legal rights are as parents to access information about school expenditures and operations, and what sanctions communities can bring to bear on under-performing schools.

Energy

- Increase the transparency of energy transactions and budgets, and increase the accountability of institutions and decision makers who control and regulate energy.
- In cases that involve international companies, formulate codes of conduct, monitor foreign partners and their collaborators, train employees and establish organizational structures to monitor and enforce these codes of conduct.
- Establish internal audit departments or other codes of conduct that represent corporate values in a consistent manner.
- Establish a legal framework and an autonomous, transparent regulatory body with sufficient authority to oversee energy transformation and distribution.
- Ensure that clear guidelines exist for accounting practices, that budgets are transparent and accessible; and that auditing systems are developed to ensure that existing guidelines and rules are followed.
- Where appropriate, unbundle power system into separate energy transformation, transmission and distribution entities.
- Establish decentralized, competitive electricity markets and decentralize payments between distribution and generation companies.
- Formulate and apply "integrity pacts" (IPs) to help government, businesses and civil society establish mutual contractual rights and obligations. Whenever possible, IPs should cover all the activities related to the contract from the pre-selection of bidders, the bidding and contracting proper, through the implementation, to the completion and operation of the business.

Environment

- Support a public awareness campaign to heighten awareness of environmental concerns and to disseminate information about the costs to the public (now and in the future) of mismanagement and corrupt management of environmental resources.

- Advocate for greater transparency in decisions on resource use and distribution.

- To identify corruption in the environmental context more effectively, actively encourage civil society to adopt a proactive role in monitoring development projects and government policies generally, and encourage civil society to advocate for stronger political action against corruption in environmental management and decision-making.

- Carry out baseline environmental analyses so that critical data can be collected to enable the subsequent creation and implementation of effective and well publicized environmental monitoring systems, coupled with effective laws, policies, and conventions. Widely publicize the findings of periodic monitoring and evaluation of environmental impacts.

Health

- Establish and encourage the use of an essential drug lists (EDLs) in public hospitals and clinics, to limit choices in procurement to the most appropriate drugs relative to the most pressing needs of the specific country.

- Encourage and support the formation of multidisciplinary groups within public hospitals to make recommendations on policies for the selection and use of drugs.

- Establish and encourage the use of standard treatment guidelines in public health care facilities, the use of codes of ethics in drug marketing, and the monitoring of purchasing patterns (drugs and medical equipment) to detect unusual deviations that might signal corruption.

- Establish and encourage the use of a government-recognized "white list" of drug and medical equipment suppliers of proven and consistent integrity.

- Widely disseminate and regularly update a government-approved list of drug prices.

- Decentralize government health services, with some degree of privatization of such services, where efficiency and improved service can be achieved.

- Allow for limited use of user fees by patients to improve the levels of remuneration by health care providers, provided safeguards are in place to prevent discrimination against patients unable to pay user fees.

- Increase and improve access to health insurance, where the capacity exists to support a viable health insurance industry.

- Restructure and rationalize secondary and tertiary levels of health care, so that an appropriate level of care is made accessible, and reliance on overcrowded, centralized medical facilities is discouraged.

Justice

- An essential attribute of successful anticorruption efforts is an objective and independent authority, able to diagnose the character and extent of corruption and empowered to act institutionally to address it in a systemic and comprehensive manner.

- Reforms cannot happen without public-spirited, ethical, and committed leaders who are respected for their integrity and competence, and their vision and leadership skills.

- Increase the independence of the judicial branch of government, including a judicial sector with control over its own budget and administration.

- In nearly all cases, the funding of the judicial sector must be increased to allow for effective and efficient administration of justice, including increasing salaries and improving working conditions.

- Appointments and promotions must be made on a merit basis and in a transparent manner, so that nepotism and political patronage become hard to hide.

- Require key justice sector officials periodically to disclose their assets (and assets of family members).

- Systematically improve the training and professionalism of justice sector officials.

- Institutionalize and stringently enforce codes of ethics.

- Improve the timely access to information on laws and legal precedent.

- Implement random assignments of cases to judges and magistrates.

- Encourage the open publication of judicial decisions.
- Make more extensive use of alternative (but legal) dispute resolution techniques.
- Promote uniformity and transparency in court procedures in the processing of cases, so that opportunities for extortion and bribery are curtailed.
- Computerize court operations (e.g., maintenance of court files) wherever appropriate.
- Hold bar associations to a high standard of integrity in exposing and preventing corrupt practices.
- Improve legal education within law schools.
- Encourage civil society organizations to become active in educating the public on their rights and assisting them in accessing legal services, and carry out oversight on the performance of the justice sector.
- Improve the quality of media coverage of the judicial system, with greater access to those court files and records that ought to be publicly accessible.

Political Parties

- Restructure political parties so that their internal structures are governed by transparency and accountability.
- Foster competitive liberal democratic regimes so active opposition parties can contribute to anticorruption oversight.
- Expand legislation governing political parties so that party laws are not limited to the role of party behavior at elections, but extend to embrace parties as central components of good democratic governance. This would include limiting the extent to which political parties can be in the pocket of special interests, possibly through some level of public funding of their activities, coupled with appropriate accountability for the use of such funding. Campaign finance legislation, if effectively drafted and enforced, would also positively influence the behavior of political parties across their whole spectrum of activities.
- Strengthen democratic practices within political parties. Rules and procedures affecting membership, election and accountability of party leadership, the selection of candidates, transparency of operations and finances, and ethical behavior

all are needed if parties are to model the democratic principles they purport to represent.

- Improve the accountability of political parties. An independent anticorruption watchdog organization (e.g., electoral
  commissions, ethics committees) should be instituted at the
  same time that anticorruption legislation is improved (or
  introduced), and this watchdog body should be granted both
  independence and the unquestioned power to prosecute corrupt activities and, where necessary, to impose sanctions.

- Realign the incentives and disincentives that influence corruption in political party behavior. To be effective in controlling corruption, the risk of being punished for corrupt
  behavior must be credible. This punishment may come at the
  ballot box, but it may also take the form of penalties, fines,
  jail sentences, or loss of a seat in parliament.

- Transform public attitudes and reduce public tolerance
  regarding corruption, and mobilize the necessary political will
  and integrity to effect positive changes in the fight against
  corruption.

Private Sector

- Provide clear standards to differentiate between private and
  public sector activities, obligations, and authorities, so that
  confusion and undesirable overlap can be prevented.

- The government, in collaboration with organizations that
  represent the interests of the private sector, should establish
  and/or encourage training programs to inculcate the values of
  ethically responsive business practices as a central component
  of corporate governance.

- The government should establish a scheme to recognize,
  honor, and publicize those private sector suppliers of goods
  and services of proven and consistent integrity.

- In cases where private sector perpetrators of corruption have
  been successfully prosecuted, establish a "name and shame"
  set of sanctions to disqualify such private sector providers of
  goods and services from contracting with any agency of government for a set period of time. Widely publicize this list,
  with regular updates.

Public Finance

- Minimize unsupervised contact between private individuals (and businesses) and tax or customs officials.

- Institute staff rotations within tax, customs, and other appropriate departments, and improve oversight by senior managers.

- Encourage the progressive computerization of tax and customs administrations.

- Improve public sector accountability through the use of public sector audits by independent public sector auditors.

- Simplify those tax laws that are too complex and too open to various interpretations by those holding positions in which they can exercise powers of official discretion, often with little or no accountability.

- Ensure that high-incentive arrangements for corruption are avoided, e.g. so that the same official is not both tax inspector and tax collector.

Sectors and an Anticorruption Framework

USAID's Handbook on Fighting Corruption (1999) proposes a useful framework for curbing corruption that relies on three main initiatives: (1) limiting authority by reducing the role of government in economic activities; (2) improving accountability by strengthening transparency, oversight, and sanctions; and (3) improving incentives by redesigning terms of employment in public service. The nine sector chapters generally support this framework. Sectoral remedies to fighting corruption basically apply these same three approaches.

On the issue of privatization of some of the government's responsibilities, it was noted that there are many instances in which there is a strong case to be made for privatizing certain government functions. Privatization imposes market disciplines, and generates a body of owners who demand accurate information on the changing value of their assets. Privatization is not a panacea, however, and expanding the analysis lens beyond just the public sector demonstrates this. Employees of private firms can find positions in which to demand bribes or to exert corrupt influences, particularly when internal financial controls remain weak. Public officials involved in the privatization process can also influence this process in their favor, through having a direct or indirect financial stake in the newly created private venture.

In terms of improving accountability by strengthening transparency, oversight, and sanctions, the important role of a free press and related mass media was a common theme to nearly all of the sectoral reviews. Public awareness of the nature of corruption, public access to information, and a public acceptance that corruption is a problem that can effectively be addressed all are essential to transforming existing social tolerance or apathy into a strong public demand for integrity in governance.

Accountability and transparency also can be improved through the application of information technology. The application of computer technologies to standard operations of government (e.g., taxation and customs operations, budgeting, court records, drugs procurement) has been demonstrated to be an effective tool in constraining and preventing corruption. Arbitrary discretion and lack of transparency are greatly reduced through the use of such technologies, although this is not a totally reliable cure—there are sophisticated methods available by which to subvert software programs to hide illicit activities. The periodic use of public sector audits (to establish institutionalized checks, clear lines of accountability, and improve access to information) by independent (disinterested) auditors was also noted as an affective tool in the pursuit of non-corrupt governance.

USAID's third component, improving incentives by redesigning terms of employment in public service, was almost accepted as a default position by the authors. There was a sense in many of the chapters, however, that this is the most important yet least probable strategy to curb public sector corruption. Currently there are very few effective anticorruption incentives for civil servants who do not earn a living wage—an economic situation that is more the rule than the exception in most developing countries. Until civil servants receive benefits and security of employment that allows them to achieve and sustain a reasonable standard of quality of life, and a status that commands the respect of their peers, they will continue to resort to corruption in order to meet their urgent needs. Strategies to remedy this predicament are mired in complexity, since not only must civil servants earn more, they must also perform more efficiently and demonstrate a profound change of attitude towards serving the public good. To some extent, this challenge is captured in the concept of professionalism, which appeared in many of the chapters.

Government institutions in some countries demonstrate a culture of pride in professionalism, ensuring that their officials adhere to a consistently high standard of performance and commitment to public service. The inculcation of a professional ethic rewards competence, and does not tolerate shoddy performance. In such institutions, however, there also is considerable social status and economic security attached to permanent employment with the government, and competitive pressures to perform well or risk loss of career advancement or even job termination. There is also a reasonably good package of employment benefits. Given such an environment of professionalism, and the articulation and internalization of appropriate ethical standards and codes of conduct, it becomes very difficult for corruption to become embedded, and there is a high correlation between public expenditures and the provision of high quality public goods and services.

In less developed and transitional countries, it is often difficult or even deemed impossible to make the level of economic investment necessary to create and sustain such conditions. Further research is needed to explore the potential returns from an elevated level of investment in the civil service, particularly if the hidden costs of inefficiency, poor service to the public (and consequent loss of productivity by the public), crime, and corruption are factored in to establishing the cost of current arrangements. It arguably may be worth the investment in improved benefits and standards even in conditions of relative scarcity.

Gaps in the Sectoral Analyses

The preceding nine sector chapters of this book present a broad but by no means exhaustive review of the ways in which corruption affects development. There are gaps in this analysis: key development sectors are missing from the analysis, private sector corruption has not been addressed, and there is a need to focus on development ethics.

First, there are other major public sector analyses that should be pursued, including a review of the government's role in physical infrastructure, transportation, communications, tourism, defense, and social services. The role of local governments in this era of expanding decentralization warrants close scrutiny, as well, as does the central government's role in regulating and participating in the financial sector.

Second, corruption is not limited to the public sector, although linkages between the public sector and the private and civil society sectors are often conduits for corrupt activities. Corruption occurs in all sectors—public, private, and civil society—yet most donor strategies and interventions in the developing world focus on the public sector. Isolating the public sector in this way can be misleading, as nearly all persons interact in public and private spheres that often overlap and which certainly influence each other. Identifying corruption as just a public sector problem or giving preponderant weight to the public sector context can confuse the origins and vectors through which corruption finds expression.

The focus in this volume on just the public sector both simplifies and complicates the overall conclusions, and renders any conclusions incomplete.[1] The relationships between public sector, private sector, and the civil society sector are intricate and growing in their interdependence. As the divisions become intentionally (and, occasionally, unintentionally) blurred among these three sectors, with respect to which sector performs certain public services and provides certain public goods, continual revision and modification of corruption frameworks will need to be carried out. As the private sector and NGOs begin to perform more of what was once always deemed public sector services, lines of accountability become very tenuous—an obvious concern when considering the prevention of corruption. Government cannot selectively abdicate its governance functions through subcontracting, nor can it avoid an obligation to ensure that corruption and inefficiency do not come to characterize any functions and services that have been subcontracted or otherwise come to be performed by others. This level of oversight is partially addressed by better and more transparent procurement by the public sector of goods and services provided by the private and civil society sectors, but the analysis needs to go deeper in considering how the government should best maintain a quality and integrity assurance role appropriate to its ultimate accountability to the public.

Third, as Klitgaard says, "Corruption is at its heart an ethical problem."(Klitgaard, 1991, p. 11) Analysis has to go beyond this sectoral approach to get to the core of the corruption problem and what to do about it. Klitgaard follows his observation with a quick disclaimer that his purpose is not to provide a moral analysis of corruption, and that any such analysis probably would run adrift on the rocks of moral relativism. Other noted analysts have made passing comments on the ethical dimensions of corruption; Rose-Ackerman speaks of the need for "personal honesty and a devotion to democratic ideals" (Rose-Ackerman, 1978, p. 95), while Cragg stresses a universalist argument when he says that "Bribery is *prima facie* unethical virtually everywhere judged by the standards of prevailing conventional morality" (Cragg, 1999).

If one accepts that corruption is fundamentally a problem of ethics, the lack of emphasis on the ethical dimension in the literature is puzzling. Problems of moral relativism are hardly insurmountable, as evident in widely accepted human rights principles. Despite this, there is little in the literature on corruption to suggest that a moral framework is appropriate to analysis—yet this may be due to the nature of ethics itself. Several leading moral theories (for example the human rights approach, the capabilities approach,[2] virtue ethics, various feminist moral theories, social contract theory, Kantianism, utilitarianism) all separately offer carefully reasoned contemporary ethical frameworks that would—were they applied to this pursuit—illuminate various ways in which corruption constrains essential human freedoms, limits human opportunities and choice, and thereby prevents human flourishing, fails to support the universal quest for "the life lived well," erodes compassion and concern for the plight of those less fortunate, undercuts justice and equitable treatment for all persons under the rule of law, ignores or diminishes respect for fundamental human dignity, and fails to generate maximum pleasure or utility for the greatest number of people. The application of ethics to the problems of development generally, and corruption specifically, now finds expression in the relatively new field of *development ethics*. To date, however, leading multilateral and bilateral aid institutions, such as the World Bank or USAID, seldom frame their discussions on corruption or development from a development ethics perspective.[3]

The prominent exception to this institutional disregard for development ethics now may be emerging with the recent emphasis on leadership and its role in curbing corruption. In a recent study by Kaufman of the World Bank, more than 80 percent of government officials from sixty-two countries in the sample identified the need to improve the quality of leadership as the single most important factor in the fight against corruption (Kaufmann, 1997).

Effective leadership entails more than competence, leadership skills, and a strong disposition towards developing a leadership role—high moral standards of integrity, honesty, and commitment to the common good are also needed. It is important to appreciate both the practical and the ethical qualities of leadership and the public expectations of adherence to a public trust—what some call civic virtue. A leader's effectiveness does depend in large measure on charisma, intellect, and assertiveness, but moral attributes underpin and influence the leader's actions within the political process and are arguably fundamental to mitigating successfully and preventing corruption—regardless of development sector. Corruption appears to flourish and become socially embedded in an environment devoid of integrity at the highest levels of leadership. Top leadership exerts a powerful influence on societal tolerance to and participation in corruption, for good or ill depending on the moral attributes—or virtues—being modeled.

Conclusions

The analyses undertaken by the previous nine authors emphasize the importance of transparency, accountability, access to information, and strong disincentives for engaging in corrupt behavior. Corruption must be prevented in a variety of ways, some sequenced, some simultaneous, some sectorally based, some regardless of sector. Significant advances can be made in the fight against public sector corruption provided there is the requisite political will, competent and well-trained public sector staff, and effective and civic-minded leadership.

Three additional observations warrant special mention:

- First, working for the public sector must be made economically viable so that talented, competent, and publicly minded individuals can be attracted and retained. It is simply not reasonable to expect absolute integrity and the provision of efficient, high-quality services responsive to the public interest from civil servants who typically are underpaid, undervalued, inadequately trained, and, not surprisingly, poorly motivated. The cost implications of such an investment appear to be prohibitive, but serious research should be undertaken to compare the hidden costs of corrupt public sector performance and the many lost opportunities that result from embedded corruption with the actual costs and potential returns from investing a greater proportion of available resources into the public sector, in turn demanding corruption-free standards and efficient stewardship of public resources.

- Second, the role of leadership in modeling and motivating ethical and corruption-free behavior is pivotal to any success in curbing corruption. Leaders who demonstrate integrity and demand the same from others inspire public service, and such leadership deserves more direct support and recognition.

- Finally, the public must demand integrity, effectiveness, and responsiveness from the public sector. The public should be made aware of the profoundly negative impacts of complacency in the face of growing and worsening corruption, and a public dialogue should begin on the values and qualities that ought to characterize the public sector, and how this can be made to happen. Involving the public as full participants in the fight against corruption is the most powerful and potentially effective approach available because it starts at the place where corruption hurts the most—by respecting the essential dignity and worth of every human being.

Notes

1. Although there was a "private sector" analysis conducted within this study, it focused on public sector corruption related to government-business transactions. It did not highlight the problem of business-to-business corruption.

2. An example of a capabilities approach framework for the analysis of corruption may be found in Schwenke (2000).

3. Interesting exceptions do occur. Both the United Nations Development Programme (UNDP) and the British Department for International Development (DFID) speak openly and prominently about ethical concerns associated with human rights claims and protections in the UNDP *Human Development Report 2000: Human Rights and Human Development and the UK government's 1997 White Paper on International Development,* respectively.

PART 2

APPLIED ANALYSES

Chapter 12

Corruption and the Delivery of Health and Education Services

Omar Azfar

Corruption is widespread in the health and education sectors of developing countries, and not uncommon in developed countries. Exams are sold in Indonesia and Pakistan. Some reports state that there are 20,000 ghost schools in Pakistan, the expenses for which find their way into the pockets of bureaucrats. Teachers routinely pay between US$200 and US$1,400 for jobs and then collect their monthly salaries of US$70–US$100 without working, sharing these salaries with their supervisors for turning a blind eye to their absenteeism. Consequently, as many as 32 percent of teachers in Pakistan never show up for classes (Burke,

181

2000), while many more who buy their jobs or get them as favors are incompetent or even illiterate. In Thailand, teachers pay bribes to board members for promotions and transfers, and board members in turn bribe people to vote for them. One report states that, as a rule of thumb, 70 percent of teachers fail to show up for work on a typical day in the poorest countries (Bennet, 2000). In another case, a Thai education fund of 103 billion baht (US$2.2 million) was reportedly rendered ineffective as loans meant for the poor were given to the rich and well-connected—many of whom were not even students (*Bangkok Post,* 2001). There is widespread corruption in textbook procurement, with the consequence that the prices of textbooks in some countries are many times higher than their prices elsewhere.

The health sector is scarcely better. Studies of corruption in formerly communist countries have shown that the health sector is considered one of the most corrupt sectors in Slovakia, Tajikistan, and Ukraine, with bribes routinely demanded for treatments that are supposed to be free (Lewis, 2000). Large leakages are reported for health expenditures in Uganda and Tanzania (Reinikka and Svensson, 2002). The dilution of vaccines in Uganda has allegedly led to the emergence of resistant strains of bacteria (Ruzindana, 1998). In Colombia and elsewhere, corruption has allegedly led to the bankrupting and closure of hospitals. Studies of hospitals in various Latin American counties have uncovered indicative evidence of theft, absenteeism and kickbacks for procurements (Di Tella and Savedoff, 2001). Nor is corruption in the health sector exclusive to developing countries. Some studies have estimated numbers as high as US$100 billion for hospital fraud in the United States—this is more than the GDP of most developing countries. Doctors in the United States and Germany routinely get valuable gifts from drug companies whose drugs they prescribe. Nor are not-for-profit organizations immune—even in relatively well governed countries like the United States, prestigious organizations have been accused of accepting large donations and recommending drugs without proper scrutiny.

Given the prevalence of these various practices it is hardly surprising that there are some statistically significant relationships between corruption and health and education outcomes. To some extent it is not surprising that corruption—the abuse of office for personal gain—would affect outcomes. I can think of three reasons why it might not affect outcomes, but none seem to be true in practice:

1. Governments cannot do anything to improve health or education outcomes.

2. Corruption is a minor concern in health and education.

3. The form of corruption is efficiency-enhancing or efficiency-neutral in the health or education sectors.

Because reason 1 is patently false, this chapter will review empirical evidence on points 2 and 3. The evidence suggests that corruption is a major concern in the delivery of health and education and the form of corruption is often efficiency-reducing.

Still there may be other valid reasons why corruption may not affect service delivery and it is important to examine evidence on whether health and education outcomes are in fact worse in places with more corruption. I shall also review the evidence, which suggests that corruption does appear to undermine service delivery, although the results are inconclusive on this score.

The chapter begins with a description of the nature of corruption in the health and education sectors and then summarizes the results on the relationship between corruption and health and education outcomes. The causes of and possible remedies for corruption in the health sector are then examined, looking at evidence from Latin American hospitals. (No such empirical evidence is currently available for the education sector.) Several data sets are described as well that are currently available or being created, which can help identify the causes, consequences and remedies for corruption in the health and education sectors. Finally, some policy recommendations are offered.

The Nature of Corruption in the Health and Education Sectors

Both health and education offer plentiful scope for corruption. As described earlier in Chapters 4 and 5, corruption in each sector can take place in procurement, recruitment, the theft of money and supplies, absenteeism, induced demand for unnecessary goods and services, and the solicitation of bribes for services. Understanding the nature of corruption in these two sectors will both help evaluate the impacts of corruption on outcomes and help design more effective responses to it.

Some of these manifestations of corruption may be worse than others in terms of their effect on service delivery. To some extent one can answer the question of whether corruption affects service delivery by looking at the kinds of corruption that are more prevalent. If corruption takes the form that patients bribe nurses and doctors for services then, *if there were no wide discrepancies in incomes*, we might expect that the resulting price mechanism would improve the effectiveness of health services.[1] If incomes vary widely, the impact of bribery on health outcomes would be ambiguous, because while the bribes would deter the relatively well-off from frivolous treatments, the bribes would also deter the indigent from seeking necessary treatments. Other forms of corruption in the health sector—like the dilution of vaccines, the pilferage of refrigerators (which breaks the vaccine cold chain), or the prescription of unnecessary treatments—have clearer effects on worsening health outcomes.

Two sources that provide a good description of the nature of corruption in parts of the health sector are Di Tella and Savedoff (2001) and Cohen et al (2002). The chapter on Argentina by Schargrodsky et al. (2001) in Di Tella and Savedoff mentions the incidence of corruption in the purchase of pharmaceuticals, meals, cleaning services and physical inputs. In addition, corruption takes place in staff appointments, the theft of supplies, bribes for scheduling surgeries, absenteeism and the diversion of patients to private practices. Additionally, in Peru there is evidence of induced demand for Caesarian births, which are in excess of the medically required number of around 10 percent and highest in the private-sector hospital (Alcazar and Andrande, 2001). This highlights the possibility of more corruption in the private sector, and suggests the need for caution about thinking of privatization as a panacea for controlling corruption.[2]

The chapter by Gideon et al. in DiTella and Savedoff on corruption in Bogota hospitals categorizes corruption into doctor-patient, hospital-payer, and hospital-supplier relationships (Table 12.1 follows this format). In the first relationship, a doctor may improperly use public facilities for a private practice and also be absent or lazy during duty hours to increase demands for the private practice. In the hospital–payer relationship, it can take the form of the falsification of bills, a problem that is likely to become more important as developing countries move to more insurance and reimbursement systems. In the hospital–supplier relationship, corruption may take the form of either explicit kickbacks or more subtle gifts not explicitly tied to the awarding of contracts.

Many chapters in Di Tella and Savedoff concentrate on this last form of corruption, corruption in procurement, perhaps because data on this form is more readily available than on other forms. The hard data on corruption in procurement is not on the corruption itself, which the perpetrators are careful to conceal, but on the prices charged, which are observable. Price differences themselves do not provide conclusive evidence of corruption—a hospital may pay higher prices because of emergency purchases, poor bargaining or general negligence. In response to this concern, the authors do find evidence in the responses of health workers which link higher prices to corruption. It is also not clear how important these distinctions are: repeated emergency purchases or neglect are forms of mismanagement and, therefore, worthy of investigation or response, whether or not they are instances of corruption. Furthermore, for practical purposes, the most effective anticorruption strategy may well be to provide incentives to reduce neglect and corruption at once, rather than trying to excise corruption surgically while consciously avoiding related forms of misgovernance.

Cohen et al. (2000) divide corruption in the pharmaceutical sector into various stages: approval and registration, selection, distribution and service delivery. They provide a corruption vulnerability assessment for each stage. They demonstrate the complex scope of the problem and the possible detail of the diagnosis if one takes a hard, sector-specific look at the problem. They also produce a set of

Table 12.1. The Nature of Corruption in the Health Sector

Patient–Doctor	Payer–Hospital	Hospital–Supplier	Within Hospital/Ministry
Bribes for treatment	Fraudulent billing for fictional treatment	Kickbacks for purchase orders of drugs, equipment, supplies, meals, and cleaning services	Sale of jobs and promotions and transfers
Induced demand for unnecessary procedures (e.g. Caesarian deliveries)	Patients with coverage get prescriptions for those without	Bribes for approval of drugs	Theft of funds
Diluted vaccines		Doctors bribed by drug companies for prescribing their drugs	Theft of supplies
Absenteeism		Non-profits and other organizations accept donations for recommending drugs	Fraudulent billing for expenses
Negligence		Kickbacks for construction	
Bribes for illegal procedures like abortions			

recommendations on how to deal with the problem. With refreshing realism they categorize the possible responses both in terms of their expected effectiveness and their political feasibility.

Corruption in the education sector can also take various forms, many of which parallel those in the health sector (cf. Table 12.2). There can be corruption in the purchase of textbooks, desks, blackboards, and other supplies, as well as in the purchase of cleaning services and meals. Corruption in the procurement of school construction can make construction cost between two and eight times what similar buildings cost for private use (Bennet, 2000). There is also frequent theft of supplies and funds. On one trip with a senior official in Pakistan where textbooks and school bags were distributed to the students, I found (only because I defied protocol and went for a hike on which I met some parents) that the principal had requisitioned all materials be "returned" to him.

There is widespread corruption in many countries in the hiring of teachers —for instance, the reported hiring of ghost teachers in Pakistan. Some reports state that 32 percent of Pakistani teachers never show up to teach (Burke, 2000).

Table 12.2. The Nature of Corruption in the Education Sector

Student–Teacher	Payer–School	School–Supplier	Within School/ Ministry
Bribes for admission	Ghost schools for processing vouchers	Kickbacks for purchase orders of textbooks, equipment, supplies, meals, and cleaning services	Sale of jobs and promotions and transfers
Bribes for grades and promotions	Inflating number of students to get reimbursements	Bribes for approval of textbooks	Theft of funds
Induced demand for private tuitions	Loan officers bribed to give loans to rich students or nonstudents	Board members bribed by publishing houses for selecting their textbooks	Theft of supplies
Absenteeism	Students who stay in university for decades to collect stipends	Bribes for turning blind eye to photocopying textbooks and violating intellectual property	Fraudulent billing for expenses
Teaching badly		Kickbacks for construction	Underallocation to education
Sale of exams and bribes for letting professional exam takers take exams for students			

Other reports (e.g., Bennet, 2000) suggest that this number may be even higher in some developing countries. Absenteeism is frequent in the schools of many countries; this is often related to the sale of jobs, as mentioned above.

Teachers and principals may solicit bribes for admitting students or giving better grades. One barely disguised way of doing this is to ask students to pay for private tuitions. Teachers may teach badly to increase the demand for private tuitions. Examiners may allow students to cheat on exams or take exams for each other. Educational institutions may issue false certifications.

There is also corruption at the interface of payers and schools and universities. Student loans may be given to people who are neither needy nor students. A 103 billion baht Thai education fund was rendered ineffective by such practices.

The implementation of voucher schemes may lead to the proliferation of ghost schools that process vouchers without providing education—similar to fraudulent health reimbursement systems.

The Effect of Corruption on Education Outcomes

Several studies—notably Gupta et al., Rajkumar and Swaroop, Azfar and Gurgur, and Azfar et al.—have shown negative effects of corruption on education outcomes in cross-sectional analyses. Additionally, Mauro (1998) and Knack and Sanyal (2000) have shown that corruption reduces the share of public expenditures on education. Knack and Sanyal's results are stronger because they actually control for the general quality of government in their regression, which indicates that it is corruption itself rather than the generally poor quality of government that is leading to the under-allocation of resources to education. Azfar and Lee (2002) have also investigated the relationship between corruption and spending on health and education, and have found, like Mauro, that there is a clear relationship between corruption and education expenditures but only a fragile relationship between corruption and health expenditures—which disappears if income is controlled for.

Before discussing the results of Gupta et al. and Rajkumar and Swaroop, it is worth discussing the corruption variable they use. As a measure for corruption, they use the International Country Risk Guide's (ICRG) index for corruption in government. It is best to think of this index as a measure of integrity, as higher numbers denote more honest governments. The definition from Knack and Keefer (1995) who introduced the variable to the literature is:

> Corruption in government: Lower scores indicate "high government officials are likely to demand special payments" and "illegal payments are generally expected throughout lower levels of government" in the form of "bribes connected with import and export licenses, exchange controls, tax assessments, policy protection, or loans." Scored 0–6. High numbers denote better government.

The index is available annually for around 130 countries, beginning in the mid-1980s. Many researchers use this index because other corruption indices either have insufficient country coverage or time-series coverage, or both.[3]

Gupta et al. and Rajkumar and Swaroop's result, can only be interpreted as the impact of a governance variable on the dependent variable. The different governance variables are too highly correlated to be able to disentangle the effects of one from the other. Perhaps the best way to view the existing evidence is that it establishes the importance of good governance as a whole, one aspect of which is reducing the level of corruption. However, Anderson et al.'s microlevel findings for Georgia, (admittedly only one, possibly unrepresentative country), on the sale of jobs and on the prevalence of corruption in the law enforcement sector, do suggest that corruption would contribute to wider misgovernance.

Gupta et al. showed that in univariate regressions, corruption is correlated with each of: school enrollment, repeater (failure) rates, dropout rates, continued schooling through grade 5, and illiteracy. This equation (despite its potentially serious omitted variable problems) can be interpreted as demonstrating the total effect of corruption on education outcomes—if we accept that the level of income is endogenous to the level of corruption.[4] The coefficient of 0.36 on dropout rates implies that improving the integrity of government by two would halve the dropout rate. The coefficients on illiteracy and repeater rates are a little lower at 0.24, implying that an improvement of two points in the integrity index would reduce the dropout rate by around 40 percent. After controlling for income, corruption is correlated with repeater rates and dropout rates but not with enrollment, persistence to grade 5 or illiteracy. The coefficients on repeater rates and dropout rates each fall by about a third, implying correspondingly smaller effects of corruption on education outcomes. The coefficient of 0.20 on dropout rates implies that a two-point improvement in the quality of government would reduce dropout rates by around 33%.

Gupta et al. also conduct a multivariate analysis of dropout rates, controlling for average female education among adults, public education spending, the dependency ratio and urbanization. They find a persistently significant effect of corruption on dropout rates, but the coefficient drops to 0.13. This implies that a two-point improvement in the integrity of government would reduce dropout rates by around 22 percent.

Because the equilibrium levels of income are probably affected to some extent by the level of corruption, but also by other variables, the actual effect of corruption on dropout rates is probably somewhere between the 22 percent estimated in the multivariate regression and the 50 percent estimated in the univariate regression. It is also worth noting that the coefficients might also be biased downwards because of measurement error in the corruption variable.

At first glance, there are serious endogeneity problems in looking at the effect of corruption on education outcomes. Improving education could lead to increased civic virtue or the competency of the bureaucracy, either of which could reduce corruption. These concerns, however, are largely allayed by the inclusion of adult education levels on the right-hand side of the regression (female education levels are quite highly correlated with total adult education levels). Having controlled for the education levels of the working and voting population, it is unclear that current dropout rates would affect the level of corruption.

However, Gupta et al., like many economists, treat these concerns seriously and provide the reader with instrumental variable estimates of the effect of corruption on education outcomes. In fact it is not clear whether the instrumental variable analysis is more credible than the ordinary least squares (OLS) regressions.

The instruments they use are from Treisman's (2000) analysis of the causes of corruption: democracy, income, the share of Protestants in the population, and a unitary form of government. All of these could easily have a direct impact on education outcomes, any one of which could create spurious results in the instrumental variable analysis. For instance, valuing education may be one part of the Protestant ethic (with the exception of France, compulsory primary education was first tried in mostly Protestant countries). Democracy and income might be even more suspect as instruments. Gupta et al. do conduct the test of overidentifying restrictions to test for this concern, but this test is very weak in small samples and does not reliably demonstrate that the instruments are well chosen (Nakamura and Nakamura, 1985; Newby, 1985). One important lesson that these econometric caveats have for the policy maker is that it is generally far better to understand the mechanisms by which one variable might affect another and to collect microlevel data on these interactions than it is to rely on statistical relationships among instrumental variables, because the latter demonstrate causality only when a host of technical conditions are satisfied.

Rajkumar and Swaroop (2001) show that reducing corruption (or, improving the quality of government) improves education outcomes largely by improving the effectiveness of public expenditures. It is quite intuitively plausible that if corruption leads to large leakages in public funds allocated to education, public expenditure on education is likely to be less effective. (A discussion of public expenditure tracking surveys that find significant leakages in the delivery of education and health is presented later in the chapter.) Rajkumar and Swaroop estimate an equation of the determinants of dropout rates using data from two years, 1990 and 1997, with the aim of examining whether public expenditure on education is more effective in well-governed countries. They control for per capita GDP, the level of corruption, public education spending, female education, income inequality, a dummy for predominantly Muslim countries, a dummy for East Asia, ethno-linguistic fractionalization, access to safe water, degree of urbanization, percentage of population under five years old, the adult illiteracy rate and distance from the equator. They also include a variable (corruption rating × public education spending) that allows the impact of corruption and public education spending to vary with the level of the other variable. Their results show that while public education expenditure would have no perceptible impact on dropout rates if the integrity rating was 2, it would have a significant and meaningful effect if the integrity rating was 4. The implied coefficient of 0.6 at the higher integrity level indicates that a doubling of public expenditure would reduce dropout rates by 70 percent.

As a part of this project, Azfar and Lee have attempted to replicate these findings for other measures of education outcomes, but have been unable to do so. In fact the coefficient on the interaction term often takes the opposite sign. This might be driven by differences in the data sets or outcome variables used by the two sets of authors (Azfar and Lee use data from three years, 1990, 1995, and 1997, and use enrollment and illiteracy rates as outcome variables, as compared to Rajkumar and Swaroop who use data from two years, 1990 and 1997, and repeater rates as the outcome variable). It does, however, seem wise to caution the reader that the results of Rajkumar and Swaroop may not remain robust with changes in the sample and outcome variable.

Azfar and Gurgur (2001) and Azfar, Kähkönen and Meagher (2001) examine the effect of corruption on education outcomes across municipalities in the Philippines. Since their papers focus mostly on health, their methodology is described in greater detail in the next section on corruption and health outcomes. They use two measures of outcomes: students' scores in the National Elementary Aptitude Test (NEAT) and households' satisfaction ratings with schools. Their corruption measure is derived from surveys of education officials. With this measure, they conduct regressions at the municipality level. Of the eighty municipalities surveyed, they are able to use data on seventy municipalities for satisfaction ratings, but only forty-four for NEAT scores, as data was not available for many schools. They find a clearly significant effect of corruption on satisfaction ratings (t-stats from 2.16 to 2.64) but only insignificant effects on NEAT scores (t-stats from 1.30 to 1.64) (see Tables 12.3 and 12.4).

The Effect of Corruption on Health Outcomes

The same four papers (Gupta et al., Rajkumar and Swaroop, Azfar and Gurgur, and Azfar, Kähkönen and Meagher) also examine the effect of corruption on health outcomes (see Tables 12.5 and 12.6). These results are perhaps a little clearer for health outcomes. One of the papers (Gupta et al.) even offers panel data results on health outcomes.

Gupta, Davoodi, and Tiongson (2000) show that levels of corruption are clearly related to child mortality and other health outcomes. They find highly significant relationships in univariate regressions between corruption and all child mortality (under 5), infant mortality (under 1), births attended by health staff, immunization and low-birthweight babies (the lowest t-statistic is 5.61, dependent variables are in logs). Of course, this regression has a serious omitted variable problem since poorer countries have higher levels of corruption. If, however, we are interested in the total effect of corruption (broadly defined) on health outcomes, and accept that differences in income are largely created by differences in the quality of governance, then the coefficient does allow an interpretation of improvements in the quality of government on health outcomes. The coefficient on the log of child mortality and infant mortality is 0.37 and 0.35, implying that a two unit change in the corruption rating would halve child and infant mortality. The coefficient on low-birthweight babies is significantly lower at 0.14,

Table 12.3. The Effect of Corruption on Education Outcomes

Authors and Data	Results[a]	Significance
Gupta, Davoodi, and Tiongson *Cross country data; 72–111 observations; ICRG data but also repeat with Kaufmann et al. Graft index*	Clear univariate relationships between corruption and various education outcomes: school enrollment, repeater rates, dropout rates, persistence to grade 5, illiteracy rates (t-stats > 2.71).	Significant OLS results
	Results become weaker and generally insignificant after controlling for income (repeater and dropout rates remain significant).	
	Results for dropout rates remain significant after controlling for various other variables, including female education, public spending on health and urbanization. Result holds in instrument variable (IV) estimation using Treisman's equation to predict corruption. Results don't hold in multivariate analysis for other education variables.	Several insignificant OLS results (signs unreported)
Rajkumar and Swaroop *ICRG data; two year (1990 and 1997) panel data; 148–169 observations*	Controlling for several variables including female education, income, urbanization, and distance from the equator, they show that public education spending has a greater effect on repeater (failure) rates the higher is the quality of government, measured both as the absence of corruption and the quality of the bureaucracy. Results hold in an IV estimation using neighboring countries' expenditures and governance quality as instruments.	Significant OLS results, but Azfar and Lee could not replicate.
Azfar, Kähkönen, and Meagher (2001); Azfar and Gurgur (2001) *Cross-municipal data from the Philippines; corruption data based on education officials responses; 44 municipalities for NEAT scores, 70 for satisfaction ratings (80 sampled)*	Controlling for income, voting, media exposure, inequality, urbanization and social differences, Azfar et al. find that corruption is significantly related to satisfaction with education services but only insignificantly with NEAT scores.	One significant OLS result One insignificant OLS result

[a]Summary: four results are of the right sign; of these, three are significant at 5 percent. One result is of the wrong sign.

Table 12.4. The Effect of Corruption on Education Outcomes (t-Stats Below Coefficients)

	Authors	G, D & T	G, D & T	G, D & T	R & S	A & L
	Estimation Method	Univariate Regression	Controlled for Income	Controlled for Income, Female Education, Etc.	Controlled for Income, Female Education, Etc.	Controlled for Income, Female Education, Etc.
		3.1	3.2	3.3	3.4	3.5
Dependant Variable	**Independent Variable**					
School enrollment	Corruption	−0.03 (3.30)	0.01 (0.82)			2.33 (0.81)
	Corruption × Education Expenditure					0.25 (0.45)
Repeater rates	Corruption	0.24 (3.47)	0.15 (2.16)		0.08 (0.58)	
	Corruption × Education Expenditure				0.43 (2.44)	
Dropout rates	Corruption	0.36 (7.02)	0.20 (3.39)	0.13 (2.00)		
Persistence to grade 5	Corruption	−0.04 (4.30)	−0.00 (0.30)			
Illiteracy rates	Corruption	0.23 (2.71)	0.11 (1.34)			1.209 (0.39)
	Corruption × Education Expenditure					−0.231 (0.35)

Regressions reported in columns 3.4 and 3.5 were run with both corruption and the interaction of corruption and public expenditure as right-hand side variables.

G, D & T: Gupta, Davoodi and Tiongson; R & S: Rajkumar and Swaroop; A & L: Azfar and Lee.

implying that an increase of 2 points in the corruption score would only lower the number of low-birthweight babies by 30 percent.

Gupta et al. also estimate the effect of corruption on health outcomes after controlling for differences in income. The impact of corruption on health outcomes now becomes significantly smaller, with the coefficients falling by around 60 percent, though with the exception of immunization (t = 1.4) they remain significant. The coefficients of 0.13 and 0.14 on child and infant mortality imply that a two-point improvement in the integrity of government would reduce child or infant mortality by 40 percent. Azfar and Lee have repeated these regressions and found these effects to be significant as reported by Gupta et al.

In fact, several other variables, like female education, may also reduce child mortality (Filmer and Pritchett, 1999) and be related to the level of corruption (Swamy et al.), so a more accurate assessment of the impact of corruption on health outcomes would involve a multivariate regression controlling for income, female education, urbanization and other factors. Gupta et al. show that even controlling for per capita income, female education, public health spending, the dependency ratio and urbanization, corruption has a significant impact on child mortality, though the coefficient falls by half. The coefficient of 0.07 indicates that a two-point improvement in the integrity of government would reduce child mortality by 20 percent.

Gupta et al. also attempt an instrumental variable analysis to overcome reverse causality problems—for instance, poor health status increasing the bargaining power of health providers and hence the level of corruption. It seems unlikely that the demand effects created by poor health outcomes would really have impact on corruption ratings by international investment agencies, but Gupta et al. do find their results hold even in instrumental variable analyses.

As with education, it is not clear whether the instrumental variable analysis is more credible than the OLS regressions. As mentioned before, the instruments they use are from Treisman's (2000) analysis of the causes of corruption. All of these could easily have a direct impact on health outcomes, any one of which could create spurious results in the instrumental variable analysis. Unitary governments may, for instance, be better than decentralized governments at managing the cold chain for vaccines. Gupta et al. do conduct the test of over-identifying restrictions to test for this concern, but as mentioned above this test is weak and unreliable in small samples and does not reliably demonstrate that the instruments are well chosen.

A more serious endogeneity/omitted variable problem is suggested by the recent work of Acemoglu, Johnson and Robinson (2001) and Easterly and Levine (2002) who find that settler mortality is an important determinant of institutional quality. The story, eloquently told, is that settler mortality affected the character of colonization, with European colonists settling in low mortality areas and only expropriating from high mortality areas. Thus low mortality areas have more Protestants, more democracy and less corruption. If one is to believe this story then mortality causes corruption not vice versa. The econometric problem is serious because some of the main causes of mortality, like malaria, remain persistent to the present day. The instrumental variable methods of Gupta et al. do not resolve this concern, because the share of Protestants and democracy are also endogenous to mortality. Controlling for settler mortality in the child mortality regression seems one way of dealing with this problem. Azfar and Lee (2002) ran this regression and found that the relationship between corruption and child mortality does not change substantially when settler mortality is included in the regression.

Table 12.5. The Effect of Corruption on Health Outcomes

Authors and Data	Results	Significance
Gupta, Davoodi, and Tiongson *Cross country data; 89–116 observations; ICRG data but also repeat with Kaufmann et al. Graft index; panel data; 204–468 country-year observations for 1985–1997*	Clear univariate relationships between corruption and various health outcomes: child mortality, infant mortality, attended births, immunizations and low birth-weight babies (t-stats > 5.6).	Significant OLS results
	Results become weaker but generally remain significant after controlling for income.	
	Results for child mortality remain significant after controlling for various other variables including female education, public spending on health and urbanization. Result holds in IV estimation using Treisman's equation to predict corruption. They state that the results also hold for infant mortality and low birth weight babies but don't present the results.	Some insignificant results. Signs unreported
	Panel data results show that corruption affects child mortality (both random effects and fixed effects) and infant mortality (only random effects).	Significant panel results
Rajkumar and Swaroop *ICRG data; two year (1990 and 1997) panel data; 148–169 observations*	Controlling for several variables including female education, income, urbanization, and distance from the equator they show that public health spending has a greater effect on child and infant mortality the higher is the quality of government, measured both as the absence of corruption and the quality of the bureaucracy. Results hold in IV estimation using neighboring countries' expenditures and governance quality as instruments.	Significant OLS results, but Azfar and Lee could not replicate.
Azfar, Kähkönen, and Meagher (2001); Azfar and Gurgur (2001)	Controlling for income, voting, media exposure, and other variables finds that corruption is significantly related to knowledge of required immunizations and that knowledge of required immunizations is strongly related to immunizations and disease incidence.	Significant result

Table 12.5. (continued)

Authors and Data	Results	Significance
Cross-municipal and cross-clinic data from the Philippines; corruption data based on household and public officials' responses; 127–133 clinics (160 sampled) from 78 municipalities (80 sampled)	Effect of corruption on satisfaction with health services, waiting times is of the expected sign but not quite significant (t-stats from 1.05 to 1.88).	Insignificant/ marginally significant result
	Direct effect on immunizations and disease incidence is also of the expected sign but not quite significant (t-stats from 1.35 to 1.90).	Insignificant/ marginally significant result

Summary: Six results have the right sign; of these, four are significant at the 5 percent level.

Gupta et al. do conduct a panel data analysis, which may allay these concerns. They find that over time countries that improved their quality of governance significantly also reduced child mortality significantly. This appears less likely to be affected by the omission of a core mortality risk variable. However, some cautions are in order because child mortality data is often imputed from neighboring years, which can create a large number of artificial observations that could create spurious statistically significant relationships.

Rajkumar and Swaroop (2001) conduct an analysis of the impact of corruption on the effectiveness of health expenditures much like their analysis of education. They show that reducing corruption or improving the quality of government improves health outcomes, largely by improving the effectiveness of public expenditures. The intuition behind this is that if public funds allocated to health are stolen, or diverted to less productive uses, they are less likely to improve health outcomes. Formally, Rajkumar and Swaroop do this by estimating an equation of the determinants of child mortality using the following data from two years, 1990 and 1997: per capita GDP, the level of corruption, public health spending, female education, income inequality, a dummy for predominantly Muslim countries, ethno-linguistic fractionalization, access to safe water, degree of urbanization, percentage of population under five years of age, and distance from the equator. They also include a variable (corruption rating × public health spending) that allows the impact of corruption and public health spending to vary with the level of the other variable. Their results show that while public health expenditure would have no perceptible impact on child mortality if the integrity rating was 2, it would have a significant and meaningful effect if the integrity rating was 4. The implied coefficient at the higher integrity level of 0.22 indicates that a doubling of public

Table 12.6. The Effect of Corruption on Health Outcomes

	Authors	G, D & T	G, D & T	G, D & T	R & S	A & L
	Estimation Method	Univariate Regression	Controlled for Income	Controlled for Income, Female Education, Etc.	Controlled for Income, Female Education, Etc.	Controlled for Income, Female Education, Etc.
Dependant Variable	Independent Variable	4.1	4.2	4.3	4.4	4.5
Child mortality	Corruption	0.37 (12.26)	0.13 4.30	0.07 2.59	0.04 1.03	0.08 2.10
	Corruption × health expenditure				0.07 2.36	0.002 0.22
Infant mortality	Corruption	0.35 12.72	0.14 5.14		0.03 0.91	0.08 1.45
	Corruption × health expenditure				0.08 2.92	0.003 0.25
Attended births	Corruption	−0.13 6.06	−0.05 2.01			
Immunizations	Corruption	−0.06 5.61	−0.02 1.40			
Low-birth-weight babies	Corruption	0.14 7.20	0.06 2.87			
Life expectancy	Corruption					0.018 3.60
	Corruption × health expenditure					−0.004 2.00

Regressions reported in columns 4.4 and 4.5 were run with both corruption and the interaction of corruption and public expenditure as right-hand side variables. G, D & T: Gupta, Davoodi, and Tiongson; R & S: Rajkumar and Swaroop; A & L: Azfar and Lee.

expenditure would reduce child mortality by 30 percent. The results for infant mortality are similar.

Mauro (1998) has raised the concern that corruption may distort public expenditure away from health and education. One interpretation of the results of Rajkumar and Swaroop is that this may be rational, as public health and education expenditure is less effective in more corrupt countries. However, since all public and private expenditure could well be less productive in misgoverned economies, no such inference is possible.

What the results of Rajkumar and Swaroop do imply is that simply increasing public health spending, as is increasingly common in the conditionalities of the IMF and the World Bank, may not improve health outcomes. Rather, it may be more effective—if more difficult—to insist on reforming the quality of governance in the health and education sectors along with insisting on increasing the level of expenditures on service delivery. In fact the Bank and the Fund do now try to insist on improving governance in many countries. Both public spending on health and education, and improvements in the quality of governance will have a bigger effect on health and education outcomes, the higher is the level of the other variable.

Azfar and Lee (2002) attempted to replicate these findings but were unable to do so. The coefficient on the interaction term is clearly insignificant ($t < 1.00$) and becomes negative and significant if life expectancy is used as a dependant variable. This could be driven by differences in the data sets used by the two sets of authors (Azfar and Lee use data from 1995 in addition to data from 1990 and 1997 used by Rajkumar and Swaroop). We tentatively caution the reader that the results of Rajkumar and Swaroop might not be robust.

These sorts of studies on a cross-national level have also been conducted on a sub-national level. In a study of the Philippines, for example, researchers (Azfar et al., 2000; Azfar and Gurgur, 2001; Azfar, Kähkönen, and Meagher, 2001) examined the effect of corruption on health and education outcomes. They randomly selected four municipalities each from twenty randomly selected provinces, for a total of eighty municipalities, which allowed them to do a cross-municipal analysis.

To measure corruption, they used responses to questions about specific instances of corruption asked of public officials (stealing funds, stealing equipment, taking bribes, buying jobs, getting paid and not working), and general questions about corruption asked of municipal officials and households. Corruption indices were constructed using answers from these different questions.

The data were cleaned of respondent bias by using answers to a question about national corruption: since national corruption is the same for everyone in the sample, different ratings for national corruption must almost reflect respondent bias, and these differences can be used to filter responses about local corruption. This was an important step, as respondent bias seems to account for 15 percent of the differences in perceptions of municipal corruption.

The next step was conducting consistency checks on the data, which generally check whether municipalities deemed highly corrupt by one set of respondents are also rated highly corrupt by other respondents. Reassuringly, the data passed all consistency checks and Azfar et al. moved to the next step of the analysis where they examined the effect of these corruption measures on several health outcomes. As measures of health outcomes, they used knowledge of required immunizations by health officials, an index of satisfaction ratings and waiting times from households, and reports on increases in immunizations and decreases in diseases from health officials. In each regression they used different sources of data for the dependent and independent variables to minimize the effect of any respondent bias that was not already filtered out.

Their strongest finding was a significant and clear effect of corruption on the knowledge of required immunizations by physicians, controlling for income levels, voting rates, media exposure, delays in salary payments and the supply of medicines. They estimated the impact of corruption on satisfaction ratings and waiting times at clinics. Here, they found that the expected effects for either dependent variable was in the right direction but not statistically significant. However, a variable combining waiting times and satisfaction ratings was significantly predicted by public officials' perceptions of corruption (at 10 percent significance). Finally, with regard to increases in immunizations and reductions in diseases, the corruption variable had the right sign but was only significant (at 10 percent) for certain regressions. Nevertheless, since the knowledge of required immunizations had a clear and significant impact on the outcomes, it appears that corruption does undermine the delivery of health and education in the Philippines. Figure 12.1 summarizes these results.[5]

Figure 12.1. The consequences of corruption in the Philippines (Azfar et al., 2000).

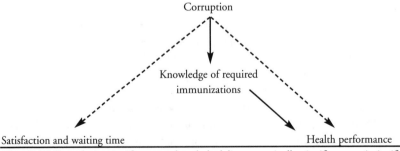

Note: Solid lines depict significant results; dashed lines marginally significant or insignificant results.

This cross-district study supplements similar findings at the cross-national level (Gupta et al.) in several important ways. First, it uses independent data focusing on one country rather than looking across countries, and two results that resonate are better than one. Second, the data were collected in a systematic and uniform way, which generally is not done at the cross-country level (few surveys systematically ask the same question in a large number of countries). Third, they were able to clean the corruption data of respondent bias, which cannot easily be done at the cross-national level. Finally, for at least some of the analysis, they were able to run regressions on almost the entire sample, which mitigates concerns about selection bias.

Thus subnational analyses, if properly conducted, can respond to questions about the quality and comparability of the data, which plague cross-national analyses. Furthermore, if there are serious concerns about omitted variables in cross-country regressions, it may be possible to collect data on these variables at the sub-national level. As decentralization proceeds around the world, an increasing number of countries have meaningful cross-jurisdictional variation in institutions, and this method can be effectively used to evaluate the effects of institutions on performance in many countries. Indeed, a number of economists are now conducting analyses using cross-jurisdictional data at the subnational level in Indonesia and other countries.

The Causes of Corruption in the Health and Education Sectors

Several studies, including Azfar et al. (2000), Kaufmann, Mehrez, and Gurgur (2002), and five papers on hospitals in Latin America, have examined the causes of corruption in the health sector. The literature on the determinants of corruption in the education sector is far more sparse. According to Klitgaard's formula, the causes of corruption may be broken down as follows:

Corruption = Monopoly + Discretion − Accountability[6]

We will discuss the findings of the various studies according to this framework.

Azfar and Gurgur and Azfar, Kähkönen, and Meagher found that the level of corruption in Filipino municipal governments is lower in municipalities where voting rates are higher. Thus, political accountability does appear to reduce corruption. Using exposure to the media as a proxy for transparency, the authors find that only exposure to national newspapers has an effect. Managerial accountability or transparency measured by the frequency of audits and evaluations appears to have no effect. Monopoly (or rather competition), proxied by the willingness of the population to migrate if health services are poor, has no perceptible effect. Urbanization does appear to have an effect, which may be due to competition from other providers, but other explanations are possible and even likely. Discretion may have an effect, though it is only significant in one regression and only at the 10 percent level. Wage effects measured by delays in salary payments are also insignificant.

Kaufmann, Mehrez, and Gurgur (hence KMG) conducted a microanalytic investigation of corruption and integrity-vulnerability in Bolivia. They collected data on corruption, service delivery, transparency, meritocracy, voice and other variables from 110 public institutions in Bolivia. The institutions include the top executive agencies, ministries, line agencies (e.g., tax and customs), autonomous agencies (e.g., central bank), departmental institutions and sixteen municipal governments. They lost twenty-one observations due to missing variables and ran their regressions with eighty-nine observations.

Their data consists of the following variables: service performance, bribery, corruption, transparency, enforcement, meritocracy, politicization, autonomous agency dummy, resource adequacy, values, voice, education, and wage satisfaction.

Their empirical analysis yielded two sets of results. First, bribery and a broader measure of corruption each appear to have a negative effect on service delivery. Second, transparency and meritocracy appear to reduce corruption, whereas politicization appears to increase it. Government wages have a marginally significant effect (at 15 percent) on reducing corruption.

One important concern with such an analysis is that different ministries and agencies fulfill very different functions and therefore there can be serious omitted variable biases in the estimation of the causes and consequences of corruption.

There are of course important causality issues relating almost any governance variable to almost any other. KMG try to resolve this concern by performing instrumental variable analysis (they try both two-stage and three-stage least squares). As usual, the believability of such instrumental variable results depends on the validity of the instruments (i.e., identifying restrictions). For instance they appear to assume that the education levels of public officials could only affect bribery, corruption or the quality of service delivery by increasing the level of transparency. If, as is possible, education levels had a direct effect on corruption or service delivery, their instrumental variable results would not be valid.

One useful extension of their work would be a repetition of this estimation methodology but with a merged data set from many countries. This exercise, which would allow controls for various agencies, would reduce concerns about omitted variables and the larger data sets may allow reasonable tests to be conducted on the identifying restrictions.

A recent book edited by Di Tella and Savedoff (2001) represents an important advance in the study of corruption in the health sector. First, it examines the incidence of corruption at the micro level (i.e., the level of the hospital). This is relatively innovative, though as discussed above, Azfar et al. have also attempted it. Second, it tries to examine "hard" data on corruption like hospital prices and excessive Caesarian deliveries. Such "hard" data on corruption is useful for several reasons. First, it allows researchers to check the data they get from subjective responses—which is subject to different forms of biases. If the two variables are correlated, this provides some reassurance that each is measuring corruption—though there remains the concern that knowledge of higher prices being paid by the hospital might be affecting the subjective responses on corruption. Second, if similar results were found on the causes or consequences of corruption using both hard and soft data, this would provide the reader with some reassurance that a real rather than a spurious relationship has been uncovered.

The chapter by Gray-Molina, Perez de Rada, and Yanez (2001) examines corruption in 30 Bolivian hospitals. The authors collected data on corruption perceptions; informal payments from patients, nurses and doctors; and procurement prices. They find that the data on informal payments and corruption perceptions are highly correlated. However, data on corruption perceptions are only weakly correlated with price data. Looking at their graph it appears that there would be a relatively strong correlation but for one outlier. This highlights one drawback of the various studies in the book. The sample of hospitals ranging from twenty to thirty-five is simply too small in each country to allow for any reasonable econometrics to be conducted and is small enough that one outlier can negate or create statistically significant effects. The other drawback in this particular comparison of hard and soft data is that the soft data on perceptions did not ask about corruption perceptions in that particular hospital; rather, it asked about corruption perception in public hospitals. While a person's perceptions about corruption in public hospitals are likely to be influenced by experience in one's own hospital, they may also be influenced by other factors, which would reduce the correlation between the perception questions and the procurement prices. In fact, the best questions may focus on perceptions about corruption in the procurement department of the hospital and compare the responses to the procurement prices.

There may also be other ways to collect information on procurement. If researchers find evidence that certain suppliers do not supply pharmaceuticals to the more corrupt hospitals, they can ask these firms why they do not bid. It may be informative if these firms respond—without being prompted—that kickbacks are routinely required at these hospitals. Performing such analyses is likely to shed more light on the value of collecting "hard" data on corruption.

Gray-Molina goes on to analyze the causes of corruption using two corruption variables, informal payments and input prices. For both input prices and informal payments they find the activism of the DILOS (a participatory planning and monitoring board consisting of community members, municipal officials, and prefectural health officials) reduces corruption. This can be thought of as an accountability variable, which they call "voice." The presence of a personnel supervision system also has the expected sign, but the effect is not quite significant—as noted before, the small sample sizes make meaningful statistical analyses difficult. They also find that the presence of a private hospital is related to lower levels of informal payments, indicating that competition does reduce corruption.

Jaen and Paravinski (2001) look at the effect of wages and penalties on corruption in Venezuelan hospitals. They also use hard and soft data for their analysis. Jaen and Paravinski find that wages have a perverse effect on corruption—higher wages are correlated with more corruption (procurement prices are higher in hospitals with higher wages). They interpret this as evidence of capture of wage setting by corrupt wage earners. The mechanisms by which corruption would raise prices and wages are quite similar. The wage earner or the seller would bribe—or perhaps influence—the buyer into paying a higher price for goods or services. Hospitals susceptible to one practice may well be susceptible to the other. In fact, the sale of jobs is a widespread practice in developing countries and reformers attempting to reduce corruption by raising wages should be aware that this practice might undermine the effectiveness of reform.

Higher wages can reduce corruption for two reasons: first, a public servant with a higher wage can more easily afford to be honest (because the marginal utility of money is lower), and second, dismissal carries larger costs in terms of foregone wages (this has clear parallels in the economic theory of crime: Becker, 1968; Ehrlich and Becker, 1973). The sale of jobs would undermine the first effect, as the wage would get capitalized in the price of the job. We do not know of any empirical study of this point, but it seems intuitively plausible. (Such an empirical study may be possible soon after wage reform.) The second effect depends on there being a non-trivial probability of detection and dismissal. Thus, especially in places where corruption has become entrenched in the practice of the sale of jobs, wage reform is only likely to be effective if combined with a realistic probability of detention and dismissal.

In fact, Jaen and Paravinski do find that greater accountability reduces two forms of corruption: theft and unjustified absenteeism. Their results on absenteeism, however, suggest an important caution. In hospitals with higher detection rates there was less unjustified absenteeism but more justified absenteeism. Raising the probability of detection for unjustified absences may simply induce people to find better justifications for being absent. In general terms, giving incentives based on one outcome is likely to improve performance on that particular outcome without necessarily improving overall service delivery; this is a broad implication of the multi-tasking literature.[7] It may, therefore, be more effective to base incentives on the ultimate objective like improvements in service delivery than exclusively on inputs like unjustified absences.

Schargrodsky, Mera and Weinschelbaum (2001) in a study of Argentinian hospitals find that prices did fall following enactment of a law on sending price information to the center, but that prices rose after agents realized that the price information was not being used for sanctions. This reminds us of a theoretically clear postulate: raising the probability of detection, or the size of salaries is only going to deter corruption if sanctions are actually implemented.

Alcazar and Andrande (2001) find interesting, if disturbing, evidence of another form of corruption in Peruvian hospitals—induced demand for Caesarian operations. The medically required number of Caesarians is around 10 percent in an average population, but all four hospitals they examined conducted significantly more Caesarians than 10 percent (the numbers varied from 21 percent to 78 percent). Alcazar and Andrande also found significant evidence of increases in Caesarian deliveries before weekends and holidays, signaling that doctor's convenience rather than patient's need was driving medical decisions. In fact, most of these Caesarian deliveries took place in private hospitals, raising some cautions about the possibility of greater corruption in the private sector. Private ownership creates incentives, and these incentives may well create more effective treatments—which patients can easily evaluate—and a better bedside manner, but they also create motives for doctors over-prescribing their own or the hospital's services. As a general point, this is another example of the possible perverse effects of incentives that we encountered above in the discussion of absenteeism in Venezuelan hospitals.

Like procurement prices, this study demonstrates the possibility of detecting corruption—or gross negligence and malpractice—by looking at large numbers of events when any one event would allow no inference. Since no one piece of information implicates anyone, the information may be relatively easy to get—this would be especially true if even the aggregate information could not implicate any one person. Still, the aggregation of the information can allow relatively clear inferences of the incidence of corruption. This principle could reasonably be applied to detecting misgovernance in other spheres. For instance, it may be worthwhile examining if the performance of students worsens when they get a particular teacher. Of course, this does not necessarily imply that there is "an abuse of office" taking place, but if the performance is bad enough it may make sense to replace the teacher whether or not they are abusing their office. Civil punishments starting from censures and small fines all the way up to dismissal can be used to improve performance and will probably reduce corruption too. Of course, no criminal charges are either possible or desirable without clear evidence of the abuse of office (Azfar, 2002b).

Alcazar and Andrande also found that doctors on fixed terms, who can be disciplined more easily than permanent staff, are more careful about prescribing Caesarians. This is further evidence that accountability matters for reducing corruption.

Gideon, Morales and Acosta (2001) conduct an analysis of variations in purchase prices across thirty-two Bogota hospitals. Like Alcazar and Andrande, they find a relationship between nonpermanent staff and integrity. They find hospitals with more non-permanent staff pay lower prices. The mechanism is frankly not that clear: it would be better to examine the effect on prices of the purchasing officer having non-permanent employment status. They do find that hospitals with female purchase managers pay lower prices for purchases. This resonates with the results of Swamy et al. (2001) and Knack and Azfar (2002), who show that women disapprove more of corruption than men in most countries and that countries with more women in parliament have lower levels of corruption.

Gideon et al. find that the existence of formal hierarchical controls increases purchase prices. This is not entirely surprising. Hierarchical controls can create a vertical chain where each member must be paid a bribe, which can increase prices. In fact this is one of the reasons cited for the harmfulness of corruption in Shleifer and Vishny's (1993) classic article on the subject.

One study was found that examined the effect of corruption on the education sector—an evaluation of El Salvador's EDUCO program by Jimenez and Sawada. Jimenez and Sawada find that being in a community program appears to reduce teachers' absences but the effect becomes insignificant when school effects are controlled for. The number of visits to the school however does appear to reduce absences. Table 12.7 summarizes the findings from many of these studies.

Emerging Data Sets and Ongoing Studies

As mentioned earlier, the most promising avenue of new research on the effect of corruption (and more generally misgovernance and management practices) on service delivery is the collection of primary data at the local government or service delivery (school, clinic, university, hospital) level and the analysis of this data. The World Bank is undertaking a number of such studies in several countries.[8]

In Indonesia, the World Bank sponsored a study that spanned across approximately 150 of the 360-plus kabupaten (districts within provinces) approximately one year after the large-scale devolution of authority to the kabupaten in January 2001. The surveys covered households (approximately 50 per kabupaten), firms (about 20 per kabupaten), and various branches of government including the health and education departments. The surveys include explicit questions about corruption. The data has only recently been collected and no results are available for review, but preliminary results are expected soon.

Quantitative Service Delivery Surveys (QSDS)

A World Bank team led by Ritva Reinikka is leading a set of Quantitative Service Delivery Surveys (QSDS) in Chad, Madagascar, Mozambique, Nigeria, and Uganda. Several other people at the World Bank are working on a number of other countries. The Bank and collaborating institutions will produce survey instruments, data sets, diagnostic reports and research and policy-oriented

Table 12.7. The Causes of Corruption: Corruption = Monopoly + Discretion
– Accountability

Monopoly	Discretion	Accountability
Cross-country results		
Ades and Di Tella find that more open economies—which may face more competition— are less corrupt. Knack and Azfar show these results may be driven by sample selection.		Treisman finds that continuous democracy deters corruption across countries. Lederman et al. corroborate this finding with a panel data analysis.
		Weder and van Rijkehem find that higher wages are correlated with less corruption. Rauch and Evans and Lederman et al find this result is not robust
Cross-municipality results from the Philippines		
Azfar et al. find that citizens' willingness to leave the municipality has no effect on corruption	Azfar et al. find that discretion is weakly correlated with corruption across Philippine municipalities	Azfar et al. find that voting rates in local elections are correlated with less corruption. However the frequency of audits and evaluations has no perceptible effect.
Results from Latin American hospitals		
Gray-Molina et al. show that the presence of a private hospital in the city is correlated with lower corruption in Bolivian hospitals.	Jaen and Paravinski find more corruption in larger hospitals.	Gray-Molina et al. show that the activism of an oversight board is correlated with lower corruption in Bolivian hospitals
		Jaen and Paravinski show that higher probabilities of detection are correlated with lower corruption (theft and absenteeism) in Venezuelan hospitals
		Andrande and Alcazar find that physicians without permanent contracts (who can be disciplined more easily) over-prescribe Caesarians less often in Peruvian hospitals.
		Gideon et al. find that hospitals with more non-permanent staff pay less for purchases.

results. These are surveys of frontline service providers (i.e., schools and clinics). The surveys have been completed in Uganda, Zambia and Papua New Guinea but results are not yet available. In the other countries, the data are still being collected.

The architects of these studies have various aims: first, they hope to uncover evidence of actual management practices in the frontline service-providing institutions, including information on corruption. Second, they hope to link these management practices to "upstream" administrative and political structure, in order to understand the causes of poor management practices. This may allow some analysis of the causes of corruption, as carried out by Azfar et al. and the various chapters in Di Tella and Savedoff. Third, they want to examine the impact of these management practices on corruption and the quality of service delivery. This they hope to do by merging data from users and providers at the clinic level, along the lines of work by Azfar et al. and some of the authors of the papers in Di Tella and Savedoff. One set of users will be surveyed as they exit the service center. There are potentially important selection issues here, as those with the best information about shortfalls in service delivery might not use the services. This concern may be mitigated by the surveys of private and not-for-profit service providers, where the surveyors may find users avoiding public services. In some countries, including Chad and Zambia, the various authors will merge the facility data with household surveys. This seems the most promising way of getting selection-free data.

These studies would, in principle, be able to examine the causes and consequences of corruption in the health and education sectors. However, we should raise an important caution. Data on corruption is presumptively suspect and should only be used after it passes reliability checks. For example, consider a country where respondents are so afraid in the most misgoverned districts that they feign ignorance of corruption. Corruption rankings of the various districts in this country based on these responses would rank the most misgoverned districts as the most honest. Any subsequent analysis of the data could easily find that corruption improved health outcomes when in fact it worsened outcomes.

Reinikka and colleagues also hope to compare management practices in the public, private and not-for-profit sectors. This is a welcome step and could allow comparisons of management practices and misgovernance across sectors. Perhaps subsequent to the study, policy prescriptions on privatization and other policy approaches will be made based on (admittedly imperfect) evidence rather than on presumptive beliefs. Still, cautions are in order. Even if less corruption is uncovered in private schools, this does not mean that there will be less corruption in *publicly financed* private schools. Corruption, which often occurs on the boundaries of the public and private spheres, might emerge in the form of ghost schools that process vouchers without providing education.

Public Expenditure Tracking Surveys (PETS)

A related effort being undertaken by the World Bank is on public expenditure tracking surveys (PETS). These were pioneered by Ritva Reinikka and Jakob Svensson in Uganda and are now being implemented in several countries (see Table 12.8 for results from several countries). Public expenditure tracking surveys monitor public expenditures down the chain from the central government, to the provincial government, to the district government, to the subdistrict governments all the way to delivery points (i.e., schools and clinics—though there is no fundamental reason why the surveys should be restricted to health and education services). If one level of government reports distributing more funds than the level below receives, it may be possible to pinpoint the leakage (by theft or diversion) of public funds.

Table 12.8. Results from Public Expenditure Tracking Surveys. Percentage Leakage of Public Funds.

Country	Year	Health Wage	Health Non-wage	Education Wage	Education Non-wage
Uganda	1993	—	—	20	85
Tanzania	1999	—	41	—	57
Ghana	2000	20	80	20	50

Summarized from Reinikka and Svensson (2002) (original sources: Reinikka and Svensson, Price Waterhouse Coopers, and World Bank).

Reinikka and Svensson found that 87 percent of non-wage expenditures allocated to education in Uganda were leaked in the transfer from districts to schools over the period 1991–1995 (though the leakage steadily declined over the period). In Tanzania, Price Waterhouse Coopers found that 57 percent of non-wage expenditure in education and 41 percent in health was leaked before reaching delivery points. In Ghana, 50% of non-wage expenditures in education and 80 percent in education were similarly lost. Although reported leakage was lower in wage expenditures (20 percent in both Uganda and Ghana), this may simply be an artifact of accounting. Leakage in "wage" expenditures may consist of people getting paid but not working, which would not necessarily show up in a purely expenditure tracking survey. A study to track such absenteeism was conducted in Honduras and found that there was substantial absenteeism—14 percent in education and 27 percent in health. Adding these figures to the observed leakage of around 20 percent in wage expenditures brings the total leakage closer to that in non-wage expenditures.

One interesting question for reformers is whether PETS can reduce the leakage of public funds. As with accounting systems, if the flow of money is better tracked, it may make it more difficult for agents to steal from principals.

Nevertheless, in our conversations about public expenditure tracking with civil servants, we have been reminded that accounting systems can also be rigged to hide theft—it just takes some effort to do so. As a rule of thumb, one should expect the agent to be craftier than the principal. In the immediate aftermath of implementing a public expenditure tracking survey, theft may well decline. Business might return to usual, however, if bureaucrats observe that sanctions are not applied when discrepancies are found—or only applied selectively. Recall the study of Argentinian hospitals by Schardorsky et al. (2001), which found that procurement prices did drop in the immediate aftermath of implementing the reporting system but reverted to near their original level over time.

Over time, it is also likely that corrupt officials will find other ways of siphoning off money, like paying more for procurement and getting kickbacks. Money that was once stolen easily will now be stolen in cleverer and subtler ways. (As a parallel case, one may recall Jaen and Paravinski's study of absenteeism in Venezuela, where increasing the probability of detection for unjustified absences reduced unjustified absences but increased "justified" absences by almost as much.) A recent study of Pre-Shipment Inspections on customs revenue in the Philippines has also found that smugglers find other ways of avoiding duties and tariff revenues do not increase.

For a PETS to be effective, it must be followed by a tracking of procurement practices and other dimensions of public administration to cover other avenues for corruption that become more lucrative when expenditure tracking is introduced. Ultimately, it is unclear whether all such avenues can be identified and blocked. The most effective reform of the system may require a measurement of ultimate outcomes—literacy rates and exam scores directly measured by outsiders, vaccination rates measured by collecting and testing blood samples from randomly selected individuals who have reportedly been vaccinated, and so forth. Incentives based on such measures, which are difficult to manipulate, may be more effective at reducing corruption than measures that seek to reduce specific instances of corruption.

There may be some synergies from implementing PETS and QSDS at the same time. PETS produces "hard" data on corruption. QSDS produces data on management practices, outcomes and soft data on corruption. Taken together, these surveys would provide reliability tests and examinations of the causes and consequences of corruption. Indeed, they are being undertaken together in many countries.

Recommendations

What does our imperfect state of knowledge allow us to recommend to the policy maker? While not persuasive on either account, the evidence does suggest that various forms of accountability might reduce corruption and that corruption undermines health and education outcomes. Therefore, better accountability may indirectly improve health and education outcomes.

Starting with reforms that reduce corruption itself, we recommend that policy makers make educated guesses about various reforms and try these out in pilot studies and then adopt the more successful ones. For instance, if the aim is to reduce teacher absenteeism and improve student performance, policy makers may want to try out two reforms: fines for unjustified absences and rewards for good performance of students on tests. A pilot study may divide 200 schools into four groups—50 who get no reforms, 50 where fines are implemented, 50 where rewards for good performance are implemented, and 50 where both reforms are tried. Such prospective random evaluations are described in more detail in Kremer (2002) and Azfar and Zinnes (2002).

Data should be collected on several outcome variables, for example, unjustified absences by teachers, total absences by teachers, number of times teachers are late for school, students' performance on the tests being used for the rewards, students' performance on other tests, students' satisfaction with teachers, and parents' satisfaction with the school. External evaluators, not the teachers themselves, should carry out the tests. An evaluation of these outcome variables before and after the trial period in the four groups of schools would allow an assessment of which of the reforms was more successful and whether there was any synergy between the reforms (i.e., whether fines for absences were more or less effective if rewards for student performance were also being given). In general, it is likely that incentives based on outcomes (like test scores) would do better than punishments for narrowly defined misdemeanors like unjustified absences (which might just lead to more resources being expended on finding justifications for absences).

A certain amount of unpredictability in the evaluation procedures may also be helpful in improving performance. If the evaluation protocol is too predictable it can probably be manipulated by the service provider to increase scores without actually improving service delivery. However, too much unpredictability might just dishearten providers, who may stop trying to do well. Designing an evaluation procedure is a bit like setting an exam: the evaluator must be predictable enough to provide incentives for providers, but unpredictable enough that the incentives are for genuine improvements, not artificial ones.

Several different kinds of reforms can be tried in different contexts, these include:

1. Increasing media coverage of service delivery by training journalists.
2. Making public officials aware of preferences—this is likely to be more effective for education which appears to be more widely demanded than health services (Azfar et al.).

3. Improving the transparency of financial flows (e.g., PETS).

4. Requiring public declarations of the assets of public officials.

5. Imposing fines and suspensions for consequences which probably result from corruption or mismanagement.

6. Surveying users about the quality of service delivery and rewarding service providers on the basis of these reports.

7. More ambitiously, users can be scientifically sampled and reexamined—in the case of education by asking students to take new tests, and in the case of vaccinations by collecting blood sampled to examine whether the antigens were in fact present.

8. Setting up competitions between different delivery points and local governments for improved performance.

9. Privatization or "NGOization" of service delivery.

10. Reducing staff and increasing wages.

11. Requiring detailed documentation of public procurements, how bids were solicited, which ones were received and the basis on which the awards were made

12. Implementing an IT system to track multiple prescriptions, shadow patients, and so forth.

13. Implementing a system of statistical forensics that analyzes exam scores to detect cheating and collusion of students with teachers.

14. Introducing standardized treatment guidelines.

15. Increasing community oversight of schools and clinics.

In all cases, it is important for there to be a setup to evaluate the reforms, best done with foreknowledge of the reform even if randomization is politically or administratively infeasible. In none of the cases above can we be confident *a priori* that the reform will reduce corruption or improve performance. For instance, standardized treatment guidelines could result in inappropriate and inflexible treatments; private or NGO suppliers could be as venal as public officials; increased wages may be dissipated in higher prices paid for jobs; and fines and suspensions might be politically applied and result in the outflow of some of the best practitioners.

The widespread decentralization of authority in many countries might allow policy makers to learn which reforms work. In the United States, one of the main arguments for decentralization is experimental federalism, the idea that states try "experiments" that, if successful, are emulated by other states. This relies on the ability of local governments to learn from each other, which is sadly absent in many developing countries, either because there is insufficient analytical capacity, or because there is insufficient media attentiveness and coverage of the programs. Creating the capacity to conduct such evaluations of reforms in developing countries will be an important step in learning about which reforms actually work.

Identifying the impact of corruption on health and education outcomes requires larger and more rigorous studies of the kind attempted by Azfar et al. Establishing the negative effects of corruption on health and education outcomes is important not only as a scientific question, but also important for policy makers to widen and solidify the political support for anticorruption reforms. Azfar et al. were hampered by budgetary restrictions, which forced them to interview only fourteen households in each municipality, and only one public official in each department, school or clinic. In addition, they had to rely on survey-based data and could not conduct interviews etc. in the 80 municipalities to collect other kinds of data. The consequence of these restrictions was that there was a fair amount of noise in the data. If such a study was replicated with larger samples interviewed in each municipality, more detailed questions about corruption in the various questionnaires, and perhaps, more importantly, the use of non-survey methods like in-depth interviews, and data on prices paid and vaccinations received, then it is possible that clearer results could be found on the links between corruption and service delivery.

Conclusions

This chapter reviewed evidence on the nature of corruption in the health and education sectors, evidence on the extent to which corruption undermines the delivery of health and education, and, finally, evidence on the determinants of corruption in these sectors. The results seem to suggest that corruption does in fact undermine the delivery of health and education services and that increasing accountability reduces corruption. The evidence for the first of these propositions, that corruption undermines the delivery of health and education, is clearer than the second.

Where does this leave the policymaker? My basic recommendation is that various reforms need to be tried out in scientifically rigorous pilot projects and the more successful of those reforms need to be widely implemented. If advice must be given without the benefit of such experience, I would propose the alignment of incentives of those delivering services with broad measures of outcomes, like test scores and vaccination rates (which should be measured by people other than those delivering services). Evidence from private sector studies in other contexts suggests that such measures might improve outcomes. They are likely to improve the effectiveness of service delivery. They may well reduce corruption, too.

Notes

1. Even in this case, informal payments may not be efficient for several reasons as pointed out by Lewis (2000). Bribes for doctors rather than payments to hospitals may lead to underinvestment in equipment (which is shared by other doctors). Bribes are often given in the form of gifts rather than money in some countries, which can lead to deadweight losses. The presence of lucrative opportunities for corruption can delay reform (as shown in another context by Lee and Azfar, 2001).

2. As a general point, this raises the issue of perverse effects of incentives on behavior: paying doctors for each procedure may give them incentives to improve both their performance and their bedside manner, but also induces them to recommend unnecessary procedures.

3. Some examples may help clarify the impact that a two-point gain in integrity represents. In Uganda, the replacement of Obote by Museveni was accompanied by a two-point gain; in the Philippines, the movement from Marcos to Aquino brought the same; Bolivia's market-oriented reforms of the 1980s and 1990s also brought about a two-point improvement in integrity, as did the lifting of military rule and the introduction of a market economy in Poland in the late 1980s and early 1990s.

4. A recent paper by Easterly and Levine (2002) makes the point that differences in institutions explain the vast majority of differences in incomes

5. A survey of this magnitude costs around US$100,000 to conduct and it costs as much again to analyze the data and write up the results. Such studies are probably the most effective way of uncovering the relationship between corruption and service delivery.

6. Klitgaard offers *Corruption = Monopoly + Discretion − Accountability* using a broad definition of accountability. Azfar (2003) found it useful to divide accountability into transparency, wages, and a narrower definition of accountability.

7. See Holmstrom and Milgrom (1991), and see Azfar (2002a) for a survey.

8. The interested reader can contact Kai Kaiser for more information on the Indonesian study. The contact person for various other studies is listed in Dehn, Reinikka, and Svensson (2002).

Chapter 13

Learning Across Cases: Trends in Anticorruption Strategies

Bertram I. Spector, Michael Johnston, and Phyllis Dininio

Many of the lessons learned about the effectiveness of anticorruption programs around the world have been derived from descriptive assessments of particular cases taken one at a time. Policymakers and practitioners would be better served, though, by knowledge culled and analyzed from the experience of many cases under a variety of circumstances. A new analytical approach is needed to accomplish this. The research described in this chapter is a first step toward creating a systematic methodology that develops valid generalizations about what works and what does not work in controlling corruption under different conditions based on actual cases.

Often, decision makers draw serious conclusions from particular historical cases despite the fact that the success or failure of the case might have been strongly influenced by political, economic, and social factors that were idiosyncratic and may not be transferable to other countries. On the other hand, implementation of anticorruption programs, as described in case studies, is one of the few sources of practical data that we have to judge effectiveness of various strategies. In this study, we have designed and conducted a pilot test of a systematic comparative methodology that facilitates drawing valid conclusions from a large sample of cases where anticorruption strategies have been implemented while not losing the detail and richness of the individual cases.

This type of analytical approach can yield several results. First, by drawing valid conclusions and lessons learned across a large number of anticorruption cases, knowledgeable programmatic decisions can be made for future anticorruption campaigns in targeted countries. Such decisions can be made by matching the existing conditions in the targeted country with those that are favorable to progress in reducing or controlling corruption in the database of cases. Second, the methodology can produce a data gathering and evaluation mechanism for analysts and managers in the field, allowing them to capture key information about ongoing and completed anticorruption programs. This information can be evaluated separately and compared to the larger set of cases in the database.

Researchers in the hard sciences and psychology, faced with the need to compare experimental findings in closely related fields, developed what is called a *meta-analysis approach* that categorizes independent and dependent variables so systematic analyses across experiments can be conducted. Each experiment becomes a case and key factors about each experiment are categorized and coded, making each one comparable to the next.

In the social sciences, researchers also have experimented with the development of coding systems that facilitate the systematic and quantitative comparison of a wide variety of cases, so that generalizations can be drawn. This has been done, in particular, in the analysis of conflict and negotiation cases (see Druckman, 1994). Certainly, comparing case studies on a qualitative level can provide in-depth understanding of historical situations. However, this quantitative analysis approach permits analysts to make comparisons across numerous cases, strengthen the validity of the results, and examine relationships among key factors in more detail.

Analytical Design

Data for this analysis were collected by reviewing written accounts of anticorruption interventions conducted in a wide range of countries.[1] The information gathered from the cases was used to answer detailed questions concerning the intervention itself, the outcome of the intervention, and the context within which the intervention was implemented. The results were translated into coding categories for use in statistical analysis. In this section, we describe briefly the procedures used to collect and analyze the data. The discussion is organized into three parts: the coding and scoring methods, the case studies, and the analysis methods.

Descriptive and Scoring Methods

Two methodologies to code cases of anticorruption interventions were tested in this study. Both methods, in their own way, categorize the key factors in each anticorruption case so that they can be compared in a systematic fashion. The first—*the Descriptive Method*—simply codes each case into a series of categories that captures the key elements of anticorruption cases. It starts with a series of thirty-two open-ended questions that allow the coder to summarize each case into major categories defined by the conceptual literature on corruption. The categories describe (a) the intervention, (b) the specific corruption that is targeted by this intervention, (c) the outcome of the intervention, (d) the general corruption situation in the country, and (e) the overall political, economic and social context. These free-text answers are then coded into thirty-two specific variables that are fact-based, requiring little judgment on the part of the coder.

The second method—*the Scoring Method*—asks the coder to respond to 156 questions about each case on an ordinal scale from 5 (definitely yes) to 1 (definitely no). In most instances, the questions are factual, but in some cases the coder is asked to make an educated guess about some aspects of a given corruption case or reform intervention. The questions are grouped into several categories: (a) what happened? (b) what was the setting for this case? (c) who won and who lost? (d) what was at stake? (e) what were the social responses to this case? (f) what anticorruption interventions resulted? and (g) the overall outcomes. The actual scoring is implemented on a spreadsheet. As scores to the 156 questions are entered, the answers are aggregated and averaged into evaluation ratings—or score indexes—for each case along several dimensions (the ratings range from 5 [high] to 1 [low]). The dimensions include:

- The significance of political, economic, bureaucratic or social corruption in the case
- The scope of corruption
- The entrenchment of corruption
- The opposition to corruption
- The beneficiaries of corruption
- The losers from corruption
- Transparency problems
- Accountability problems
- Awareness problems

- Prevention problems
- Enforcement problems
- The overall effectiveness of the intervention
- The targeting and emphasis of the intervention (on transparency, accountability, awareness, prevention, or enforcement; on high or low levels; and on public or private sector)
- Support or local ownership of the intervention
- Resources committed to the intervention
- Design elements of the intervention
- Implementation of the intervention
- Country trends for the future (in terms of the economy, governance, corruption, and anticorruption capacity)

The Case Studies

The *unit of analysis* for this study is the discrete anticorruption program or strategy that has been implemented in a particular country. Thus, to be useful for this analysis, written case studies have to highlight the implementation of a distinct anticorruption program or strategy. The case write-ups also have to include information about the context within which the intervention was conducted, how it was conducted, and the results of the program.

Thirty-five written case studies were selected for this pilot test. Although they represent a wide range of anticorruption intervention types in a wide range of countries, they should not be considered a representative sample of all intervention cases; rather, since this study is a pilot test of these methodologies, we settled for an "availability" sample. All thirty-five cases had sufficient information to be coded using the "descriptive method," whereas only thirty-one had sufficient information to be coded using the "scoring method." A list of the cases used in the analysis appears in the Appendix.

We found that the quality of case studies generally available in the literature is widely variable and in many situations unimpressive. There is a need for more careful and critical observation and for case studies that are less closely linked to the interests of the observers and program sponsors.

Analytical Approach

The data derived from the two methodologies were formulated into SPSS data sets and analyzed statistically. Because the "descriptive method" data is primarily categorical in nature, the analysis involves cross-tabulation tables. The "scoring method" data are the aggregated evaluation ratings, which are ordinal scales; correlational analysis (Spearman rank-order correlations) is feasible for this data set.

Results

The analytical results are presented in this section. First, the case sample is described. Second, results for a selection of questions using the "descriptive method" data set are presented. Third, questions answered by the "scoring method" data are offered.

Description of the Case Sample
How can these thirty-five cases be characterized? Do they appear to be a representative collection of anticorruption intervention cases? The following discussion presents the results.

Overall
1. Do the cases represent anticorruption activities from all regions?
Of the tirty-five cases, approximately one third are in African countries (31.4 percent) and another one third are in Asia and Near East countries (34.3 percent), whereas only 20 percent are in Latin American and Caribbean countries, and 14.3 percent are in Europe and Eurasian countries. This distribution represents an "availability" sample of written and published cases; that is, cases that were available from publicly accessible sources and contain the appropriate information needed by our coding systems. It does *not* necessarily reflect the frequency of anticorruption programs implemented region-by-region. To produce a more representative distribution in the sample, a much larger database that draws from additional information sources would be needed. However, for the purposes of pilot testing our methodology, this sample is adequate.

Nature of the Corruption Problem in the Case
2. What types of corruption are targeted in the sample?
In 47 percent of the cases, petty bureaucratic corruption is targeted, while in 41% of the cases, grand corruption is targeted. In the wide majority of cases, this corruption is viewed as extremely widespread and pervasive. The beneficiaries of this corruption are evenly split between low/mid-level bureaucrats and high-level officials.

3. What is the general condition of corruption in the sampled countries?
In 79 percent of the cases, corruption, in general, is seen as widespread throughout the country. In the majority of cases, grand corruption is viewed as the major culprit (55 percent), whereas 27 percent have major difficulties with petty bureaucratic corruption.

The Context for Corruption
4. How vulnerable is the country to corruption?
In about half of the cases (46 percent), the country is facing a particular economic, social or political crisis or transition that makes it particularly vulnerable

to corrupt practices. In 50 percent of the cases, general worsening economic, social or political trends make the country prone to increasing levels of corruption.

5. Who are the stakeholders affected by corruption and how available are they to engage in anticorruption activities?
In 81 percent of the cases, a reformist-minded government is in power and interested in fighting corruption. In 57 percent of the cases, civil society organizations are extremely active in policy debates. In 83 percent of the cases, the business community is extremely active in policy issues. And in 92 percent of the cases, the mass media is viewed as an active and independent force.

6. How is public tolerance toward corruption characterized?
In 44 percent of the cases, public tolerance for corruption is moderate to high. In 22 percent of the cases, the public is frustrated with the problem. In 35 percent of the cases, the public is visibly angered by the problem of corruption.

7. What are the principal effects of corruption?
In 67 percent of the cases, corruption is seen as slowing economic development.

The Nature of the Intervention
8. What anticorruption intervention was applied?
In the sample, 24 percent of the cases are enforcement programs, 38 percent are prevention programs, and another 38 percent are public awareness programs. Categorized in a different way, 44 percent deal with increasing transparency, 21 percent with increasing governmental accountability, 18 percent with increasing integrity, and another 18% with reducing opportunities for corruption to emerge.

9. Who are the key implementers of these interventions?
The government implemented 34 percent of the interventions, civil society implemented 63 percent, and the mass media implemented 3 percent.

10. Was there a major catalyst that can be credited with stimulating the intervention?
By far, domestic pressure was the catalyst for most of the cases in our sample (56 percent), and the political will of the leadership stimulated 38 percent of the cases. Only 6 percent were motivated by external sources.

11. What types of preparatory activities were conducted to support the anticorruption initiative?
When there was preparatory activity prior to implementing an anticorruption intervention, it usually took the form of survey research (65 percent) or coalition building (13%).

12. What was the process by which these anticorruption programs were implemented?

Forty-nine percent involved mobilizing or educating the public, 34 percent involved mobilizing or educating government officials, and 14 percent involved changing procedures and regulations to reduce opportunities for corruption.

Outcome of the Intervention

13. How can the results of the interventions by characterized?

As a result of the intervention, 85 percent of the cases were seen as being successful: 47 percent due to institutional and legal reforms implemented, 18 percent due to visible behavioral changes, and 20 percent due to increased awareness of the problem. Some 6 percent of the cases demonstrated failure—characterized by a lack of enforcement and political will. In 9 percent of the cases, the outcome could not be determined.[2] Looking at the nature of the reforms implemented, 47 percent resulted in a mobilization of civil society and the business community, 32 percent resulted in the implementation of new governmental procedures, and 18 percent resulted in new laws and regulations.

14. Was the intervention successful in keeping corruption under control?

As a result of the intervention in the cases, 63 percent are seen as having controlled the corruption problem effectively, whereas 37 percent are viewed as having failed to bring corruption under adequate control.

15. Were new institutions implemented to sustain the anticorruption programs?

In 49 percent of the cases, new institutions were created—primarily in civil society organizations, public-private partnerships, or enforcement-related institutions.

Analysis of the "Descriptive Method" Dataset

Analysis of the descriptive database takes the form of cross-tabulation tables. The cells with prominent percentages are presented in the following discussion. The key quantitative findings are summarized in Tables 13.1 to 13.4. Implications drawn from the results are presented in italics.

1. What are the typical outcomes of each anticorruption intervention?
    a) The majority of enforcement strategies yielded new laws and were viewed as successful. They yielded institutional and legal reforms and generally brought corruption under control (Table 13.1).
    b) The majority of preventive strategies yielded successful procedural and institutional reforms. They were also effective keeping corruption under control (Table 13.1).

Table 13.1. Key Findings by Type of Anticorruption Intervention[a]

Correlated Factors	Sample Size	Intervention Type		
		Enforcement Strategy	Preventive Strategy	Public Awareness Strategy
Reforms implemented	33	New laws (63%)	New procedures (58%)	Civil society and business mobilized (85%)
Intervention results	33	Success—institutional and legal reforms (75%)	Success—institutional and legal reforms (69%)	Success—awareness raised (50%). Success – behavioral changes observed (33%).
Control of corruption	19	Under control (83%)	Under control (67%)	Inadequate control (57%)
Corruption type	33	Petty bureaucratic corruption (63%)	Grand corruption (39%). Petty bureaucratic corruption (31%).	Petty bureaucratic corruption (58%)
Tolerance of corruption	22	High tolerance (40%)	Anger (50%)	High tolerance (43%)
General context/trends	23	General worsening trends (100%)	Particular crisis (80%)	General worsening trends (63%)
Key implementers	34	Government (63%)	Civil society (69%)	Civil society (77%)
Stimulus	33	Political will of domestic leadership (88%)	Domestic pressure (69%)	Domestic pressure (75%)

[a]Percentages denote the percent of cases using the identified strategy.

c)   Public awareness strategies resulted in mobilization of civil society and the business sector and were viewed as successes because they raised awareness levels and produced behavioral changes. However, they were not viewed as yielding adequate *longer-term* checks on corrupt practices (Table 13.1).

Table 13.2. Key Findings by Goal of Anticorruption Interventions[a]

Correlated Factors	Sample Size	Greater Transparency	Greater Accountability	Greater Integrity	Reduced Opportunities
General context/trends	23	Particular crisis (67%)	General worsening trends (75%)	General worsening trends (100%)	General worsening trends (60%)
Control of corruption	19	Inadequate control (57%)	Under control (80%)	Under control (67%)	Under control (75%)

[a]Percentages denote the percent of cases using the identified strategy.

d) Strategies that promoted greater accountability, greater integrity, and reduced opportunities for corruption tend to bring corruption under significant control. Strategies that promoted greater transparency, on the other hand, tend to result in inadequate control over corrupt practices (Table 13.2).

The implications of these findings contend that public awareness and transparency strategies, as currently conceived, may not be as effective as other strategies over the longer run in terms of sustained control of corruption; their effects appear to be transitory. Perhaps the long term effectiveness of these types of anticorruption responses can be enhanced through institutionalization and proceduralization of their mechanisms. These kinds of results, even at a level of first approximations, seem quite useful. Too many discussions in the literature consist of drawing up long lists of good ideas and seeking to apply them all; these results seem to indicate priorities and important distinctions among interventions.

2. Which anticorruption strategies are used to deal with different types of corruption?

Enforcement and public awareness strategies tend to target petty bureaucratic corruption. Preventive strategies tend to be used to attack both petty bureaucratic corruption *and* grand corruption cases (Table 13.1).

3. Under what general situational contexts and what conditions of public tolerance are different anticorruption strategies selected?

Enforcement and public awareness strategies tend to be chosen under conditions of generally worsening economic, social or political trends. Preventive programs tend to be selected when there is a particular economic, social or political crisis (see Table 13.1). Looking at the question from another perspective, programs that emphasize greater accountability and integrity are selected under generally worsening trends, and yet they seem to be effective! Transparency programs are chosen under crisis conditions and thus the initial conditions driving them are likely to lose impetus over time (Table 13.2).

Enforcement and public awareness strategies tend to be applied when there is high public tolerance for corruption. Preventive strategies appear to be used when the public demonstrates anger over the persistence of the corruption problem (Table 13.1).

The criteria by which anticorruption strategies are chosen must include situational factors—such as public tolerance and economic trends—as well as likely effectiveness, so that they are tailored appropriately to the country context.

4. Do general situational conditions influence success?
Under generally worsening political, economic or social trends, interventions tend to fail to effectively control corruption. However, when implemented under crisis situations, anticorruption strategies tend to be successful in keeping the problem under control (Table 13.3).

Table 13.3. Key Findings by Control of Corruption[a]

Correlated Factors	Sample Size	Control of Corruption	
		Corruption Under Control	Corruption Inadequately Controlled
Stimulus	18	Political will (88%)	Domestic pressure (67%)
General context/trends	14	Crisis situation (71%)	Generally worsening trends (57%)

[a]Percentages denote the percent of cases using the identified correlated factors.

These findings suggest that crisis and transitional periods are the best times to initiate anticorruption programs. During such periods, leaders and the public in general may be jolted into seeking fixes that will resolve the crisis or transition and, the costs of corruption are most difficult to ignore then.

5. Who are the principal implementers of different anticorruption interventions?
Do outcomes vary significantly depending on who implements the anticorruption strategy (see Table 13.4)?
Enforcement strategies tend to be implemented by government agencies, as would be expected. Preventive and public awareness strategies tend to be implemented by civil society organizations.

For government-led interventions, there are a variety of outcomes—new laws, new procedures, and civil society awareness—that are viewed as successful.

Table 13.4. Key Findings by Implementer[a]

Correlated Factors	Sample Size	Implementer		
		Government	Civil Society	Media
Reforms implemented	34	New laws or regulation (33%) New procedures (33%) Civil society and business mobilized (33%)	Civil society mobilized (52%)	Civil society mobilized (100%)
Intervention results	34	Success—institutional or legal changes implemented (58%)	Success—institutional or legal changes implemented (43%)	Success—awareness raised (100%)

[a]Percentages denote the percent of cases using the identified implementer.

For civil society-led strategies, the majority of cases yield a mobilized civil society that produce successful institutional reform, behavioral change, and heightened awareness.

6. What factors motivate anticorruption interventions?
Enforcement strategies tend to be stimulated by the political will of government leaders. Preventive and public awareness strategies, on the other hand, tend to be catalyzed by the application of domestic pressure on governmental authorities.

These findings suggest the important role played by civil society, business and the mass media as advocates for change. Their targeted domestic pressure activity can take the form of media campaigns, lobbying, and watchdog monitoring of government agencies and functions, for example. Donor support for these kinds of activities by local groups should be encouraged.

7. How important is political will? (see Table 13.3)
When the leadership has the political will to fight corruption, the interventions tend to be successful in keeping the problem under control. However, when the stimulus for reform is domestic pressure, the outcome of anticorruption programs often produces inadequate control over the problem.

These findings suggest the critical role of political will in sustaining anticorruption results. Active agitation against public corruption in civil society can be effective in initiating programs, but may not have the staying power to achieve solutions that can stand the test of time. If the political leadership does not have the ownership and motivation to make these reforms work, early successes may only foreshadow later backsliding and recorruption.

Analysis of the "Scoring Method" Data Set

This pilot analysis of the scoring method database provides preliminary insights on several additional dimensions of anticorruption programming. These data take the form of indices that measure the intervention, the situation, and the outcome of anticorruption programs. Analysis is conducted using rank-order Spearman correlations. The results are compelling and suggest that expanding the research beyond this initial study is worthwhile.

1. What aspects of the corruption problem influence the effectiveness of anticorruption initiatives?

This pilot study points to some interesting aspects of the corruption problem that are likely to impact the effectiveness of anticorruption initiatives. The seriousness and political nature of the problem in these cases clearly reduces the success of the initiative. Specifically, the entrenchment and political significance of the corruption, with correlations of –0.57 and –0.37, respectively, and the high status of beneficiaries to corruption, with a correlation of –0.36, reduce the effectiveness of the intervention. At the same time, the economic, bureaucratic and social significance of corruption and opposition to corruption have no significant relationship to the intervention's effectiveness (see Tables 13.5 and 13.6).

Table 13.5. Correlation of Effectiveness of Initiative with Significance of Corruption

		Significance of Corruption			
		Political	Economic	Bureaucratic	Social
Effectiveness	Correlation	–0.37	–0.11	0.03	–0.02
	significance	0.04*	0.55	0.87	0.93

* Correlation is significant at the 0.05 level (2-tailed).

2. Are some kinds of initiatives generally more effective than others?

Each of the five kinds of initiatives—transparency, accountability, awareness, prevention, and enforcement—has a positive and significant relationship with overall effectiveness (see Table 13.7). Initiatives that emphasize accountability perform the best for this group of cases, with a correlation of 0.68, whereas initiatives that emphasize enforcement and transparency perform relatively less well, with correlations of 0.44 and 0.46, respectively, and initiatives that emphasize prevention and awareness falling in between, with correlations of 0.58 and 0.56, respectively. If the dataset were more robust, it would be interesting to examine what combination of initiatives generally performs better. For example, do the

Table 13.6. Correlation of Effectiveness of Initiative with Entrenchment of Corruption, Opposition to Corruption, and Status of Beneficiaries to Corruption

		Entrench-ment	Opposition	High-level Beneficiaries	Mid-level Beneficiaries	Low-level Beneficiaries
Effectiveness	Correlation	-0.57	0.26	-0.36	0.17	-0.18
	significance	.00**	0.16	0.05*	0.36	0.34

**Correlation is significant at the 0.01 level (two-tailed).

* Correlation is significant at the 0.05 level (2-tailed).

Table 13.7. Correlation of Effectiveness of Initiative with Type of Initiative

		Trans-parency	Account-ability	Awareness	Prevention	Enforcement
Effectiveness	Correlation	0.46	0.68	0.56	0.58	0.44
	significance	0.01**	0.00**	0.00**	0.00**	0.01**

**Correlation is significant at the 0.01 level (two-tailed).

other four initiatives generally work better on their own or in combination with awareness-raising initiatives?

3. Are there aspects of the reform process that impact the initiative's effectiveness? Aspects of the reform process itself clearly have an impact on the initiative's effectiveness. The commitment of resources for the initiative has a large positive impact on an initiative's effectiveness, with a correlation of 0.67. Support for the reform and a good reform design also tend to increase overall effectiveness of reforms, with correlations of 0.47 and 0.41, respectively (see Table 13.8).

While these findings are not surprising in and of themselves, they do lend support to the overall validity of the data and to the soundness of the methods we have employed.

Table 13.8. Correlation of Effectiveness of Initiative with Aspects of the Reform Process

		Resources	Support	Good Design
Effectiveness	Correlation	0.67	0.47	0.41
	significance	0.00**	0.01**	0.02*

**Correlation is significant at the 0.01 level (two-tailed).
*Correlation is significant at the 0.05 level (two-tailed).

4. Does the focus of initiatives correspond with the specific problem areas? Curiously, for this database, there was very little correlation between the five kinds of problem areas–transparency, accountability, awareness, prevention, and enforcement–and their corresponding initiatives (see Table 13.9). There was just

one positive correlation between a problem area and an initiative, and that was in law enforcement, with a correlation of 0.42. The correlation between prevention as a problem area and prevention as the initiative's emphasis was negative, −0.40, which may suggest either that the reform designers were misguided or that preventive strategies are used as frequently to address problems in transparency, accountability and awareness as they are to address prevention problems. One could read this set of results as suggesting that while we have the right basic ideas there is a lot of work needed to turn them into specific actions and to implement them.

Table 13.9. Correlation of the Kind of Initiative by the Kind of Problem Area

	Transparency x Transparency	Accountability x Accountability	Awareness x Awareness	Prevention x Prevention	Enforcement x Enforcement
Correlation	0.10	0.26	0.07	-0.40	0.42
Significance	0.59	0.15	0.72	0.03*	0.02*

*Correlation is significant at the 0.05 level (two-tailed).

5. What general factors increase support for an anticorruption initiative?

As one would expect, support for an anticorruption initiative tends to go hand in hand with adequate resources for the work and a well-designed program, with correlations of 0.62 and 0.47, respectively (see Table 13.10). The causality in these relationships probably operates in both directions: a well-supported initiative would be more likely to get adequate resources and a good design, and a well-funded, well-designed initiative would be more likely to garner support. Perhaps a more compelling finding in this pilot study is the negative relationship between support for an initiative and awareness as an underlying problem area, with a correlation of −0.37. This finding suggests that awareness-raising programs may increase support for anticorruption efforts.

Table 13.10. Correlation of Support for Initiative with Resources, Design and Awareness

		Adequate Resources	Good Design	Awareness Problems
Support for	Correlation	0.62	0.47	-0.37
initiative	significance	0.00**	0.01**	0.04*

**Correlation is significant at the 0.01 level (two-tailed).
*Correlation is significant at the 0.05 level (two-tailed).

6. What factors influence opposition to corruption?

The data show that the political significance and entrenchment of corruption have a negative relationship with opposition to corruption, with correlations of −0.37

and –0.46, respectively (see Table 13.11). This suggests that fear of political reprisals or a sense of helplessness may constrain losers from standing up against corruption. By contrast, the economic, bureaucratic and social significance of corruption have no statistically significant relationship with opposition to corruption in this database.

Table 13.11. Correlation of Opposition to Corruption with Political Significance and Entrenchment of Corruption

		Political Significance	Entrenchment
Opposition to	Correlation	-0.37	-0.46
corruption	significance	0.04*	0.01**

**Correlation is significant at the 0.01 level (two-tailed).
*Correlation is significant at the 0.05 level (two-tailed).

Discussion

Analysis of these pilot data produces findings that are both reassuring—expected relationships are borne out—as well as compelling—new insights into the effectiveness of anticorruption programs are suggested. Some of the highlights of the analysis include:

- Enforcement, preventive, and public awareness strategies typically yield the expected results of legal reform, procedural and institutional reform, and awareness and behavioral change, respectively. However, public awareness programs are less likely to yield sustainable control over the corruption problem for the long term. All of these results are, of course, influenced by situational factors.

- Anticorruption initiatives that were targeted at grand corruption—where high-level officials were involved and where the scandal was particularly political and serious—have a tendency not to succeed. Apparently, new and innovative anticorruption strategies to counter high-level, entrenched corruption are required.

- When the political will to fight corruption resides in leadership, the initiatives are more likely to be effective. If the catalyst for anticorruption programs relies on domestic pressure alone, on the other hand, the results are less likely to endure.

- Effectiveness of anticorruption programs is influenced strongly by the availability of resources, public support for reform, and good policy design.

- Enforcement, public awareness and accountability strategies tend to be implemented when there are general downward trends in the economy and there is public malaise in opposing corruption. On the other hand, prevention and transparency strategies tend to be implemented when there are economic and political crises or major transitions. Anticorruption programs that are implemented under these crisis or transitional conditions tend to be more successful in managing corruption over time.

- Awareness raising programs tend to be good first steps to develop public support for more intrusive anticorruption programs.

What are some of the implications and lessons that can be drawn from these findings? First, the availability of political will and domestic pressure groups in a country is important, not only to stimulate the initiation of reform programs, but to produce effective and enduring anticorruption outcomes over the longer term. But an emphasis on institutionalizing and proceduralizing reform packages appears to be critical as well, to avoid the potential for backsliding due to personalization of the reforms, lack of persistence by pressure groups, or lack of a sense of ownership by high government officials.

Second, the decisions to initiate an anticorruption reform program and the form that it takes should be determined based on a variety of criteria, including likely effectiveness, stakeholder interests, public tolerance toward corruption, situational factors, and the general economic and political conditions in the country. Decisions to formulate anticorruption programs should not be made based solely on what has worked in other countries, most likely under very different conditions.

These findings tend to argue against the "tool kit" approach to reform, in which good ideas are pulled "out of the box" and expected to work. Whether they will work at all and how they might interact with each other are very complicated questions. Sequencing of reforms and using some (e.g., accountability) to build foundations for others (e.g., transparency) needs careful consideration.

Third, external donors can play an important role in producing effective anticorruption results. Support in the democracy and governance arena that encourages responsible pressure groups, advocacy and lobbying activity, citizen watchdogs, and responsible mass media might substitute for the absence of political will on the part of a country's leadership, and stimulate program initiation. Providing resources for reform programs and technical assistance in designing well-conceived initiatives were shown to be important factors that yield enduring outcomes.

Conclusions

This experiment to develop a comparative methodology appears to be successful. It has facilitated the drawing of lessons and generalizations about what makes anticorruption initiatives work or fail. If developed further, it holds out the promise of providing both researchers and practitioners with useful conclusions—drawn from experience—that are valid across a wide and representative sampling of cases, not just a few cases.

Based on this pilot test, several next steps are suggested to improve and expand the methodology:

- A larger sample of cases will facilitate more sophisticated analyses and more valid generalizations on anticorruption interventions. For example, it would enable the assessment of how various interventions impact reductions of corruption, region-by-region, under different economic conditions, or under different conditions of public tolerance for corruption.

- We found that the data that can be extracted from written case studies is highly limited. Much data of interest are missing. Instead, conducting face-to-face interviews with the government or nongovernment implementers of anticorruption interventions might yield more complete and insightful data entries. In particular, such interviews will yield more detailed information about the general context of the case and better information about the sustainability of intervention outcomes.

- Based on what we have learned from this pilot test, the two data gathering protocols can be adjusted to support data collection by country analysts in the field. They can be trained easily to collect information about previous and ongoing anticorruption programs. Their results can be added to a growing database for comparative analytical purposes. In addition, the very activity of collecting the data can provide new insight into the effectiveness of specific programs by focusing on critical factors that make a difference.

One problem that has become clear to us in the course of this project is that the quality of case studies varies widely and many of them speak more to the agendas of the individuals or organizations compiling them than to corruption and reform as general concerns. Nonetheless, we did find a number of cases that appeared to be complete and objective descriptions of the activity under examination. Undoubtedly, many more exist with further search.

The most important immediate need, with respect to this methodology, is to continue testing it and to gather feedback on all aspects of the process. Some additional questions can be included in the protocols. For example, many anticorruption programs consist of multiple initiatives—some preventive, some transparency, some enforcement, and some public awareness. We need to develop approaches to capture this and measure the degree of emphasis placed upon the various components of those strategies. In other cases, we may be able to reduce the number of questions, as a result of further analysis.

Appendix

List of Cases

Country	Intervention	Source	Scoring Method	Descriptive Method
1. Benin	Country program involving a multipronged strategy to combat corruption	IRIS (1996)	X	X
2. Niger	A campaign to prevent illegal road payments	IRIS (1996)	X	X
3. Uganda	Civil service reform and strengthening transparency	IRIS (1996)	X	X
	Country program focusing on strategy to reform public service	Stapenhurst and Kpundeh (1999)	X	X
4. Bolivia	Reforming institutions (La Paz)	IRIS (1996) Klitgaard (2000)	X	X
5. Mauritius	Citizen's Charter (awareness raising)	TI Toolkit (2001)	X	X
6. Morocco	Annual National Anticorruption Day	TI Toolkit (2001)		X
7. Paraguay	Teaching "values" project in elementary schools	TI Toolkit (2001)		X
8. Morocco	Anticorruption comics workshop at the university level	TI Toolkit (2001)		X
9. Colombia	Integrity pacts underwritten by parties involved in a contract process funded by public resources	TI Toolkit (2001)	X	X

Country	Intervention	Source	Scoring Method	Descriptive Method
10. Nepal	Integrity pact at municipal level, public pledges by officials	TI Toolkit (2001)	X	X
11. Bulgaria	Monitoring privatization of the telecommunications company	TI Toolkit (2001)	X	X
12. Argentina	Monitoring procurement process for waste collection services	TI Toolkit (2001)	X	X
13. Bangladesh	Development of a corruption database of corruption stories from local newspaper archives	TI Toolkit (2001)	X	X
14. Bulgaria	Monitoring and analysis of draft legislation by experts and the public	TI Toolkit (2001)	X	X
15. Bangladesh	Committees of Concerned Citizens comprising members of the public undertake to rate municipal services	TI Toolkit (2001)	X	X
16. Kenya	Research on corruption in the Kenyan institution of "Harambee"	TI Toolkit (2001)	X	X
17. Russia	Rating the attitude of Russian political parties toward corruption by monitoring their voting on various laws meant to curb corruption	TI Toolkit (2001)	X	X
18. India	Report cards as an aid to assess public accountability by public services organizations	TI Toolkit (2001)	X	X
19. Bangladesh	Report cards as an aid to assess public accountability by public services organizations	TI Toolkit (2001)	X	X
20. Latvia	Survey of access to information	TI Toolkit (2001)	X	X
21. Australia	National Integrity Systems Assessment of the integrity system in the country	TI Toolkit (2001)		X
22. Zimbabwe	Monitoring of general elections	TI Toolkit (2001)	X	X
23. Argentina	Programme for the monitoring financing of election campaigns	TI Toolkit (2001)	X	X
24. Venezuela	Campo Elias Action Plan involving a mix of political will, technical capacity and partnership with civil society to curb corruption	World Bank Prem Note (2000b)	X	X
25. Ghana	Anticorruption coalition	Johnston-Kpundeh (2000)	X	X

Country	Intervention	Source	Scoring Method	Descriptive Method
26. India	Bangalore Anticorruption Coalition	Johnston-Kpundeh (2000)	X	X
27. Tanzania	Country program whereby a presidential commission appointed to evaluate corruption and suggest recommendations	Stapenhurst and Kpundeh TI Toolkit (2001)		X
28. Sierra Leone	Country program involving a multi-pronged strategy to combat corruption	Stapenhurst and Kpundeh (1999)	X	X
29. Hong Kong	ICAC—an independent agency solely dedicated to fighting corruption	Stapenhurst and Kpundeh (1999)	X	X
30. Singapore	Country program involving a multipronged strategy to combat corruption	Quah (1999)	X	X
31. Italy	Media coverage of corrupt practices of politicians and the nexus between government and business	Giglioli (1996)	X	X
32. Hungary	Financial sector governance reform	IRIS (2001)	X	
33. Bolivia	Customs reform	IRIS (2001)	X	X
34. Nepal	Local governance reforms	IRIS (2001)	X	X
35. Ghana	Anticorruption Agency	UNPAN Web site	X	X
TOTAL			31	35

Notes

1. The authors would like to thank Ruchi Yadav and Naomi Spector for collecting and coding the cases for this study.

2. It would be valid to ask about the objectivity of the case studies—are sponsors framing results in the most optimistic way?

Chapter 14

The Risks of Recorruption

Phyllis Dininio

This chapter examines the tendency, over time, for anticorruption reforms to break down and corruption to reemerge.[1] By analyzing case studies, it aims to identify features of anticorruption initiatives that help to resist the phenomenon of recorruption and make reforms more sustainable. It distinguishes between anticorruption reforms where political will resides primarily in the executive branch of government and anticorruption initiatives where political will resides primarily outside the executive branch. This classification suggests different challenges and reform strategies based on the locus of political will.

The findings are directly relevant to the growing number of efforts to fight corruption under way in all parts of the world. As a new awareness of the costs of corruption has emerged, citizens and their governments are demanding an end to business as usual. Increasingly democratic politics and global markets have provided openings for reformers to combat corruption and lay the foundation for more equitable, just, and prosperous communities. Although some reforms have made headway against corrupt practices,[2] sustainability is clearly an issue. Yet if early gains in reducing corruption are reversed, cynicism about the feasibility of controlling corruption can be worse than before, hurting future opportunities to mobilize the political capital for significant reforms. Understanding the factors that make recorruption possible is therefore critical for designing enduring reform strategies that use national, international and donor resources effectively to achieve sustained results.

The sustainability of anticorruption reforms is of vital importance to the economic, environmental, political and social welfare of communities where corruption is pervasive. New research shows that there is a strong causal effect running from control of corruption to higher income levels[3] and to such development outcomes as lower infant mortality rates and higher rates of literacy (Kaufmann, 2000, p. 143). Corruption retards economic growth through a number of channels: it leads to the inefficient allocation of resources, increases the cost of business, decreases investor confidence, reduces competition, and raises the cost and decreases the quality of public projects and services. Corruption also jeopardizes efforts to protect the environment as payoffs derail the formulation or implementation of effective policies. The political consequences of widespread corruption, while less tangible, are no less real. Corruption undermines the legitimacy of elected officials and democratic values, reduces representation in policymaking, erodes rule of law, and impairs performance of public institutions. For these reasons, corruption increases social polarization and, in extreme cases, can trigger social and political upheaval.[4]

The phenomenon of recorruption needs to be distinguished from reform efforts that fail because of poor strategies or insufficient support. *Recorruption involves a reemergence of corrupt practices—backsliding—after an initial reduction in corruption as reforms break down.* This differs from "pseudo reforms,"[5] which are more rhetoric than substance. Kpundeh notes that governments often employ pseudo reforms to de-legitimate the previous regime, purge the opposition, or respond to scandals, popular discontent, or challenges from a counter-elite (1997, p. 2). The cosmetic nature of many reform strategies points to their political rather than substantive objective. Anticorruption campaigns in postindependence Sierra Leone, for example, were primarily pseudo reforms as new governments there regularly proposed commissions of inquiry, anticorruption squads and tough legislation, but did not provide specific enforcement measures or adequate resources for these initiatives (Kpundeh, 2000). Similarly, Doig contends that Mexican politicians used anticorruption rhetoric in the 1980s to deflect attention from economic difficulties and rejuvenate popular faith in the government (1999, p. 24).

The definition of corruption has received a great deal of attention in academic and policy circles (Heidenheimer, 1978). The notion that corruption is culturally relative has worked against universal definitions. Nonetheless, many practitioners have adopted a minimalist definition of corruption as the abuse of public office for private gain.[6] A more encompassing approach changes "public" to "trusted," thereby defining corruption as the abuse of trusted office for private gain.[7] As this study does not focus on corruption in the private sector, but rather examines corruption in the public sector (including corruption between public and private actors), it uses the minimalist definition of corruption.

The Question of Measurement

The analysis of recorruption poses a methodological challenge. How does the analyst know that corruption levels dropped in response to reforms and subsequently rose as reforms broke down? Many scholars have explicated the difficulty of measuring levels of corruption (Johnston and Kpundeh, 2002; Treisman, 2000, p. 400). Golden and Chang write, for example, "By its nature, corrupt activity tends to be secret, and those involved have incentives to keep it that way" (2001, p. 597). An increase in press reports and prosecutions related to corruption may reflect, for example, increased freedom of the press or independence of the judiciary rather than increased levels of corruption. Leaving aside press reports and prosecutions because of their questionable reliability, analyses of corruption levels can draw upon opinion and experiential surveys, technical studies, and expert opinion for more reliable measures, although data limitations remain.

Reflecting the growing interest in the phenomenon, a range of corruption surveys is now available for analysis. These include public opinion surveys (such as the Southeast European Legal Development Initiative's Regional Corruption Monitoring System), opinion surveys of business leaders (such as World Economic Forum's Global Competitiveness Report and PriceWaterhouseCoopers' Opacity Index), service delivery surveys (such as the Public Affair Center's report cards in Bangalore, India, and the World Bank expenditure tracking surveys in Uganda), experiential surveys of business leaders (such as the World Bank and European Bank for Reconstruction and Development's Business Environment and Enterprise Performance Survey), experiential and opinion surveys of public officials, enterprise managers, and households (such as the World Bank diagnostic surveys) and composite indexes (such as Transparency International's Corruption Perceptions Index and the World Bank Institute's Governance Indicators).

Although providing a wealth of information, these data pose several problems for measuring recorruption. First, to the extent that they reflect public perceptions more than experience, opinion surveys contain a bias related to public reporting on corruption. For example, when respondents assess the level of corruption across state institutions (the agency for foreign investment, say, as opposed to the army), their response may reflect news reports, which may not be accurate or representative of the situation, rather than personal experience with those institutions. Second, to the extent that the surveys aggregate data for a country, they may not capture changes in corruption levels for a locality, specific agency, or type of corruption (such as administrative rather than political corruption) that were the focus of reform. Third, some surveys (such as the World Bank's diagnostic surveys) provide a single snapshot of corruption and do not enable analysis over time unless subsequent surveys are conducted. Fourth, because of the methodology for constructing composite indexes, it is not always possible to compare corruption levels across time, as each year the number of surveys included in the index changes.

In some cases, technical studies can provide data for measuring corruption levels in specific sectors or agencies. For example, Poder Ciudadano, the Argentine chapter of Transparency International, was able to record the monthly expenditures of public hospitals in Buenos Aires. The data generated a way to monitor the variation in prices paid and conditions given for purchasing standard medical supplies. The results revealed enormous discrepancies in the prices paid for specific items, such as syringes, suggesting corruption in some of the hospital procurement offices (Paul and de Michele, 2002). To be useful for the study of recorruption, however, this kind of data needs to be gathered over ensuing intervals, and this has not often been done to date.

Expert opinion can also provide a way to measure changes in corruption levels. Expert opinion includes independent analysis (such as Freedom House's *Nations in Transit*), mutual evaluation of compliance with an international agreement (such as the Stability Pact Anticorruption Initiative for South Eastern Europe, the Council of Europe's Group of States against Corruption, and the Organization of American States' Inter-American Convention against Corruption), and participatory diagnosis, which involves bringing together relevant public officials and stakeholders to ascertain key aspects of the corruption problem, including its incidence. Again, expert opinion needs to be compiled over regular intervals to be useful for the study of recorruption, which can pose a problem in some cases.

For the case studies in this analysis, data limitations on corruption levels pose a problem. Quantitative data on changes in corruption levels are only available to show the initial drop in corruption in Campo Elias, Venezuela and the more sustained decrease in corruption levels in Hong Kong. I rely on expert opinion of analysts and insiders to otherwise identify changes in corruption levels in these cases.

Conceptual Framework for Recorruption

I use a political economy framework for this analysis of recorruption. The political economy literature focuses attention on the structures and calculations sustaining corrupt equilibria, such as opportunities, probability of detection, incentives, and attitudes. Using basic insights from economics, this framework stresses reforms that reduce the benefits or increase the costs of corruption (Klitgaard, 1988; Dininio, Kpundeh, and Leiken, 1999; Rose-Ackerman, 1999). In this approach, reforms aim to change the cost-benefit calculus for engaging in corruption by individuals in the public and private sectors. Drawing from new institutionalism, I treat a person's analysis of costs and benefits as deriving not just from a rational calculation of self-interest, but also from behavioral norms and notions of identity that arise from the context (Hall, 1986; Scharpf, 1987; March and Olsen, 1989; Thelen and Steinmo, 1992). For example, social mores, religious taboos, esprit de corps, and professionalism may deter some public officials and their counterparts in the private sector from engaging in corruption (Meagher, 1999, pp. 10–13). Accordingly, reforms should aim to improve attitudes and professional incentives as well as to strengthen accountability and reduce opportunities for corruption. A well-known strategy conveys the same points in a slightly different formulation, advocating education, prevention and enforcement as the pillars to anticorruption reform.[8]

The political economy and new institutionalism literature also show how the selection of a specific institutional reform, from among many that might be chosen, depends on the distribution of group-specific costs and benefits associated with each, and on the way in which existing institutions apportion power among competing groups. The presence of civil and political liberties, the structures of horizontal accountability, the coherence of the state, the cohesiveness of the party system, the concentration and organization of the business sector, and the strength of civil society organization all shape the way anticorruption efforts can assist the efforts of reformers and defuse the opposition of detractors. This politically determined approach to reform is critical, and underscores the role of political will and coalitions in anticorruption reform.

The distributional consequences of anticorruption reform can mobilize powerful forces to protect vested interests. As detailed by Brinkerhoff and Kpundeh, political will for anticorruption reform may wax and wane with changing political circumstances, and reform strategies must work to bolster leaders' resolve (Brinkerhoff and Kulibaba, 1999; Kpundeh, 1999). Coalition building, in particular, strengthens and links political will and civil society (Johnston and Kpundeh, 2001). The participation of civil society organizations, businesses, the media, and a broad array of officials from all branches of government complements top-level political commitment for reforms. Such broad input into reforms improves their content as well as prospects for implementing them. Ways to foster coalitions and increase channels for participation include awareness raising campaigns, surveys, support to civil society organizations, citizen monitoring, workshops, and public-private partnerships.

Case Studies

This study examines three cases of recorruption. The first two case studies focus on anticorruption initiatives where the political will for reform resided primarily in the executive branch of government. These include the reforms of Ronald Maclean-Abaroa in La Paz, Bolivia, and Elba Soto in Campo Elias, Venezuela, which succeeded in reducing corruption under their leadership, but unraveled after their departure from office. For purposes of comparison, the study also reviews the successful anticorruption reform in Hong Kong, which benefited from more institutional resources and political autonomy.

The third case study focuses on an anticorruption initiative where the political will for reform resided primarily outside the executive branch of government. It focuses on the Clean Hands judicial investigation in Italy, which broke up collusive relations between business and party bosses within the Christian Democrats in the early 1990s but did not eliminate the more pervasive clientelistic networks, organized crime influence, and structural inefficiencies in the public administration, which is allowing political corruption to reemerge under Prime Minister Berlusconi. For purposes of comparison, the study also reviews the pattern of alternating reform and machine governments that characterized New York City politics for almost a century until the Tammany machine's ultimate defeat.

This selection of case studies includes both local and national level reform efforts. By examining reforms at both levels, I aim to address the concern that strategies used at one level may not be replicable at the other. For instance, anticorruption reforms at the local level cannot be as encompassing as those at the national level, for they need to take the legislative and regulatory framework as a given. Alternatively, anticorruption reforms at the national level, because of their scale, cannot be as participatory as those at the local level. Staying attuned to these issues, I examine reform efforts at both levels and conclude that the similarities far outweigh the differences between them.

La Paz, Bolivia

Ronald MacLean-Abaroa took office in September 1985.[9] He was the first elected mayor of La Paz, Bolivia, in almost 40 years. He found the city of 1 million people in crisis: the payroll stood at 120 percent of its revenues, salaries were nonetheless eroded by hyperinflation, and corruption was rampant throughout the city administration.

MacLean-Abaroa moved aggressively to ameliorate these problems. He secured a US$1 million loan from the World Bank, which allowed him to attract capable professionals with higher salaries, and to hire consultants (including Robert Klitgaard) to help carry out anticorruption reforms. The reform process started with a number of diagnostic activities, including workshops with senior officials, interviews with secretaries, and technical studies (such as systems analyses of procurement). Next, Mayor MacLean-Abaroa worked with employees to develop a strategy to fight corruption that reduced constraints to collective action, improved incentives, and increased transparency and the probability of detecting corrupt acts.

His reforms were wide-ranging. In public works, the mayor used surveys of local groups and cost-benefit analyses to establish priorities for public works, eliminating the discretion of city employees to locate public works where they could collect a pay off. He also redefined the city's mission to focus primarily on emergency repairs and to contract out major projects, limiting workers' ability to steal parts and gasoline. To increase tax collection, he focused on property taxes, which had been a main source of city revenue before hyperinflation had eroded property values. Rather than giving civil servants the discretion to determine new property values and the attendant opportunity for corruption, he asked citizens to self-evaluate the value of their own properties under the threat that the city could purchase their properties for 1.5 times the declared value. To further reduce opportunities for corruption, he eliminated some licenses and permits, streamlined application processes, published a manual, which described each process in detail so citizens knew their rights, and developed a single register of all applications so progress could be monitored. In procurement, he simplified the process and increased monitoring of each step. Regarding personnel, he developed a comprehensive program with employees that included firing the last 2,000 employees that were hired by the outgoing administration, increasing training and salaries, and establishing a meritocratic system of recruitment and promotion.

The results were impressive. Within three years, revenues were eighteen times higher (Galtung, 1998, p. 115) and investment was ten times higher than when he had come to office. Corruption decreased by all reports, and Mayor MacLean-Abaroa was reelected for two more two-year terms.

MacLean-Abaroa left office in 1991, but returned in 1995. He found a staggering amount of recorruption. Public works officials were demanding bribes of 10 to 15 percent for awarding contracts and for paying the city's bills. The single registry for permit and license applications had broken down, and speed money (bribes to facilitate government processing) of about US$40 was routine for the "revision of paperwork." Political appointments had usurped meritocracy, as the first administration after MacLean-Abaroa had replaced an estimated 70 percent of the city's managerial and technical staff and the following administration replaced a further 40 percent of staff. Moreover, resistance by city employees had derailed the system of integrated financial management, which was still unfinished, and the self-evaluation of property values had broken down when the threat to buy property for a multiple of its declared value turned out to be illegal. In a February 1996 survey, 50 percent of citizens agreed "the level of corruption with respect to the past is worse," another 43 percent said it was the same, and the other 7 percent said, "don't know." As of June 2002, two of the mayors who ran the city between 1991 and 1995 were in jail for corruption and a third was facing charges for corruption but was still at large.

Nonetheless, some reforms from MacLean-Abaroa's earlier administrations were still in place. The elimination of some permits and licenses had permanently removed the corruption that had attended their enforcement. As well, the amount of construction undertaken by the city was still down (and with it the opportunities for corruption), although the procurement process for contracting out major projects was a growing source of corruption.

Campo Elias, Venezuela

In 1996, Elba Soto was elected mayor of Campo Elias, Venezuela.[10] At that time, corruption impaired the city's provision of services and its 125,000 citizens were not motivated to participate in government. The following year, Soto participated in a World Bank workshop on institutional reform, and requested assistance to improve governance and reduce corruption in the city. From April 1998 to December 1999, the World Bank Institute worked with the municipal government and civil society to develop a transparent and participatory system of government.

The initiative began with a diagnosis of the city's governance problems. The diagnosis featured a survey, which asked citizens and businesses about the delivery of services and the integrity of the municipal government, workshops with community organizations, and meetings with representatives of civil society. The diagnosis pointed to two key deficiencies: complex and unpredictable administrative procedures for granting permits and paying taxes; and the absence of public information and ways for citizens to hold officials accountable. At a subsequent workshop, government officials and citizens discussed these findings and devised an action plan for addressing them. Implementation of the action plan proceeded quickly with technical assistance from the World Bank.

To address the first problem, Soto's government wrote a manual to simplify and standardize administrative procedures, and integrated all financial and administrative information into a data system. These changes reduced discretion, eliminated duplication of efforts, improved coordination among offices, and sped up the approval process (e.g., from three months to three to five days to obtain a construction permit).

To address the second problem, her government created a number of channels for citizen participation. It established an Office for Development and Citizen Participation to respond to citizen requests and complaints, and to keep citizens informed about municipal services, officials and procedures. At the same time, the city began holding participatory budget hearings each July, which allowed citizens to evaluate the government's performance and to help establish priorities in the city budget, which was finalized in December. A Tripartite Municipal Commission, comprised of three citizens, three city officials, and one representative of the municipal council, was also established to approve the community's requests in the budget and to approve the schedule and plan for executing public works. Soto's outreach program also included the addition of a citizen representative on bidding committees and on control and monitoring committees, quarterly meetings with community organizations, guaranteed access to public documents, and access to data systems through the Internet or the Office of Information.

After taking these steps, the city conducted a second survey of citizens and businesses. According to those surveyed, corruption levels had fallen from 39 percent in 1998 to 16 percent in 1999, a drop of more than 50 percent. Moreover, the reforms enhanced the effectiveness and credibility of government, and empowered citizens to participate in government.

Soto did not run for reelection in 2000 for political reasons but worked with the new administration to ensure continuity of the reforms. She arranged a workshop with the new team to explain the background and the dynamics of these reforms. Nonetheless, the new mayor dropped many of the initiatives that fostered transparency and participation, and corruption levels climbed.

What sets this case study apart from the La Paz case study is that in 2002, local citizens demanded a return to the procedures established under Mayor Soto. Community organizations collected a large number of signatures requesting the government to reactivate the systems of transparency and participation. The new mayor, a populist aligned with President Chavez, acceded to this petition from the people. He contacted Soto for advice, and she explained that the municipal government would need to start the governance and anticorruption program anew, because new problems required a new diagnosis and action plan. As of this writing, the new mayor plans to move forward with the reform.

Analysis of Reforms Led by the Executive

These two case studies feature reforms led by a committed leader that nonetheless broke down upon their departure from office. Although the source of the reform effort is similar, the substance and the outcome of the reforms differ in meaningful ways. Mayor MacLean-Abaroa had implemented a technically sound, preventative strategy to curb corruption. This strategy did not, however, incorporate citizens in any systematic way and so lacked a vital basis of support and sustainability beyond his administration. Mayor Soto, by contrast, made the introduction of participatory processes a pillar of her governance and anticorruption strategy, along with preventative measures. This approach contributed to accountability during her tenure, but as important, provided the key challenge to the abandonment of these reforms after she left office. While we should not be too sanguine about the prospects for thoroughgoing reform under a mayor whose commitment is questionable, the mobilization of civil society creates a chance for some continuity of reform and sustained momentum in the work, rather than a complete break from a committed leader's efforts after a change in administration.

Reference to the sustained anticorruption reform in Hong Kong reinforces this point (de Speville, 1997; Klitgaard, 1998; de Speville 1999). Corruption was a very serious problem for this city of 4 million when a scandal triggered the governor of Hong Kong to establish in 1974 an Independent Commission Against Corruption (ICAC), which replaced the Anticorruption Office in the police force.[11] The ICAC was given strong investigatory powers in its operations department, but also was given responsibility for prevention and community relations. Its corruption prevention department has worked to eliminate opportunities for corruption in public and private systems, each year conducting roughly 100 studies for government offices and providing advice to an average of 75 companies. Its community relations department, with about 200 officers, has sought to involve the community in fighting corruption by changing attitudes toward corruption and encouraging the public to report corruption to the ICAC. To increase public awareness about the costs of corruption and mobilize support for the ICAC's mission, the community relations department uses the media to broadcast press releases, public announcements, interviews, documentaries, court reports, and statistics, and distributes posters and leaflets on the topic. Department officials also speak publicly on fighting corruption and help integrate anticorruption lessons into school curricula and government training programs. The community also played a monitoring role in the ICAC's work: the governor established citizen advisory committees to provide a check on the far-reaching powers of the ICAC, and, in particular, its operations department.

Over its tenure, the ICAC has struck a significant and sustained blow to corruption. The first survey of public opinion conducted in 1977 found that 38 percent of respondents thought corruption was widespread. In 1994, by contrast, only 7.8 percent thought corruption was widespread. This decrease in the perception of corruption levels is complemented by the growing trust and confidence in the ICAC: only one-third of informants were willing to identify themselves in 1974, but more than two thirds did so in 1994. And while the transfer of sovereignty in 1997 was a cause of concern for ICAC's work, corruption has not increased under Chinese rule.[12]

Admittedly, Hong Kong's ICAC benefited from factors that are not necessarily replicable in other settings. Its success, at least in part, comes from a large budget (e.g., it was US$14 million in 1982), and a skilled, well-paid staff of 1,300. Its sweeping legal prerogatives also have facilitated prosecutions, including the reverse burden of proof, the ability to arrest suspects, the powers of search and seizure without a warrant in some cases, the power to issue restraining orders to freeze assets and properties, and the right to seize travel documents. What is more, the ICAC has enjoyed autonomy from corrupt networks in the public and private sectors. The insulation of the executive[13] from electoral politics or other imperatives to secure power has meant that the independent agency, which reports directly to the executive, has indeed remained independent.

Nonetheless, the Hong Kong experience supports the notion that a participatory, inclusive strategy is a key feature of sustainable anticorruption reforms. The participation of civil society fosters the integrity and accountability of government by monitoring the decisions and activities of public officials. More broadly, the engagement of civil society as partners in this endeavor elicits their demand for good governance in the ballot box, petitions, demonstrations, public discourse, and high-level meetings. As a change in leadership is to be expected in most contexts, sustainability of anticorruption initiatives rests in large part on the participation of civil society in the systems of governance.

The participation of civil society is equally important at the local and national levels, but the particular forms of participation may need to be adapted for scale. The participatory budget hearings that Mayor Soto used in a city of 125,000 people are probably not replicable on a national scale and may need to give way to a transparent, participatory process involving organized rather than individual interests. However, the citizen oversight committees and public outreach programs that ICAC used in a city of 4 million are replicable on a national scale.

How relevant is this lesson to reform initiated primarily from outside the executive branch of government? Are there other lessons that are more pertinent in that context? To explore this possibility, I turn to the Clean Hands investigation in Italy, which relied on the resolve of judges and the support of civil society to curtail the corruption emanating from the executive.

The Clean Hands Investigation

The Clean Hands investigation began February 17, 1992, with the arrest of a Socialist city councilor in Milan for accepting a small bribe.[14] His subsequent collaboration with the Milanese assistant prosecutor set off a chain of confessions that resulted in the investigation of 3,000 public officials and businesspeople in the following four years. Although the investigations started in Milan, they spread to other Italian cities, including Naples and Palermo. About 450 defendants were eventually found guilty, including Bettino Craxi, party secretary of the Italian Socialist Party and former prime minister, and Arnaldo Forlani, party secretary of the Christian Democrats. The investigations revealed an extensive system of corruption in which business leaders paid bribes to party officials for preferential treatment in public contracts, privatization, nationalization, regulation, and taxes. In the south, many of the investigations revealed the mediating role of the mafia in the corrupt exchange. The revelations led to the demise of the country's largest party, the Christian Democrats, and its partner in the ruling coalition, the Socialists, and with this, to the break-up of the corrupt networks emanating from those parties.

The impetus for this unprecedented campaign to clean up the political system rested with the magistrates. Although clearly dangerous to the political class, they were able to shelter themselves from political interference throughout these investigations. Their independence from the executive was a key feature of their success. Indeed, the judiciary in Italy is not accountable to the Minister of Justice, but to an independent council of the judiciary, two-thirds of which is elected by the judiciary and one-third of which is appointed by political nomination. The judicial system thereby allows individual magistrates to investigate and prosecute cases without obtaining the permission of politicians.

Given that corruption was not a new phenomenon in Italian politics, why didn't the prosecutors take such action before? In part, the answer lies in the weakness of the judicial system, which only allows prosecutors to act on the basis of information revealed during an investigation. At the same time, however, public support gave them the additional protection and motivation to pursue the investigations with rigor. With the end of the Cold War and the demise of the Communist Party, the motivation to support the Christian Democrats dropped away, and the public was more interested in accountability. The Maastricht Agreements also heightened citizens' expectations about the country's performance within Europe and raised a fear among business about not being able to withstand international competition. A close relationship with the media also helped the magistrates win the public's support. Media outlets, especially those controlled by opposition parties, provided extensive coverage of the investigations that was favorable to the magistrates.

By most accounts, the incidence of political corruption fell in the wake of the Clean Hands campaign. The investigations increased the probability of being caught, and disrupted a more or less stable network of corrupt exchanges. Political financing had been a major source of corruption, and campaign expenditures plummeted in the following years to as little as one-tenth of previous expenditures. A Transparency International survey suggested that the costs of public contracting dropped by 45 percent (Pope, 2002).

Sadly, this decrease in corruption appears short-lived.[15] The election of Silvio Berlusconi in May 2001 revealed a public ambivalence to the Clean Hands campaign. Berlusconi had come under investigation for corruption when he was prime minister in 1994, which led to his resignation. He has dodged criminal investigations ever since, but claims that the corruption charges were politically inspired. Indeed, right-wing politicians characterize the investigations as a plot by left-wing magistrates to help the left to power and in 2001 passed a motion in parliament condemning the Milan prosecutors as biased. Since coming to office, Berlusconi has proposed reforms to limit the independence of the judiciary, interfered in the trials against him and his allies, reduced false accounting from a crime to a misdemeanor, halved the statute of limitations to seven and one-half years, and pushed through a toothless conflict of interest law, which opponents claim is designed to protect him. His media networks have devoted little attention to these machinations or to new allegations of bribery involving his Forza Italia party. As of this writing, two experts on corruption in Italy, della Porta and Vannucci, are writing a paper on its reemergence, noting its altered form within different types of networks.[16]

Analysis of Reforms Driven from Outside the Executive

This outcome is not surprising. The judicial campaign against corruption in Italy centered primarily on enforcement. There was an element of public education in the media's focus on the investigations, but the more informed, analytical and normative treatments of the subject were not common in public meetings, training seminars, talk shows or similar fora. Nor did this campaign provide effective channels of citizen involvement in anticorruption efforts. Preventative elements were similarly weak. A referendum introduced majority electoral law and transparency in party financing in 1993, but little other reforms were taken to eliminate the more pervasive clientelistic networks, organized crime influence and structural inefficiencies in the public administration.

Reference to the eventual reform of machine politics in New York City is instructive to the Italian case. The Democratic political machine in New York City, known as Tammany,[17] came to dominate politics in the middle of the nineteenth century. The machine held power through patronage, providing jobs and other assistance to immigrants in exchange for votes. Flagrant abuses during the reign of William "Boss" Tweed prompted a group of leading citizens, including lawyers and publishers, to form a "Committee of 70" to oust him. Investigations and court trials led to his eventual conviction, while publications of his corrupt dealings and cartoons portraying his methods aroused public indignation and led to the election of a new slate of reform candidates in 1871. In his study of Boss Tweed, Nathan Miller notes the importance of the free press, the judiciary, public interest groups, and elections in challenging the system (Miller, 1992).

Nonetheless, Tammany returned to power not long after and ruled until corruption under Richard Croker provoked new investigations and the election of another reform mayor in 1901. This pattern of alternating reform and machine governments characterized New York City politics for almost a century until the Tammany machine's ultimate demise by 1970. Scholars credit immigration restrictions, social programs of the New Deal, and upward mobility for finally reducing demand for the machine, as well as civil service reform that ended the spoils system of job placement and eliminated a key source of patronage (Wilson, 1978, p. 301; Columbia Encyclopedia, 2001).

What this cursory look at Tammany shows is the difficulty of achieving sustained corruption control when reforms are driven from outside the executive and focus primarily on enforcement. The mobilization of reformers in other branches of government and outside it can succeed in forcing a corrupt administration from power as illustrated in the two cases discussed here. Once this significant task is accomplished, however, the reformers may be less well poised to push through political and administrative reforms that help to prevent backsliding. As well, a new government and its backers may not appreciate the imperative to implement preventative measures to fight against recorruption, resting instead on their temporary success of bringing a corrupt government to justice. The push and pull of successive machine and reform governments can continue over a long period.

The challenge for reforms driven from outside the executive is to push through stronger reforms that are more difficult to undo and, to the extent possible, to defuse opposition to reforms, particularly within the administration. One way to broaden support for reforms is to co-opt detractors with carefully crafted inducements. Rose-Ackerman notes, for example, that civil service reform in the United States worked, in part, because it converted patronage appointees to civil servant status rather than firing them or subjecting them to a test (Rose-Ackerman, 1999). Along these lines, anticorruption strategies should start with "low-hanging fruit" and use early wins to build support for interventions that will likely elicit greater political fallout.

Of course, reforms originating outside the executive can take other paths. Rather than the judicial branch, the legislative branch may be aligned with citizen groups in fighting corruption and may pursue a prevention-based rather than an enforcement-based reform strategy. In the United States, for example, Senators John McCain (Republican, Arizona) and Russ Feingold (Democrat, Wisconsin) advocated campaign finance reform and worked closely with a number of citizens groups over seven years until passage of a campaign finance bill in June 2002. The Federal Election Commission's subsequent rulings on the law's implementation have weakened its provisions against big donations to political parties, however, and highlight the threat of forcing reform legislation on a reluctant executive. The key challenge in this case is to protect legislation, to the extent possible, from capricious implementation and to broaden its support within the administration by including targeted inducements for that purpose.

Another scenario for reforms originating outside the executive involves conditionality or other arm-twisting by aid donors or peers in international agreements. Political will in this context clearly lies with external actors, even though the executive is responsible for taking the steps to put reforms in place, an arrangement that underscores the fragility of the reform effort. The establishment and demise of the Kenya Anticorruption Authority (KACA) illustrates this point. In 1997, international aid donors, notably the International Monetary Fund and the World Bank, had suspended lending to Kenya because of corruption and had required progress in tackling governance problems as a condition for further aid. After President Moi established KACA in 1999, the donors resumed lending and made grants to KACA. Yet just as KACA was prosecuting three influential people for corruption in December 2000, the constitutional court ruled that the existence of KACA undermined the authority of the attorney general and the commissioner of police and therefore declared it illegal (Githongo, 2001). Most experts regard this decision as politically driven by the Moi regime to protect the system of patronage on which it depends.[18] The lesson here is the importance of a prevention- and education-based strategy that provides inducements for support and only secondarily provokes opposition to anticorruption reform by prosecuting powerful individuals.

Conclusions

Recent scholarship on corruption has produced a number of studies on the causes of corruption. Treisman, for example, has found that countries with a history of British rule, Protestant tradition, high per capita GDP, unitary state structure, uninterrupted democracy and openness to imports are less corrupt (Treisman, 2000, pp. 399–457). This research is important in tracing the historical development of less corrupt states, and in postulating conditions that may be more or less favorable to reducing levels of corruption. In fact, it is analogous to the preconditions work in the democracy literature. Huntington, among others, has delineated the economic, social, external, and cultural preconditions that are more likely to foster democracy (Moore, 1966; Dahl, 1971; Huntington, 1984, pp. 193–218; Huntington, 1991).

What these causal studies fail to consider, however, is human agency and the crafting of institutions to further desired ends. In the case of fighting corruption, committed reformers and strategic reforms can make inroads against corruption despite unfavorable conditions. Admittedly, corruption levels may drop further where favorable background conditions facilitate these efforts and may drop less where unfavorable conditions impede the work. But anticorruption efforts can shift corruption levels down in both contexts.

To be effective, anticorruption reforms must include prevention, education, and enforcement. They must create incentives for good behavior, but also set up systems of external accountability, using citizen monitoring as well as government oversight institutions. Supporting these structures, anticorruption efforts must foster a broad coalition of reformers both inside and outside the government. Such coalitions are critical to sustaining reforms in the face of political fallout or fatigue. Indeed, fighting corruption is not a one-time proposition: it requires constant vigilance and sustained commitment. But with effective systems and incentives in place, and a broad coalition backing reforms, local and national government can succeed in lowering corruption levels and limiting the prospect of recorruption.

The typologies laid out in this study suggest a number of lessons for sustaining anticorruption reforms. In the context of reforms driven by the executive, the key challenge is to secure a base of support outside the government, by creating channels for citizen participation in government. In the context of reforms driven from outside the executive, the key challenge is to deepen reform efforts primarily by stressing prevention and education, and to broaden support, particularly from those within the administration. Designing preventative measures that carry inducements for those in the administration to support these efforts is often a necessary measure to defuse opposition and sustain reforms from backsliding.

Notes

1. This study benefited greatly from interviews with and written comments from the following experts: Joel Barkan, Donatella della Porta, Maria Gonzalez de Asis, Miriam Golden, Michael Johnston, Robert Klitgaard, Sahr Kpundeh, Ronald MacLean-Abaroa, Melanie Manion, Madalene O'Donnell, Susan Rose-Ackerman, Elba Soto, Bert Spector, Mike Stevens, John Sullivan, and Jack Titsworth.

2. For an overview of anticorruption reforms that have been initiated in recent years, see the following Web sites: http://www.transparency.org; http://www.worldbank/org/wbi/governance; http://www.respondanet.com/english; and http://www.nobribes.org.

3. According to Mauro, a country with widespread corruption is likely to lose about half a percentage point of gross domestic product growth per year. See Mauro (1996).

4. For example, the kleptocracy under Mobutu Sese Seko in Zaire can be seen as a contributing factor to the civil war that followed his ouster. Grand corruption in Liberia also led to the populist revolution and public execution of President William Tolbert in 1980.

5. I thank Michael Johnston for this point and use his terminology.

6. For example, the World Bank (http://www1.worldbank.org/publicsector/anticorrupt/) and USAID (http://www.usaid.gov/democracy/anticorruption/index.html), among others.

7. For example, Transparency International (http://www.transparency.org).

8. Hong Kong's Independent Commission Against Corruption, for example, has championed this strategy.

9. This case draws principally from Klitgaard, MacLean-Abaroa, and Parris (2000); Klitgaard (1996); and a presentation by and conversation with Ronald MacLean-Abaroa, World Bank, Washington, DC, June 17, 2002.

10. This section is based on Gonzales de Asis (2000) and a presentation by and discussion with Elba Soto, World Bank, Washington, DC, June 17, 2002.

11. The chief superintendent of police, Peter Godber, had been indicted on charges of unexplained enrichment but escaped to England prior to his trial. This prompted student rallies and other public demands for a response. The governor appointed a one-man commission of inquiry in addition to introducing anticorruption measures such as the ICAC.

12. I thank Melanie Manion for clarifying this. She contends, however, there was a surge of corruption prior to the transfer of sovereignty as people tried to make a quick buck in the shadow of uncertainty, but this can be seen as a temporary exogenous shock, which the system withstood.

13. Until 1997, Hong Kong's executive was the governor, and thereafter has been the chief executive of the special administrative region.

14. This section draws principally from della Porta and Vannucci (1999); Colazingari and Rose-Ackerman (Fall 1998); Savona (1995); Meldolesi (2000) "Italy: 'Operation Clean Hands'" (1996); and della Porta and Vannucci (2000).

15. This account draws primarily from press clippings. In December 2004, Berlusconi was acquitted of corruption charges in a Milan court related to allegations of bribing judges in a 1985 trial. A 1991 charge that he again bribed a judge was nullified because the statute of limitations had come into effect.

16. Correspondence with Donatella della Porta.

17. Formed in 1786, the Tammany Society was originally a social and patriotic society but became a political force under Aaron Burr at the turn of the nineteenth century.

18. Interviews and correspondence with Mike Stevens, Jack Titsworth, and Joel Barkan.

Contributors

Bertram I. Spector is the Director of Management Systems International's Center for Governmental Integrity in Washington, DC, and Executive Director of the Center for Negotiation Analysis. He has more than thirty years of consulting, research, and practical field experience in anticorruption and integrity programs, transparency and accountability programs, public policy mediation and negotiation, and conflict resolution and decision-making support in countries in Eastern Europe, the former Soviet Union, Africa, Latin America, and Asia. Dr. Spector has designed and conducted many corruption surveys, assessments and implementation activities, and has coordinated closely on anticorruption programs with the World Bank, US Agency for International Development, US State Department, OECD, Transparency International, UNDP, and the Council of Europe. Dr. Spector is the Editor-in-Chief of *International Negotiation: A Journal of Theory and Practice* (Martinus Nijhoff Publishers). His most recent book is *Getting It Done: Post-Agreement Negotiation and International Regimes* (Washington, DC: United States Institute of Peace Press, 2003, co-edited with I. W. Zartman). He holds a Ph.D. in political science from New York University.

Omar Azfar is a Research Associate at the Center for Institutional Reform and the Informal Sector (IRIS) at the University of Maryland. He joined the IRIS Center after receiving his Ph.D. in Economics from Columbia University and teaching for the University of Pittsburgh in Bratislava, Slovakia. Dr. Azfar conducts research and provides technical assistance to various international development organizations such as USAID and the World Bank. He has written several papers on the causes and consequences of corruption, examining the links between corruption and women's empowerment; corruption and trade reform; corruption and health and education outcomes; and corruption and crime rates.

Verena Blechinger is Assistant Professor of Government at Hamilton College (New York). She earned an M.A. in Japanese studies, political science, and law in 1991, and a Ph.D. in political science from the University of Munich (Germany) in 1997. Since then, she has served as a lecturer at Münster and Tokyo Universities and as a research fellow at Harvard University. From 1997 to 2002, she was a research fellow and then the Deputy Director of the German Institute for Japanese Studies in Tokyo. The author of many journal articles and book chapters, she is currently preparing for publication a book manuscript on political corruption in Japan. She will begin as professor of Japanese politics and political economy at the Free University of Berlin, Germany in 2005.

David W. Chapman is Professor of Comparative and International Development Education and Chair of the Department of Educational Policy and Administration at the University of Minnesota. He has worked in more than forty-five countries for the World Bank, the US Agency for International Development, UNICEF, the Asian Development Bank, the InterAmerican Development Bank, and UNESCO, among others. He has authored or edited 7 books and more than 100 journal articles, many of them on issues related to the development of education systems throughout the world.

Phyllis Dininio is Scholar-in-Residence at American University's Transnational Crime and Corruption Center. A recognized expert on corruption, she is a governance advisor for the Development Gateway, has advised the US National Security Council on corruption issues, and served as the lead social scientist in the United States for the Center for Public Integrity's Global Integrity Project to assess the accountability and transparency of governments. She wrote the *USAID Handbook for Fighting Corruption,* co-edited *Improving Governance and Controlling Corruption* (forthcoming), and authored several scholarly articles on corruption as well as the regional report on the United States for TI's *Global Corruption Report 2003* and *2004.*

Rodney J. Fink earned his Ph.D. in agronomy from the University of Missouri. He worked for Iowa State University as an Extension Specialist after which he moved to the University of Missouri and Western Illinois University where he served for sixteen of twenty-five years as the Dean of the College of Applied Science. During the past fifteen years, he participated in numerous foreign assignments, many involving project evaluations in countries throughout the world, in addition to completing more than eighty published works. He is a retired Naval Reserve officer, and he and his wife have led volunteer work groups to Panama, Brazil, Haiti, Mexico, and Cuba.

Michael Johnston, who earned his Ph.D. at Yale University in 1977, is the Charles A. Dana Professor of Political Science and Director of the Division of Social Sciences at Colgate University in Hamilton, New York. Current research projects include a comparative study of contrasting syndromes of corruption in the context of globalization and an edited anthology on civil society and reform. He has been a consultant to many international organizations and development agencies, including the World Bank, the Asia Foundation, the New York State Commission on Governmental Integrity, and the US Agency for International Development, and recently completed a project on democratic governance for the United Nations.

Mary Noel Pepys is a senior attorney with a specialization in international legal and judicial reform. With more than twenty-five years of legal experience in the judicial, legislative, diplomatic, and private sectors, Ms. Pepys has lived and worked abroad within Central and Eastern Europe, the former Soviet Union, and Western Europe. With her knowledge of common law and civil law principles, Ms. Pepys has successfully developed, managed, and implemented effective legal reform projects promoting transparent and fair justice systems. Ms. Pepys has extensive domestic governmental experience, having worked for local, state, and federal governments in the areas of diplomacy, peacekeeping, legislative drafting, judicial process, and governmental transparency.

Matthias Ruth is Professor and Director of the Environmental Policy Program at the School of Public Policy, University of Maryland. His research focuses on dynamic modeling of natural resource use, industrial and infrastructure systems analysis, and environmental economics and policy. His theoretical work heavily draws on concepts from engineering, economics, and ecology, and his applied research uses methods of nonlinear dynamic modeling as well as adaptive and anticipatory management. Professor Ruth has published six books and more than eighty papers and book chapters. He collaborates extensively with scientists and policy makers in the USA, Canada, Europe, Asia, and Africa.

Michael Schaeffer has more than eighteen years of experience in more than sixty countries in private public partnerships, decentralization, governance and knowledge sharing (management) in developing countries, e-government, performance monitoring and evaluation, public expenditure management and budgeting, and accountability in financial management. Mr. Schaeffer has assessed a water utility private sector partnership and improved its cost recovery elements (Jordan); evaluated decentralization, municipal budgeting, and equalization transfer formulas (Republic of Georgia); and assisted the joint assessment mission in various aspects of designing effective treasury, financial management, and national/subnational budgeting systems in Georgia.

Stephen Schwenke is a specialist in good governance and integrated development planning. His experience spans a range of diverse and complex national, regional and local planning, governance, anticorruption, conflict, ethics, and participatory projects. He is currently active in a major decentralization project in Uganda and has recently led projects on ethics training for government officials in Tanzania and a four-country assessment of good local governance in Eastern Europe for USAID. Although Africa has been his geographic focus, Dr. Schwenke has also had extensive project experience in Asia, the Middle East, Latin America, Europe, and North America. Dr. Schwenke received his Ph.D. in international public policy studies from the School of Public Affairs at the University of Maryland.

Taryn Vian is Assistant Professor of International Health at Boston University School of Public Health, where she is Faculty Coordinator of Certificate Education Programs and teaches courses in health care management and corruption prevention. As a management consultant with Abt Associates Inc. and Management Sciences for Health, Ms. Vian has worked in more than twenty countries, including two years managing a decentralized child health and family planning project in the Philippines. A returned Peace Corps volunteer from Cameroon, Ms. Vian holds an M.S. degree in health policy and management from the Harvard School of Public Health and a B.A. degree in philosophy from Colgate University.

Russ Webster has twenty-three years of professional international development experience in forty countries worldwide. His areas of specialization include private sector development, economic policy reform, and public sector management. He has advised government agencies, business associations, think tanks, NGOs and donor organizations on methods and approaches for increasing transparency, reducing corruption, improving efficiency, promoting dialogue, and monitoring policy change processes. In addition to being a skilled facilitator, trainer, and speaker, Mr. Webster has prepared numerous reports and related documents on effective program strategies for private enterprise development and market-led economic reforms. He holds an M.P.A. degree from Michigan State University (1981) and a B.A. (cum laude) in philosophy from Albion College (1976). Formerly a Technical Director at Management Systems International, he is currently Practice Manager for Institutional and Policy Reform at Development Alternatives, Inc.

Svetlana Winbourne has more than ten years of experience conducting research and practical assignments in the field of environment and sustainable development and ten years of worldwide experience in the areas of good governance and anticorruption. She has conducted work for many international organizations and development agencies, including the United States Agency for International Development and the US State Department, the World Bank, the Organization for Economic Cooperation and Development, and NATO. Her most recent activities in the anticorruption area include country-specific projects in Russia, Ukraine, and Albania, regional projects for Eastern Europe and the Former Soviet Union, and several corruption assessment and evaluation projects in Romania, Russia, Indonesia, Bangladesh, and Kosovo. Dr. Winbourne worked on environmental programs at a research institute in Ukraine, the UN Development Program, and USAID. She currently is an Associate Technical Director at Management Systems International. Dr. Winbourne earned her Ph.D. in geography at Kiev State University in 1990.

Bibliography

Ablo, Emmanuel, and Ritva Reinikka. 1998. *Do budgets really matter? Evidence from public spending on education and health in Uganda. Policy research working paper 1926.* Washington, DC: Africa Region, Macroeconomics 2, The World Bank.

Abramson, WB. 2001. Monitoring and evaluation of contracts for health service delivery in Costa Rica. *Health Policy and Planning* 16: 404–411.

Abt Associates Inc. 2001. *Transport in primary healthcare: a study to determine the key components of a cost effective transport system to support the delivery of primary health services.* Bethesda, MD: SAFI Program.

Ades, Alberto, and Rafael Di Tella. 1999. Rents, competition, and corruption. *American Economic Review* 89 (4): 982–993.

Alcazar, Lorena, and Raul Andrande. 2001. Induced demand and absenteeism in Peruvian hospitals. In *Diagnosis corruption: fraud in Latin America's public hospitals.* Rafael Di Tella and William D. Savedoff, editors. Washington, DC: Inter-American Development Bank.

Alexander, Herbert E., and Rei Shiratori, editors. 1994. *Political finance among the democracies.* Boulder: Westview Press.

Allen, Richard, and Daniel Tommasi, editors. 2001. *Managing public expenditure: a reference book for transition countries.* Paris: OECD Press.

American Bar Association/CEELI. 2001. *Judicial reform index for Bosnia and Herzegovina.* October, Washington, DC: USAID.

————. 2002. *Judicial reform index for Serbia.* February, Washington, DC: USAID.

Anderson, James H., Omar Azfar, Daniel Kaufmann, Young Lee, Amitabha Mukherjee, and Randi Ryterman. 1999. *Corruption in Georgia: survey evidence.* Mimeo. Washington, DC: World Bank.

Andvig, Jens Chr., Odd-Helge Fjeldstad, Inge Amundsen, Tone Sissener, and Tina Soreide. 2000. *Research on corruption - a policy oriented survey.* Commission by NORAD, December. Bergen, Norway: Chr. Michelsen Institute.

Angell M. 2000. Investigators' responsibilities for human subjects in developing countries. *The New England Journal of Medicine* 342: 967–969.

Anti-corruption gateway for Europe and Asia. <http://www.nobribes.org>

Arabic News Weekly Edition. 2002. Ministry of Agriculture Official Arrested for Corruption. 26 August. Available at <http://www.arabicnews.com>.

Asian Development Bank 2000a. *Developing best practices for promoting private sector investment in infrastructure—power.* Washington, DC: ADB.

_____. 2000b. *Lao people's democratic republic education development sector development plan*. Manila: Asian Development Bank and Vientiane: Ministry of Education.

Asibuo, K. Sam. n.d. *Role of an anti-corruption agency in the struggle against corruption—the case of serious fraud in Ghana*. Available at <http://unpan1 .un.org/intradoc/groups/public/documents/cafrad/unpan002272.pdf>.

Association of International Pharmaceutical Manufacturers. 2001. *AIPM position paper on counterfeit drugs in Russia*. Moscow, Russia: AIPM, April.

Azfar, O. n.d. *Corruption and the delivery of health and education services*. Preliminary paper, limited circulation. College Park, MD: IRIS Center, University of Maryland.

_____. 2002. Corruption. *Encyclopedia of public choice* Draft. University of Maryland, College Park: IRIS.

_____. 2002a. *The NIE approach to economic development: an analytical primer*. Mimeo. IRIS Center, University of Maryland.

_____. 2002b. *Fighting corruption with evidence of mismanagement*. Mimeo. IRIS Center, University of Maryland.

_____, and Anand Swamy. 2001. The causes and consequences of corruption. *Annals of the American Association of Political and Social Science*, 573: 42–57.

_____, and Clifford Zinnes. 2002. *Prospective evaluation procedures (PEP Toolkit)*. Mimeo. IRIS Center, University of Maryland.

_____, and Tugrul Gurgur. 2001. *Does corruption affect health and education outcomes in the Philippines?* Mimeo. IRIS Center, University of Maryland.

_____, and Young Lee. 2002. *Corruption and social development*. Mimeo. IRIS Center, University of Maryland.

Azfar, O., Satu Kahkonen, Anthony Lanyi, Patrick Meagher, and Diana Rutherford. 1999. *Decentralization, governance and public services: the impact of institutional arrangements*. University of Maryland, College Park: IRIS Center.

Azfar, O., Satu Kähkönen, and Patrick Meagher. 2001. *Conditions for effective decentralized governance: A synthesis of research findings*. Mimeo. IRIS Center, University of Maryland.

Banfield, Edward. 1975. Corruption as a feature of governmental organization. *Journal of Law and Economics* 18 (December): 587–605.

Bangkok Post. 2000. Vote buying provides windfalls: elections to help economy. 3 February.

Bangkok Post. 2001. Corruption blights the learning curve: Poor monitoring means funds do not reach those in genuine need. 24 July.

Barber, Charles Victor, Emily Matthews, David Brown, Timothy H. Brown, Lisa Curran, Catherine Plume, and Liz Selig. 2002. *State of the forest: Indonesia*. Washington, DC: World Resource Institute.

Bardhan, Pranab, and Dilip Mookherjee. 1998. *Expenditure decentralization and the delivery of public services in developing countries.* IED Discussion Paper, Boston University.

Barnes, Grenville, David Stanfield, and Kevin Barthel. 2000. Land modernization in developing economics: a discussion of the main problems in Central/Eastern Europe, Latin America and the Caribbean. *URISA Journal* 12, 4. Available at <http://www.urisa.org/journal/protect/Vol12%20No4barnes/10–10barnes%20extract.pdf>.

Bartlett, Kathy. 2000. *Supporting NGOs working in education: Nurturing ideas and approaches and mainstreaming these through partnership.* Paper presented at the annual meeting of the Comparative and International Education Society, 8–12 May, San Antonio.

Bates, J.A., Y. Chandani, K. Crowley, J. Durgavich, and S. Rao. 2000. *Implications of health sector reform for contraceptive logistics: a preliminary assessment for Sub-Saharan Africa.* Arlington VA: Family Planning Logistics Management Project (FPLM)/John Snow Inc. (JSI).

Bates, Robert, Avner Greif, Margaret Levi, Jean-Laurent Rosenthal, and Barry Weingast. 1998. *Analytic narratives.* Princeton: Princeton University Press.

Batra, Geeta, Daniel Kaufmann, and Andrew H.W. Stone. 2000. *Voices of the firms 2000: investment climate and governance findings of the world business environment survey (WBES).* May. Washington, DC: The World Bank Group.

Becker, Gary. 1968. Crime and punishment: An economic approach. *Journal of Political Economy* 76: 169–217.

Bennet, Nicholas. n.d. *Corruption in education systems in developing countries: What is it doing to the young.* Available at <http://www.10iacc.org/content.phtml?documents=112&art=126>.

Berenbeim, Ronald E., and Jean-François Arvis. 2002. Implementing anti-corruption programs in the private sector. *PREM-notes Public Sector, Number 66.* April, Washington, DC: The World Bank.

Berman, P.A., and T.J. Bossert. 2000. *A decade of health sector reform in developing countries: what have we learned?* Boston MA: Harvard School of Public Health, Data for Decision Making Project. Available at <http://www.hsph.harvard.edu/ihsg/publications/pdf/closeout.pdf>

Bhargava, V., and Emil Bolongaita. 2003. *Challenging corruption in Asia: Selected case studies and a framework for improving anti-corruption effectiveness (Directions in Development).* Washington, DC: World Bank.

Bicknell, W.J., A.C. Beggs, and Van P. Tham. 2001. Determining the full cost of medical education in Thai Binh, Vietnam: a generalizable model. *Health Policy and Planning* 16: 412–420.

Bies, A.L., A. Moore, and J. DeJaeghere. 2000. *Consultancies and capacity-building: considerations of mutual fit, mutual learning, and mutual benefit.* Paper presented at the annual meeting of the Association for Research on Nonprofit Organizations and Voluntary Action, New Orleans.

Bird, Richard, Robert Ebel, and Christine Wallich. 1995. *Decentralization of the socialist state: intergovernmental finance in transition economies.* Washington, DC: The World Bank.

Black, Bernard S., and Anna S. Tarassova. 2002. *Institutional reform in transition: a case study of Russia.* John M. Olin Program in Law and Economics Working Paper No. 238, August, Palo Alto: Stanford Law School.

Blechinger, Verena. 1998. *Politische korruption in Japan: ursachen, hintergründe und reform* [Political corruption in Japan: causes, consequences, and reform]. Hamburg: Institute for Asian Affairs

_____. 1999. Changes in the handling of corruption scandals in Japan since 1994. *Asia-Pacific Review* 6 (2): 42–64.

_____. 2000. Cleaning up politics and revitalizing democracy? A European view of the new system of political finance in Japan. *European Review* 8 (4): 533–551.

_____, and Karl-Heinz Nassmacher. 2001. Political finance in non-western democracies: Japan and Israel. In *Foundations for democracy. Approaches to comparative political finance.* Karl-Heinz Nassmacher, editor. Baden-Baden: Nomos.

Brainard, Lael, Carol Graham, Nigel Purvis, Steven Radelet, and Gayle Smith. 2003. *The other war: global poverty and the millennium challenge account.* Washington, DC: Brookings Institution Press.

Bransten, J. 2001. World: corruption said to be flourishing in education. *Radio Free Europe* 10 October. Available at <http://www.rferl.org/features/2001/10/10102001114001.asp>

Brinkerhoff, Derick W., and Nicolas P. Kulibaba. 1999. Identifying and assessing political will for anti-corruption efforts. *Implementing Policy Change Project Working Paper No. 13.* January, Washington, DC: USAID.

Brudon P, J-D. Rainhorn, and M.R. Reich. 1999. *Indicators for monitoring national drug policies: a practical manual,* 2nd ed. Geneva: World Health Organization.

Brugha, R., M. Starling, and G. Walt. 2002. GAVI, the first steps: lessons for the global fund. *The Lancet* 359: 435–438.

Bures, L. *Citizen report cards.* 2002. Washington, DC: World Bank. Available at <http://worldbank.org/poverty/empowerment/toolsprac/tools16.pdf>.

Burke, Jason. 2000. Where state fails, others give poor a chance. *The Guardian* 28 February: 15.

Burki, Shahid Javed, Guillermo E. Perry, and William R. Dillinger. 1999. *Beyond the center: decentralizing the State.* Washington, DC: The World Bank.

Buscaglia, E. 2002. *Judicial corruption in developing countries: its causes and economic consequences.* Stanford, CA: Hoover Institution.

Business World. 2001. Corruption busting in Philippines: officials pick up a guide to preventing graft in government. 23 March.

Callister, Debra J. 1999. *Corrupt and illegal activities in the forestry sector: current understandings, and implications for World Bank forest policy.* Draft Paper prepared for the World Bank Forest Policy Review.

Campos, Edgardo J., and Sanjay Pradhan. 1996. Budgetary institutions and expenditure outcomes: binding governments to fiscal performance. *Policy Research Working Paper No. 1646.* Washington, DC: World Bank.

Cashin, C., and F. Feeley. 2002. *How much to spend for health? How do nations decide how much to spend?* Paper prepared for the ZdravPlus Project of USAID, 20 November. Boston, MA: Boston University School of Public Health.

Chang, Eric C., and Miriam A. 2001. Competitive corruption: factional conflict and political malfeasance in postwar Italian Christian democracy. *World Politics* 53 (July): 597.

Chapman, D.W. 1991. The rise and fall of an education management information system in Liberia. *Journal of Educational Policy* 6 (2): 133–143.

_____. 2000. Trends in educational administration in developing Asia. *Educational Administration Quarterly* 36 (2): 283–308.

_____, E. Barcikowski, M. Sowah, E. Gyamera, and G. Woode. 2002. Do communities know best? Testing a premise of educational decentralization: community members' perceptions of their local schools in Ghana. *International Journal of Educational Development* 22: 181–189.

Chon, Soo-Hyun. 2000. The election process and informal politics in South Korea. In *Informal Politics in East Asia.* Lowell Dittmer, Haruhiro Fukui, and Peter N.S. Lee, editors. Cambridge, New York: Cambridge University Press.

Chren, M.M., and C.S. Landefeld. 1994. Physicians' behavior and their interactions with drug companies: a controlled study of physicians who requested additions to a hospital drug formulary. *Journal of the American Medical Association* 271: 684–9; quoted in Coyle, S. 2002. Physician-industry relations. Part 1: individual physicians. *Annals of Internal Medicine* 136: 397.

Cohen, Jillian, et. al. 2002. *Improving Transparency in Pharmaceutical Systems: Strengthening Critical Decision Points against Corruption.* Mimeo. Washington, DC: World Bank.

Colazingari, Silvia, and Susan Rose-Ackerman. 1998. Corruption in a paternalistic democracy: lessons from Italy for Latin America. *Political Science Quarterly* 3 (Fall): 113.

Collins D.H., J.D. Quick, S.N. Musau, and D.L. Kraushaar. 1996. *Health financing reform in Kenya: the fall and rise of cost sharing, 1989–1994.* Boston, MA: Management Sciences for Health.

Columbia Encyclopedia. 2001. Tammany. In *The Columbia Encyclopedia, Sixth Edition.* Available at <http://www.bartleby.com/65/ta/Tammany.html>.

Contreras-Hermosilla, Arnoldo. 2001. *Law compliance in the forestry sector. An overview.* Paper presented at the East Asia Ministerial Conference on Forest Law Enforcement and Governance (FLEG), Indonesia, September 11–13.

Corruption in Bangladesh Surveys. 2002. Dhaka: TI Bangladesh.

Corruption in Slovakia: Results of Diagnostic Surveys. 2000. Washington, DC: World Bank.

Corruption Prevention Council of Latvia. *Registered crimes and sentenced persons 1994–2001.* Available at <http://www.pretkorupcija.lv/En/statistics/statistika_anglu.doc>.

Coyle, S. 2002. Physician-industry relations. Part 1: individual physicians. *Annals of Internal Medicine* 136: 396–402.

Cragg, A.W. 1999. Bribery, globalization and the problem of dirty hands. Paper presented at conference *Corruption: Ethical Challenges to Globalization,* November 5. Georgetown University, Washington, DC.

Dahl, Robert A. 1971. *Polyarchy: participation and opposition.* New Haven: Yale University Press.

De Speville, Bertrand. 1997. *Hong Kong's war on corruption.* Presentation to UNDP-PACT and OECD Development Centre Workshop, Paris, October.

———. 1998. Hong Kong's quiet revolution. *Governance* I, 1 (January): 29–36.

———. 1999. The experience of Hong Kong, China, in combating corruption. In *Curbing corruption: toward a model for building national integrity.* R. Stapenhurst and S. Kpundeh, editors. Washington DC: The World Bank.

De Michele, Roberto, and Samuel Paul. 2002. Monitoring corruption. In *Improving Governance and Controlling Corruption.* D. Kaufman, M. Gonzalez de Asis, Dininio, (eds.). Washington, DC: World Bank Institute.

Dearden, Stephen J.H. 2000. Corruption and economic development. *DSA European Development Policy Study Group discussion Paper No. 18.,* October.

Dehn, Jan, Ritva Reinikka, and Jakob Svensson. 2002. *Survey tools for assessing service delivery.* Available at <http://www.worldbank.org/research/projects/publicspending/tools/survey.tools.for.assessing.sd.june2002.pdf>.

DeJaegher, J. 2000. *NGO partnerships in education: a framework of opportunities and obstacles.* Paper presented at the annual meeting of the Comparative and International Education Society, San Antonio.

Delcheva, E., D. Balabanova, and M. McKee. 1997. Under-the-counter payments for health care: evidence from Bulgaria. *Health Policy* 42: 89–100.

Della Porta, Donatella, and Alberto Vannucci. 1999. *Corrupt exchanges: actors, resources, and mechanisms of political corruption.* New York: Aldine de Gruyter.

———. 2000. *Corruption and political financing in Italy.* Paper presented for a Transparency International workshop on corruption and political party funding, La Pietra, Italy, October.

Department of State For Education. 2001. *Education management project: output to purpose review.* Government of Gambia, 17–19 January.

Diagnostic Surveys of Corruption in Romania. 2001. Washington, DC: World Bank.

Di Tella, R., and W. Savedoff, editors. 2001. *Diagnosis corruption: fraud in Latin America's public hospitals.* Washington, DC: Inter-American Development Bank.

Di Tella, R., and E. Schargrodsky. 2002. *Controlling corruption through high wages.* Available at <http://www.people.hbs.edu/rditella/papers/high_wages.pdf.>.

Dininio, Phyllis, Sahr John Kpundeh, and Robert Leiken. 1998. *USAID handbook for fighting corruption.* Washington, DC: U.S. Agency for International Development, Center for Democracy and Governance.

Doig, Alan. 1999. Corruption, good government, good governance, and economic development. In *Curbing corruption: toward a model for building national integrity.* R. Stapenhurst and S. Kpundeh, editors. Washington, DC: The World Bank.

———, and Robin Theobald, editors. 2000. *Corruption and democratisation.* London, Portland, OR: Frank Cass

Druckman, Daniel. 1993. Situational levers of negotiating flexibility. *Journal of Conflict Resolution* 32 (2): 236–276 (June).

———. 1994. Determinants of compromising behavior in negotiation: a meta analysis. *Journal of Conflict Resolution* 33 (3): 507–556.

Dukes, M.N.G. 2002. Accountability of the pharmaceutical industry. *The Lancet* 360: 1682–1684.

Duncan, F. March 2002. *Corruption in the health sector,* draft paper. Washington, DC: USAID E&E Bureau.

Easterly, William, and Ross Levine. 1997. Africa's growth tragedy: Policies and ethnic divisions." *Quarterly Journal of Economics* 12 (4): 1203–1250.

———. 2002. *Tropics, germs and crops: How endowments affect economic development.* Mimeo. University of Minnesota.

Economic Freedom of the World. 2001. *2001 Annual Report.* Vancouver: Fraser Institute.

Economist, The. 2002. *Black gold: Sub-Saharan African oil.* 26 October: 59.

Economist Intelligence Unit. 2002. *Country Report Mexico*. London: The Economist.

Edwards, M. 1999. International development NGOs: agents of foreign aid or vehicles for international cooperation. *Nonprofit and Voluntary Sector Quarterly* 28 (4): 25–37.

Eichler, R., P. Auxila, and J. Pollock. 2002. *Performance based reimbursement to improve impact: evidence from Haiti*. Presentation to the Commercial Market Strategies Project, Washington DC, October.

Elliott, Kimberly, editor. 1997. *Corruption and the global economy*. Washington, DC: Institute for International Economics.

Falkenberg, T., and G. Tomson. 2000. The World Bank and pharmaceuticals. *Health Policy and Planning* 15: 52–58.

Feeley, F.G., I.M. Sheimann, and S.V. Shiskin. 1999. *Health sector informal payments in Russia*. Boston: Boston University Department of International Health.

Filmer, Deon, and Lant Pritchett. 1999. The impact of public spending on health: does money matter? *Social Science and Medicine* 49 (10): 1309–1323.

Fischer, Charles. 2000. *U.S.-Russia Business Council's Ag Committee*. Available at <http://www.dowagro.com/newsroom/speeches/101200sp.htm>.

Fisheries Action Coalition Team. 2002. *Feast of famine? Solutions to Cambodia's fisheries conflicts. A report by the Fisheries Action Coalition Team in collaboration with the Environmental Justice Foundation*. Available at <http://www .oxfammekong.org/documents/Fisheries policy reform cam1.doc>.

Fisman, Ramond, and Roberta Gatti. 1998. *Decentralization and corruption: evidence across countries*. Washington, DC: The World Bank.

———. 2000. *Decentralization and corruption: evidence across countries*. World Bank Policy Research Working Paper 2290: Washington, DC

Fiszbein, Ariel. 1997. The emergence of local capacity: lessons from Colombia. *World Development* 25 (7): 1029–1043.

Fitzgerald, D.W., C. Marotte, R.I. Verdier, W.D. Johnson, and J.W. Pape. 2002. Comprehension during informed consent in a less-developed country. *The Lancet* 360: 1301–1302.

Freedom House. 2001. *Freedom in the World 2000–2001*. Washington, DC: Freedom House.

Fukui, Haruhiro, and Shigeko N. Fukai. 2000. The informal politics of Japanese diet elections: cases and interpretations. In *Informal politics in East Asia*. Lowell Dittmer, Haruhiro Fukui, and Peter N. S. Lee, editors. Cambridge, New York: Cambridge University Press.

Galtung, Fredrik. 1998. Criteria for sustainable corruption control. In *Corruption and development*. Mark Robinson, editor. London: Frank Cass Publishers.

George, Alexander. 1991. *Forceful persuasion.* Washington, DC: United States Institute of Peace Press.

Gibson, Clark C. 1999. *Politicians and poachers: the political economy of wildlife policy in Africa.* Cambridge, UK: Cambridge University Press.

Giedion U, L. Gonzalo Morales, and O. Lucia Acosta. 2001. The impact of health reforms on irregularities in Bogotá hospitals. In *Diagnosis corruption: fraud in Latin America's public hospitals.* Rafeal Di Tella and William D. Savedoff, editors. Washington, DC: Inter-American Development Bank.

Giglioli, Pier Paolo. 1996. Political corruption and the media: the Tangentopoli Affair. *International Social Science Journal* 48: 381–394.

Githongo, John. 2001. Graft so entrenched in Kenya, KACA was doomed. *The East African.* 11 January. Available at <http://allafrica.com/stories/2001 01110425.html>

Giyduem, A.W., and D. Stasavagem. 1997. *Corruption: the issues. Technical paper No 122.* Paris: OECD Development Centre.

Gonzales de Asis, Maria. 2000. Reducing corruption: lessons from Venezuela. *PREMnote* 39 (May). Washington, DC: The World Bank.

Gordon, Roger. 1983. An optimal tax approach to fiscal federalism. *Quarterly Journal of Economics.* 98 (4): 567–586.

Goudie, Andrew W., and David Stasavage. 1997. *Corruption: the issues.* OECD Development Centre, Technical Papers No. 122. Available at <http://www .oecd.org/dev/Technics>.

Gray-Molina, G., E. Perez de Rada, and E. Yanez. 1999. Transparency and accountability in Bolivia: does voice matter? Working paper number R-381. *Latin American Research Network, Office of the Chief Economist.* Washington, DC: Inter-American Development Bank.

———. 2001. Does voice matter? Participation and controlling corruption in Bolivian hospitals. In *Diagnosis Corruption: Fraud in Latin America's Public Hospitals.* Rafael Di Tella and William D. Savedoff, editors. Washington, DC: Inter-American Development Bank.

Grey, Cheryl W., and Daniel Kaufman. 2000. *Corruption and development.* Washington, DC: The World Bank.

Gruen, R., R. Anwar, T. Begum, J.R. Killingsworth, and C. Normand. 2002. Dual job holding practitioners in Bangladesh: an exploration. *Social Science and Medicine* 54: 267–279.

Guluzadeh, A., E. Bakeer-zadeh, O. Minayeva, and D. Chapman. 2002. *Subregional cooperation in managing education reforms, country study: Azerbaijan.* Manila: Asian Development Bank.

Gupta, Sanjeev, Hamid Davoodi, and Rosa Alonso-Terme. 1998. *Does corruption affect income inequality and poverty, International Monetary Fund Working Paper.* Washington, DC: International Monetary Fund.

Gupta, Sanjeev, Hamid Davoodi, and Erwin Tiongson. 2000. *Corruption and the provision of health care and education services.* Working Paper No. 00/116. Washington, DC: International Monetary Fund.

Hall, Peter. 1986. *Governing the economy: the politics of state intervention in Britain and France.* New York: Oxford University Press.

Hammergren, Linn. 2002. *Do judicial councils further judicial reform? Lessons from Latin America.* June. Washington DC: Carnegie Endowment for International Peace.

Harrison, Graham. 1999. Corruption as 'boundary politics': the state, democratisation, and Mozambique's unstable liberalisation. *Third World Quarterly* 20 (3): 537–550.

Heaton, A, and R. Keith. 2002. *A long way to go: a critique of GAVI's initial impact. Briefing analysis.* United Kingdom: Save the Children/UK.

Heemink, I., M. Melero-Montes, E. Tabit, B. Waning, and R. Laing. 1999. Review of the functioning of P&T committees in Boston area hospitals, Parts 1 and 2. *Pharmacy and Therapeutics* May-June.

Heidenheimer, Arnold J., editor. 1978. *Political corruption: readings in comparative analysis.* New Brunswick, NJ: Transaction Books.

Heimann, Fritz F. 1997. Combating international corruption: the role of the business community. *Corruption and the world economy.* Kimberly Ann Elliott, editor. Washington, DC: Institute for International Economics.

Hellman, Joel S., Geraint Jones, and Daniel Kaufmann. 2000. *Seize the state, seize the day. Policy research working paper 2444, September.* Washington, DC: The World Bank, World Bank Institute, Governance, Regulation, and Finance Division and Europe and Central Asia Region, Public Sector Group and European Bank for Reconstruction and Development, Office of the Chief Economist.

Hellman, Joel. 2002. Strategies to combat state capture and administrative corruption in transition economies. Prepared for *International conference on economic reform and good governance: fighting corruption in transition economies.* April 11–12. Sponsored by the Graduate School of Public Policy and Management of Qinghua University and Carnegie Endowment for International Peace.

Henry, D., and J. Lexchin. 2002. The pharmaceutical industry as a medicines provider. *The Lancet* 360: 1590–1595.

Hirose, Michisada. 1993. *Seiji to kane* [Politics and money]. Tokyo: Iwanami Shinsho.

Holmstrom, Bengt, and Paul Milgrom. 1991. Multitask principal-agent analyses: incentive contracts, asset ownership, and job design. *Journal of Law, Economics and Organization* 7: 24–52.

Huang, Peter, and Ho-Mou Wu. 1994. More order without more law: a theory of social norms and organizational cultures. *Journal of Law, Economics and Organization* 10 (2): 390–406.

Huntington, Samuel. 1968. Modernization and corruption. In *Political order in changing societies*. A. Heidenheimer, M. Johnston, and V. Levine, editors. New Haven: Yale University Press.

———. 1984. Will more countries become democratic? *Political Science Quarterly* Summer: 193–218.

———. 1991. *The third wave: democratization in the late twentieth century.* Norman: University of Oklahoma Press.

Ilibezova, E., L. Ilibezova, N. Asanbaev, and G. Musakojaeva. 2000. *Corruption in Kyrgyztan.* Bishkek: Center of Public Opinion Studies and Forecasts. Available at <http://www.undp.kg/english>.

International Monetary Fund. 1998. *Code of good practices on fiscal transparency.* Washington, DC: International Monetary Fund.

INDEM Foundations. 2002. *Diagnosis of Russian corruption: sociological analysis.* Moscow: INDEM Foundations.

International Anti Corruption Newsletter. 2000. *D.C.EC Botswana: Botswana's approach to fighting corruption and economic crime.* January. Available at <http://www.icac.org.hk/text/eng/newsl/issue1/D.C.ec1.html>.

International Federation of Pharmaceutical Manufacturers Associations. IFPMA Code of Pharmaceutical Marketing Practices. Available at <http://www.ifpma.org>.

International Institute for Educational Planning. 2001. *Background document, expert workshop on ethics and corruption in education.* Paris: UNESCO.

International Rivers Network, IRN's Lesotho Campaign. Available at <http://www.irn.org/programs/lesotho/index.html>.

IRIS. 1996. *Governance and economy in Africa: tools for analysis and reform of corruption.* College Park, MD: Center for Institutional Reform and Informal Sector.

Isham, Jonathan, Daniel Kaufman, and Lant Pritchett. 1997. Civil liberties, democracy, and the performance of government projects. *World Bank Economic Review* 11 (2): 219–242.

Isham, Jonathan, and Satu Kähkönen. 1998. *Improving the delivery of water and sanitation: a model of co-production of infrastructure services. IRIS Working Paper Series, No. 210.* University of Maryland: IRIS Center.

Italy: 'Operation Clean Hands.' 1996. Case study. In Respondacon III, Third Inter-American Conference on the Problems of Fraud and Corruption in Government, 13 June.

Iwai, Tomoaki. 1992. *Seiji shikin no kenkyû* [Studies in political finance]. Tokyo: Nihon Keizai Shinbunsha.

Jaen, Maria, and Daniel Paravisini. 2001. Wages, capture and penalties in Venezuela's public hospitals. In *Diagnosis corruption: fraud in Latin America's public hospitals*. Rafeal Di Tella and William D. Savedoff, editors. Washington, DC: Inter-American Development Bank.

Johnson, S., D. Kaufmann, and P. Zoido-Lobatón. 1999. *Corruption, public finance, and the unofficial economy*. Washington, DC: The World Bank.

Johnston, Michael. 1993. *The political costs of corruption*. Paper presented at the Primera Conferencia Latinoamerica de Lucha Contra La Corrupcion Administrativa, Bogota, 17 November.

———. 1996. Public officials, private interests and sustainable democracy: when politics and corruption meet. *Conference of corruption in the world economy*. Institute of International Economics, Washington, DC

———. 1997. Public officials, private interests, and sustainable democracy: when politics and corruption meet. In *Corruption and the Global Economy*. Kimberly Ann Elliott, editor. Washington, DC: Institute for International Economics.

———. 2000. Controlling corruption in local government: analysis, techniques and action. Washington, DC: Management Systems International.

———, and Sahr J. Kpundeh. 2000. *Building the clean machine: anti-corruption coalitions and sustainable reform*. Washington, DC: World Bank Institute. Available at <http://people.colgate.edu/mjohnston/personal.htm> and <http://www.worldbank.org/wbi/governance>.

———. 2001. *Anti-corruption coalitions and sustainable reform*. Unpublished manuscript.

———. 2002. *The measurement problem: a focus on governance*. Unpublished manuscript.

Kaddar, M., A. Levin, L. Dougherty, and D. Maceira. 2000. *Costs and financing of immunization programs: findings of four case studies*. Bethesda, MD: Partnerships for Health Reform, Abt Associates Inc.

Kahkonen, S., and A. Lanyi. 2001. Decentralization and governance: does decentralization improve public service delivery? In *The development economics vice presidency and poverty reduction and economic management network, PremNotes* 55 (June).Washington, DC: The World Bank.

Kang, David C. 2002. *Crony capitalism. Corruption and development in South Korea and the Philippines*. Cambridge, New York: Cambridge University Press.

Karadnycky, Adrian. 2001. Nations in transit: emerging dynamics of change. In *Nations in Transit 2001*. Adrian Karatnycky, Alexander Motyl, and Amanda Schnetzer, editors. Washington, DC: Freedom House.

Kaufmann, Daniel. 1997. Corruption: the facts. *Foreign Policy*. 107 (Summer): 114–131.

_____. 2000. Governance and anticorruption. In *The Quality of Growth.* Thomas, V., M. Dailami, A. Dhareshwar, D. Kaufman, N. Kishor, R. López, and Y. Wang, editors. New York: Oxford University Press.

_____. 2003. Rethinking governance: empirical lessons challenge orthodoxy. Washington, DC: World Bank. Discussion draft, March 11.

Kaufmann, Daniel, and Aart Kraay. 2002. *Growth without governance.* Washington, DC: The World Bank. July.

Kaufmann, Daniel, and Paul Siegelbaum. 1997. Privatization and corruption in transition countries. *Journal of International Affairs* 50 (2) (Winter): 419–458.

Kaufman, Daniel, and Shang-Jin Wei. 1999. *Does 'grease money' speed up the wheels of commerce?* Cambridge, MA: National Bureau of Economic Research Working Paper No. 7093.

Kaufmann, Daniel, Aart Kraay, and Paolo Zoido-Lobaton. 1999. *Aggregating governance indicators.* Washington, DC: World Bank Policy Research Working Paper No. 2195.

Kaufman, Daniel, Gil Mehrez, and Tugrul Gurgur. 2002. *Voice or public sector management? An empirical investigation of determinants of public sector performance based on a survey of public officials.* Mimeo. Washington, DC: World Bank.

Kaufmann, Daniel, A. Kraay, and M. Mastruzzi. 2003. Governance Matters III: Governance Indicators for 1996–2002. Washington, DC: World Bank. Policy Research Working Paper 3106.

Kibumba, G. 2002. *Donated fluconazole stolen in Uganda.* E-drug Listserv, Posted October 4.

Kikuchi, Hisashi. 1992. *Sagawa no kane kutta akutoku seijika* [The immoral politicians who took Sagawa's money]. Tokyo: Yamanote Shobô Shinsha.

Killingsworth J.R., N. Hossain, Y. Hedrick-Wong, S.D. Thomas, A. Rahman, and T. Begum. 1999. Unofficial fees in Bangladesh: price, equity and institutional issues. *Health Policy and Planning* 14: 152–163.

Kim, Young-Jong. 1997. Corruption in South and North Korea. Paper presented at the *8th International Anti-Corruption Conference*, Lima, 7–11 September.

Kitschelt, Herbert. 2000. Linkages between citizens and politicians in democratic politics. *Comparative Political Studies* 33 (6/7): 845–879.

Klitgaard, Robert. 1988. *Controlling corruption.* Berkeley: University of California Press.

_____. 1996. Bolivia: healing sick institutions in La Paz. In *Governance and the economy in Africa: tools for analysis and reform of corruption.* Patrick Meagher, editor. College Park, MD: Center for Institutional Reform and the Informal Sector.

_____, R. Maclean-Abaroa, and H. Lindsey Parris. 2000. *Corrupt cities: a practical guide to cure and prevention.* Oakland, CA: ICS Press.

Knack, Stephen, and Omar Azfar. 2003. Trade intensity, country size, and corruption. *Economics of Governance* 4: 1–18.

Knack, Stephen, and Philip Keefer. 1995. Institutions and economic performance: Cross-country tests using alternative institutional measures. *Economics and Politics* 7 (3): 207–227.

Knack, Stephen, and Paroma Sanyal. 2000. *Making a difference: Do women in government affect health and education outcomes?* Mimeo. Washington, DC: World Bank.

Koh, Byul-Chung. 1997. South Korea in 1996: internal strains and external challenges. *Asian Survey* 37 (1): 1–9.

Korea Herald. 2000. Overwhelmed with rampant violations, CEMC calls for fundamental changes. 20 March.

Kotlobay, Anatoly. 2002. *Illegal logging in the southern part of the Russian far east: problem analysis and proposed solution. a case study on experiences of log tracking and chain of custody practices in forestry and forest products in Russia.* Moscow, Russia: WWF. Available at <http://archive.panda.org/forests4life/downloads/Case_study_for_Russia.rtf>.

Kpundeh, Sahr. 1997. *Political will.* Unpublished manuscript.

_____. 2000. Controlling corruption in Sierra Leone: an assessment of past efforts and suggestions for the future. In. *Corruption and development in Africa.* Bornwell Chikulo and Ronald Hope, editors. New York: St. Martin's Press.

Kramer, John M. 1999. *Anti-corruption research concerning eastern Europe and the former Soviet Union: a comparative analysis. Technical note no. 2, Center for Governmental Integrity.* Washington, DC: Management Systems International. Available at <http://www.nobribes.org/documents/kramer_anti corruption research report-tech2.doc>.

Kremenyuk, Victor. 1991. *International negotiation.* San Francisco: Jossey-Bass.

Kremer, Michael. 2002. *Incentives, institutions, and development assistance.* Discussion Paper No. 02/04. College Park: IRIS Center, University of Maryland.

Krueger, Anne O. 1974. The political economy of the rent-seeking society. *The American Economic Review* 64 (3): 291–303.

Kuchta-Helbling, Catherine. *Tapping hidden fortunes.* The Center for International Private Enterprise. Available at <http://www.cipe.org/pdf/informal sector/tappingEng.pdf>.

Kynge, James. 2002. Doing overtime in the workshop of the world. Five part series on China's future. *Financial Times.* 29 October: 11.

_____. 2002. Creaking economy needs stronger foundations. Five part series on China's future. *Financial Times*. 30 October: 9.

_____. 2002. Taxman heaps added burden on to farmers. Five part series on China's future. *Financial Times*. 31 October: 13.

_____. 2002. Cancer of corruption spreads through China. Five part series on China's future. *Financial Times*. 1 November: 13.

_____. 2002. Beijing's new masters face crisis of governance. Five part series on China's future. *Financial Times*. 2 November: 6.

La Porta, Rafael, Florencio Lopez-de-Silanes, Andrei Shleifer, and Robert Vishny. 1997. Trust in large organizations. *American Economic Review Papers and Proceedings* 87 (2): 333–8.

Laing R. 1999. The world health and drug situation. *International Journal of Risk & Safety in Medicine* 12: 51–57.

_____, H. Hogerzeil, and D. Ross-Degnan. 2001. Ten recommendations to improve use of medicines in developing countries. *Health Policy and Plan*ning 16: 13–20.

Lambsdorff, Johann Graf. 1999. *Corruption in empirical research—a review*. Washington, DC: Transparency International Working Paper. Available at <http://www.transparency.org/working_papers/lambsdorff/lambsdorff_eresearch.html>.

Lee, Young, and Omar Azfar. 2001. *Does corruption delay trade reform?* IRIS Center, University of Maryland.

Leff, Nathaniel. 1964. Economic development through bureaucratic corruption. *American Behavioral Scientist* 8: 8–14.

Levy, Marc A. 2001. Corruption and the 2001 Environmental Sustainability Index. In *Global corruption report 2001*. Washington, DC: Transparency International.

Lewis, M. 2000. Who is paying for health care in Eastern Europe and Central Asia? *Human development sector unit, Europe and Central Asia region*. Washington, DC: The World Bank.

Lipset, Seymor, and Gabriel Lenz. 2000. Corruption, culture and markets. In *Culture Matters*. L.E. Harrison and S.P. Huntington, editors. New York: Basic Books.

Litvack, Jennie. 1994. *Regional demands and fiscal federalism, in Russian and the challenge of fiscal federalism*. Washington, DC: The World Bank, 218–240.

_____, Junaid Ahmad, and Richard Bird. 1998. *Rethinking decentralization in developing countries*. Washington, DC: The World Bank.

Litvack, Jennie, and Jessica Seddon. 1999. Decentralization briefing notes. *World Bank Institute Working Papers*. Washington, DC: The World Bank.

Loksatta Times. 2001. Political Funding Reform. 2 (3) (May-June): 1–28.

Love, J. 2002. Plan to curb illicit medicines trade. *IP-Health Digest* 1 (976), 29 October.

Lovei, L., and A. McKechnie. 2000. *The cost of corruption for the poor: the energy sector.* Washington, DC: The World Bank Group, Private Sector and Infrastructure Network.

Lynoe, N., Z. Hyder, M. Chowdhury, and L. Ekstrom. 2001. Obtaining informed consent in Bangladesh. *The New England Journal of Medicine* 344: 460–461.

Ma, Stephen K. 2001. The culture of corruption in Post-Mao China. In *Where corruption lives.* Gerald E. Caiden, editor. Bloomfield, CT: Kumarian Press.

Management Sciences for Health. 1993. *Lessons learned from the family planning management development project, Philippines.* Manila: MSH.

_____. 1997. *Managing drug supply: the selection, procurement, distribution, and use of pharmaceuticals,* 2nd ed.. Boston, MA: Management Sciences for Health.

_____ and WHO. 2001. *International drug price indicator guide.* Boston, MA: Management Sciences for Health.

_____, *The Manager.* 2001. Using performance-based payments to improve health programs. Available at <http://erc.msh.org/mainpage.cfm?file =2.1.11.htm&module=finance&language=english>.

Management Systems International. 2000. *Integrity survey in Kharkiv, Ukraine.* Washington, DC: MSI (conducted by Kiev International Institute of Sociology, November-December 1999).

_____. 2000. *Ukraine anti-corruption support project.* Washington, DC: Management Systems International.

_____. 2003. *Civil society successes in fighting corruption in Russia's regions.* Washington, DC: MSI. Under contract to US Agency for International Development (January).

_____ and the World Bank. 2000. *Diagnostic assessment of corruption in Romania, July.* Washington, DC: MSI and the World Bank.

March, James G., and Johan P. Olsen. 1989. *Rediscovering institutions: the organizational basis of politics.* New York: The Free Press.

Marshall, I.E. 2001. *A survey of corruption issues in the mining and mineral sector, international institute for environment and development,* London: Mining, Minerals and Sustainable Development Project.

Martinez, J., and T. Martineau. 1998. Rethinking human resources: an agenda for the millennium. *Health Policy and Planning* 13: 345–358.

Mastny, Lisa, and French, Hilary. 2002. Crimes of (a) global nature. *World Watch magazine* Worldwatch Institute, September/October.

Mauro, Paolo. 1995. Corruption and Growth. *Quarterly Journal Of Economics* 110 (3): 681–712.

_____. 1996. The effects of corruption on growth, investment, and government expenditures. *International Monetary Fund Working Paper 96/98.* Washington, DC: International Monetary Fund.

_____. 1997. The effects of corruption on growth, investment and government expenditure: a cross-country analysis. In *Corruption and the global economy.* Kimberly Ann Elliott (ed.). Washington, DC: Institute for International Economics.

_____. 1997. *Why worry about corruption?* Washington DC: International Monetary Fund.

_____. 1998. Corruption and the composition of government expenditure. *Journal of Public Economics* 69: 263–79.

_____. 2002. *Corruption: causes, consequences, and agenda for further research.* Washington, DC: Mimeo, International Monetary Fund.

McPake, B., D. Asiimwe, F. Mwesigye, M. Ofumbi, L. Ortenblad, P. Streefland, and A. Turinde. 1999. Informal economic activities of public health workers in Uganda: implications for quality and accessibility of care. *Social Science & Medicine* 49: 849–865.

Meagher, Patrick. 1999. Cooperating against corruption: governance, collective action, and jurisdictional design in plural societies. Paper prepared for *IRIS Conference on Collective Action and Corruption in Emerging Economies,* May.

_____. 2000. Changing hands: a case study of financial sector reforms in Hungary's market transition. *IRIS Working Paper No. 245.* College Park, MD: Center for Institutional Reform and Informal Sector.

_____. 2000. Roads with destinations: A case study of governance and rural infrastructure in Nepal. *IRIS Working Paper No. 246.* College Park, MD: Center for Institutional Reform and Informal Sector.

Meldolesi, Luca. 2000. Corruption, accountability, and democracy in Italy: an outline. In *Combating Corruption in Latin America.* Joseph S. Tulchin and Ralph H. Espach (eds.). Washington, DC: Woodrow Wilson Center Press.

Meyer, David, and R. Hester. 2001. *Combating corruption: the case of tax reform.* Washington, DC: USAID.

Mick, T. 1991. Pharmaceutical funding and medical students. *Journal of the American Medical Association* 265 (1991): 662–664; quoted in Coyle, S. 2002. Physician-industry relations. Part 1: individual physicians. *Annals of Internal Medicine* 136: 397.

Miller, Nathan. 1992. *Stealing from America.* New York: Peragon House.

Miller, William L., Åse B. Grødeland, and Tatyana Y. Koshechkina. 1998. Are the people victims or accomplices: the use of presents and bribes to influence officials in Eastern Europe. *Crime, Law and Social Change* 29 (4): 273–310.

_____. 1999. What is to be done about corrupt officials? Public opinion in Ukraine, Bulgaria, Slovakia and the Czech Republic. *International Review of Administrative Sciences* 65: 235–249.

_____. 2001. *A culture of corruption: coping with government in post-communist Europe*. Hungary and New York: Central European University Press.

Mills, A. 1998. To contract or not to contract? Issues for low and middle-income countries. *Health Policy and Planning* 13: 32–40.

Ministry of agriculture official arrested for corruption. 2002. *Arabic News Weekly Edition*. 26 August. Available at <http://www.arabicnews.com/ansub/Daily/Day/020826/2002082616.html>.

Monge, Raúl, and Silvia Ortiz. 2001. Graft's toll on Mexico: environmental destruction. Originally in Spanish in *Proceso*, Mexico City, Mexico, 8 July. Reprinted in English in *World Press Review* 48 (10) (October). Available at <http://www.worldpress.org/1001.toc.htm>

Moore, Barrington. 1966. *Social origins of democracy and dictatorship*. Boston: Beacon Press.

Moran, Jon. 1999. Patterns of corruption and development in East Asia. *Third World Quarterly* 20 (3): 569–587.

Morris, Stephen D. 1999. Corruption and the Mexican political system: continuity and change. *Third World Quarterly* 20 (3) 623–643.

Munshi, J. 2000. *Corruption in state owned monopolies, the Bangladesh power sector*. February, Dhaka: Transparency International Bangladesh.

Murphy, Kevin, Andrei Shleifer, and Robert Vishny. 1993. Why is rent seeking so costly for growth? *American Economic Review* 83: 409–14.

Nakamura, Alice, and Masao Nakamura. 1985. On the performance of tests by Wu and Haussman for detecting the ordinary least squares bias problem. *Journal of Econometrics* 29 (3): 213–227.

Nancollas S. 1999. *From camels to aircraft: the development of a simple transport management system designed to improve health service delivery*. Paper prepared for the WHO TECHNET Meeting. Geneva: WHO.

Nassmacher, Karl-Heinz, editor. 2001. *Foundations for democracy. Approaches to comparative political finance*. Baden-Baden: Nomos.

Newey, Whitney. 1985. Generalized method of moments specification testing. *Journal of Econometrics* 29 (3): 229–256.

New York Times. 1996. Thai civics: new leader, but votes are still for sale. 19 November.

_____. 1998. Folk Hero Strips Teflon from Thailand's Corrupt. 26 April.

Noonan, John T., Jr. 1984. *Bribes: the intellectual history of a moral idea*. Berkeley: University of California Press.

North, Douglas. 1981. *Structure and change in economic history*. New York: Norton.

_____. 1990. *Institutions, institutional change and economic performance.* Cambridge, MA: Cambridge University Press.

O'Driscoll Jr., Gerald, Kim Holmes, and Melanie Kirkpatrick. 2001. *2001 Index of Economic Freedom.* Washington, DC: Heritage Foundation.

O'Rourke, P.J. 2000. The Godfather decade: an encounter with Post-Soviet corruption. *Foreign Policy* November/December: 74–80.

OECD. 1999. Principles of corporate governance. Ad hoc task force on corporate governance. *Directorate for Financial, Fiscal and Enterprise Affairs.* SG/CG (99) 5, 19 April.

_____. 2000. *No longer business as usual: fighting bribery and corruption.* Paris: Organization for Economic Cooperation and Development.

Olson, Mancur. 1996. Big bills left on the sidewalk: Why some nations are rich and others poor. *Journal of Economics Perspectives* 10: 3–24.

_____. 2000. *Power and prosperity - outgrowing communist and capitalist dictatorships.* New York: Basic Books.

Orlowski, J.P., and L. Wateska. 1992. The effects of pharmaceutical enticements on physician prescribing patterns. There's no such thing as a free lunch. *Chest* 102: 270–3.

Ostrom, Elinor, Larry Schroeder, and Susan Wynne. 1993. *Institutional incentives and sustainable development: infrastructure polices in perspective.* Boulder, CO: Westview Press.

Pabico, Alecks P. 2000. The Price of Power: The San Roque Dam in Pangasinan will displace thousands. *The Investigative Reporting Magazine.* The Philippine Center for Investigative Journalism (PCIJ). Available at <http://www.pcij.org/imag/EarthWatch/sanroque.html>.

Park, Chan-Wook. 2000. Major issues and direction of political reform. *Korea Focus* 8 (3). Available at <http://www.kf.or.kr/koreafocus/>.

Partnership for Governance Reform in Indonesia. 2002. *A diagnostic study of corruption in Indonesia. Final Report.* Jakharta: UNDP.

Paul, Samuel. 1992. Accountability in public services: exit, voice and control. *World Development* 29 (7): 1047–1060.

Pinto-Duschinksy, Michael. 1981. *British political finance 1830–1980.* Washington, London: American Enterprise Institute.

_____. 2002. Financing politics: a global view. *Journal of Democracy* 13 (4): 69–86.

Pope, Jeremy. 2000. Confronting corruption: the elements of a national integrity system. *Transparency International (TI) Source Book 2000.* Washington, DC: Transparency International.

_____. 2002. France and Italy set a bad example (comment). *International Herald Tribune.* 7 March: 6.

Pradhan, Sanjay, James Anderson, Joel Hellman, Geraint Jones, Bill Moore, Helga Muller, Randi Ryterman, and Helen Sutch. 2000. *Anticorruption in transition: a contribution to the policy debate.* Washington, DC: The World Bank.

Probe International Press Advisory. 2002. *Canadian engineering multinational to be sentenced today in world's largest corruption case.* Available at <http://www.odiousdebts.org/odiousdebts/index.cfm?DSP=content&ContentID=5544>.

Quah, S.T Jon. 1999. Singapore's experience in curbing corruption. In *Political Corruption.* Arnold J. Heidenheimer, M. Johnson, and V.T. Levine, editors. New Brunswick: Transaction Publishers.

————. 1999. Comparing anti-corruption measures in Asian countries: lessons to be learnt. *Asian Review Of Public Administration* 1 (2): 71–90.

Rajkumar, A. Sunil, and Vinaya Swaroop. 2001. *Public spending and outcomes: Does governance matter?* Mimeo. Washington, DC: The World Bank.

Rational Pharmaceutical Management Project, Latin American and Caribbean Health and Nutrition Sustainability Project. 1995. *Rapid pharmaceutical management assessment: an indicator-based approach.* Arlington, VA: RPM Project, Management Sciences for Health.

Rauch, James, and Peter Evans. 2000. Bureaucratic structure and bureaucratic performance in less developed countries. *Journal of Public Economics* 75: 49–71.

Reed, Stephen R. 1996. Political corruption in Japan. *International Social Science Journal* 48: 395–405.

Regional Corruption Monitoring: Corruption Indexes. April 2002. Sofia, Bulgaria: Vitosha Research.

Reich, M.R. 2000. The global drug gap. *Science* 287: 1979–1981.

Reinikka, R., and J. Svensson. 2002. *Assessing frontline service delivery. Draft paper.* Washington, DC: World Bank, Development Research Group, Public Services. Available at <http://www.worldbank.org/wbi/governance/assessing/pdf/reinikka.pdf>.

Renger, Jochen, and Birgitta Wolff. 2000. Rent seeking in irrigated agriculture: institutional problem areas in operations and maintenance. Deutsche Gesellschaft für Technische Zusammenarbeit. Available at <http://www.padrigu.gu.se/ED.C.News/Reviews/Renger2000.html>.

Renner, Michael. 2002. The anatomy of resource wars. *World Watch Paper 162* (October).

Respondacon III Italy. 1996. *Operation Clean Hands' case study, third Inter-American conference on the problems of fraud and corruption in government.* 13 June. Arlington, VA: Casals and Associates.

Respondanet homepage. Available at <http://www.respondanet.com/english>.

Rodrik, Dani, Arvind Subramanian, and Francesco Trebbi. 2002. Institutions Rule: The Primacy of Institutions Over Geography and Integration in Economic Development, October. CEPR Discussion Paper No. 3643.

Rose-Ackerman, Susan. 1978. *Corruption: a study in political economy*. New York: Academic Press.

_____. 1996. The political economy of corruption - causes and consequences. *Public Policy for the Private Sector*. April. Washington, DC: The World Bank.

_____. 1999. *Corruption and government. Causes, consequences, and reform.* Cambridge, New York: Cambridge University Press.

Ross, Michael. 2001. *Timber boom and institutional breakdown in Southeast Asia.* Cambridge, UK: Cambridge University Press.

Ruzindara, Augustine. 1997. The importance of leadership in fighting corruption in Uganda. In *Corruption and the global economy*. Kimberly Ann Elliott, editor. Washington, DC: Institute for International Economics.

Salmon, Pierre. 1987. Decentralization as an incentive scheme. *Oxford Review of Economic Policy* 3 (2): 24–43.

Saltman, R.B. 2002. Regulating incentives: the past and present role of the state in health care systems. *Social Science and Medicine* 54: 1677–1684.

Sarimiento, Prime. 2000. Agriculture weighed down by corruption and waste. *Philippine Center for Investigative Journalism*. Available at <http://www.pcij.org/stories/2000/agri.html>.

Savona, Ernesto U. 1995. Beyond criminal law in devising anticorruption policies: lessons from the Italian experience. *European Journal on Criminal Policy and Research* 3 (2): 21–37.

Schargrodsky, Ernesto, Jorge Mera, and Federico Weinschelbaum. 2001. Transparency and accountability in Argentina's hospitals. In *Diagnosis corruption: fraud in Latin America's public hospitals*. Rafael Di Tella and William D. Savedoff, editors. Washington, DC: Inter-American Development Bank.

Scharpf, Fritz W., translated by Ruth Crowley and Fred Thompson. 1987. *Crisis and choice in European social democracy*. Ithaca, NY: Cornell University Press.

Schiavo-Campo, S. 1999. Governance, corruption and public financial management. Manila: ADB Press. S. Schiavo-Campo and Daniel Tommasi, editors. 1999. *Managing government expenditure.* Manila: ADB.

_____, and P.S.A. Sundaram., editors. 2001. *Improving public administration in a competitive world.* Manila: ADB Press.

_____, and D. Tommasi. 1999. *Managing government expenditure.* Manila: ADB. Manila.

Schloss, Miguel. 2000. *Challenges of investing in countries seen to be the most corrupt in the world - the case of natural resources industries.* Transparency International. Annual General Meeting, Ottawa, 20 September.

Schwenke, Stephen. 2000. The moral critique: corruption in developing countries. *Journal of Public and International Affairs* 11: 137–156.

Sedigh, Shahrzad. 1999. The fight against corruption in Sierra Leone. In *Curbing corruption: toward a model for building national integrity.* R. Stapenhurst and S. Kpundeh, editors. Washington DC: The World Bank.

_____ and Alex Muganda. 1999. The fight against corruption in Tanzania. In *Curbing corruption: toward a model for building national integrity.* R. Stapenhurst and S. Kpundeh, editors. Washington DC: The World Bank.

Sedigh, Shahrzad, and Augustine Ruzindana. 1999. The fight against corruption in Uganda. In *Curbing corruption: Toward a model for building national integrity.* R. Stapenhurst and S. Kpundeh (eds.). Washington DC: The World Bank.

Sen A. 1999. *Development as freedom.* New York: Alfred A. Knopf, Inc.

Severino, Howie G. 1998. *Caught in a bind, Cerilles gets midnight ECC from the DENR.* Manila: The Philippine Center for Investigative Journalism (PCIJ). Available at <http://www.pcij.org/stories/1998/cerilles.html>.

Shell International Limited. 2002. *Dealing with bribery and corruption:* a *management primer.* Available at <http://www.shell.com/static/royal-en/downloads/dealingwithbriberyprimer_final.pdf>.

Shelley, Louise I. 1995. Post-Soviet organized crime and the rule of law. *John Marshall Law Review* 28 (4) (Summer): 827–845.

Shkolnikov, Aleksandr, editor. 2002. *Corporate governance: an antidote to corruption.* Washington, DC: CIPE.

Shleifer, Adrei. 1996. *Government in transition, HIER discussion paper no. 1783.* Boston: Harvard Institute For Economic Research.

_____ and Robert W. Vishney. 1993. Corruption. *Quarterly Journal of Economics.* 108 (August): 599–617.

Siller, Donald. n.d. *Strengthening basic education through institutional reform: linking authority, accountability, and transparency, Policy Issues Paper.* Washington, DC: USAID (draft).

Spector, Bertram. 2000a. Building constituencies for anti-corruption programs: the role of diagnostic assessments. Paper presented at the *Regional Anti-Corruption Conference,* Bucharest, Romania, March 30. Available at <http://www.nobribes.org>.

_____. October 2000b. *Anti-corruption program feasibility study in Russia: Tomsk and Samara, final report.* Washington, DC: Management Systems International.

_____. 2001. Negotiation readiness in the development context: adding capacity to ripeness. In *From Conflict Resolution to Peace Building.* Ho-Won Jong, editor. New York: Macmillan.

Stapenhurst, Rick, and Sahr Kpundeh. 1999. *Curbing Corruption: Toward a Model for Building National Integrity.* Washington, DC: World Bank.

Stein, Janice, editor. 1989. *Getting to the table: the processes of international prenegotiation.* Baltimore: The Johns Hopkins University Press.

Steiner, Achim. 2000. *Accountability and the environment: the need for a joint initiative of public, private and civil society sectors.* Introductory Remarks for Workshop On Corruption And The Environment. 9th International Anti-Corruption Conference.

Sullivan, John D. Combating corruption: a policy tool kit. Available at <http://www.cipe.org/programs/corruption/index.htm>.

Supreme Administrative Court of the Republic of Bulgaria. 2004. Available at <http://www.sac.government.bg>.

Swamy, Anand, et. al. 2001. Gender and corruption. *Journal of Development Economics* 64 (1): 25–55.

Sweetser, A.T. 1997. *BRAC's non-formal primary education: customer focused evaluation of the world's largest NGO.* Advancing Basic Education and Learning Project, Washington DC: Academy for Educational Development.

Swygert, Michael I., and Katherine Earle Yanes. 1998. *A unified theory of justice: the integration of fairness into efficiency.* Seattle: Washington Law Review Association.

Tanzi, V. 1998. *Corruption: causes, consequence, and agenda for further research.* Washington DC: International Monetary Fund.

_____. 1998. *Corruption around the world: causes, consequences, scope, and cures. International Monetary Fund Staff Papers* 45 (4): 1.

_____ and Hamid Davoodi. 1998. *Corruption, growth, and public finances.* International Monetary Fund working paper. Washington DC: International Monetary Fund.

Taylor, Ian. 2002. Crisis in Zimbabwe and death of NEPAD. *Progressive Response* 6 (8).

Thelen, Kathleen, and Sven Steinmo. 1992. Historical institutionalism in comparative politics. In *Structuring politics: historical institutionalism in comparative analysis.* Sven Steinmo, Kathleen Thelen, and Frank Longstreth, editors. New York: Cambridge University Press.

Thornton, Laura L. 2001. *Political party strategies to combat corruption. Executive summary.* Washington, DC: National Democratic Institute for International Affairs (NDI) and The Council of Asian Liberals and Democrats (CALD). Available at <http://www.ndi.org>

Toyne, Paul, Cliona O'Brien, and Rob Nelson. 2002. *The timber footprint of the G8 and China: making the case for green procurement by government.* Washington, DC: WWF International.

Transparency International. Available at <http://www.transparency.de/> (German). <http://www.transparency.org> (English).

———. 2000. *Bribes to political parties an increasing threat to democracy.* Press release, Berlin, 19 October. Available at <http://www.transparency.org/press releases_archive/2000/2000.10.19.p_funding.html>.

———. 2001. *The corruption fighters' toolkit.* Berlin: Transparency International. Available at <http://www.transparency.org/toolkits/toolkit_toc.html>.

———. 2001. *The integrity pact (TI-IP): the concept, the model and the present applications: a status report.* Available at <http://www.transparency.org/building_coalitions/integrity_pact/i_pact.pdf>.

———. 2002. *Bribe Payers Index.* Berlin: TI. Available at <http://www.transparency.org/cpi/2002/bpi2002.en.html>.

———. 2003. *Corruption Perceptions Index.* Berlin: TI. Available at <http://www.transparency.org/cpi/2003/cpi2003.en.html>.

Treisman, Daniel. 2000. The causes of corruption: a cross-national study. *Journal of Public Economics* 76: 399–457.

United Nations. 2001. *Human development report, 2001.* New York: United Nations Development Programme.

UNDP. 2001. *An economic and jurimetric analysis of official corruption in the courts.* Washington, DC: UNDP, CICP-12, May.

US Department of Energy. 2000. *International energy annual.* Available at <http://www.eia.doe.gov/emeu/iea/table29.html>.

USAID. 1988. *Liberia education and human resources sector assessment, improving the efficiency of education systems project.* Tallahassee: Florida State University and Washington DC: USAID.

———. 1999. *A handbook on fighting corruption, technical publication series.* Washington, DC: Center for Democracy and Governance, Bureau for Global Programs, US Agency for International Development.

———. 2002. *Strengthening basic education through institutional reform: linking authority, accountability, and transparency.* Washington DC: USAID.

———. 2003. *Fighting Corruption.* Available at <http://www.usaid.gov/democracy/anticorruption/index.html>.

——— and World Bank. 2000. *Corruption in Slovakia: results of diagnostic surveys.* Washington, DC: USAID and World Bank.

Vian, T. 2001. *Low- and middle-income country perspectives on collaborative quality improvement: can the breakthrough series work?* Buenos Aires, Argentina: paper presented at the November Meeting of the International Society for Quality Assurance.

———. 2002. *Corruption, accountability and decentralized health systems: keeping the public's trust.* Presentation prepared for the 130th Annual Meeting of the American Public Health Association, Philadelphia, 13 November.

_____, and J. Bates. 2002. *Recent trends and developments for logistics management in essential drugs, vaccines and contraceptives: implications for contraceptive security.* Arlington, VA: The Deliver Project, October.

Wall, L.L., and D. Brown. 2002. Pharmaceutical sales representatives and the doctor/patient relationship. *Obstetrics & Gynecology* 100: 594–599.

Washington Conference on Corruption. 1999. *Fighting corruption in developing countries and emerging economies: the role of the private sector.* February, Washington, DC Under the auspices of the Development Center of the OECD. In cooperation with PriceWaterhouseCoopers.

Wedel, Janine R. 2001. *Clans, cliques, and captured states: rethinking 'Transition' in Central and Eastern Europe and the Former Soviet Union.* Helsinki: United Nations University, World Institute for Development Economics Research.

Wedeman, Andrew. 1997. Looters, rent-scrapers, and dividend-collectors: corruption and growth in Zaire, South Korea, and the Philippines. *The Journal of Developing Areas* 31: 457–478

Wei, Shang-Jin. 1997. *Why is corruption so much more taxing than tax? Arbitrariness kills.* Cambridge, MA: National Bureau of Economic Research.

_____. 2000. *Natural openness and good government.* Cambridge, MA: National Bureau of Economic Research Working Paper No. 7765.

Werner, C. 2000. Gifts, bribes and development in Post-Soviet Kazakhstan. *Human Organization* 59:11–22.

Weyland, Kurt. 1998. The politics of corruption in Latin America. *Journal of Democracy* 9 (2): 108–121.

Wilson, B. 2002. Global disease fund postpones Tanzania grant. *National Public Radio Morning Edition Audio Report.* 25 November. Available at <http://www.npr.org/archives/index.html>.

Wilson, James Q. 1978. Corruption: the shame of the states. In *Political corruption: readings in comparative analysis.* A. Heidenheimer, editor. New Brunswick, NJ: Transaction Books.

Woodle, D. 2000. Vaccine procurement and self-sufficiency in developing countries. *Health Policy and Planning* 15:121–129.

World Bank Institute Governance and Anti-corruption Sector. Available at <http://www.worldbank/org/wbi/governance>.

World Bank Public Sector Governance/Anti-corruption. Available at <http://www.worldbank.org/publicsector/anticorrupt/>.

World Bank and Corruption Prevention Council of Latvia. 1998. *Corruption in Latvia: survey evidence.* Washington DC: World Bank.

World Bank. 1990. *Basic education study in Indonesia.* Washington DC: World Bank.

_____. 1998. New frontiers in diagnosing and combating corruption. *Prem Notes: The World Bank* 7 (October).

_____. 1999. An anticorruption strategy for revenue administration. *Prem Notes: The World Bank* 33 (October).

_____. 2000a. Reforming tax systems: lessons from the 1990s. *Prem Notes: The World Bank* 37 (April).

_____. 2000b. Reducing corruption: lessons from Venezuela. *Prem Notes: The World Bank* 39 (May).

_____. 2000c. Computerizing tax and customs administrations. *Prem Notes: The World Bank* 44 (October).

_____. 2000d. *World development report: the state in a changing world.* Washington, DC: The World Bank.

_____. 2000e. *Bosnia and Herzegovina: diagnostic surveys of corruption.* Washington, DC: World Bank.

_____. 2000f. *Technical note: the procurement of health sector goods.* Washington, DC: World Bank.

_____. 2000g. *Anticorruption in transition. A contribution to the policy debate.* Washington, DC: World Bank.

_____. 2000h. *Helping countries combat corruption: progress at the World Bank since 1997.* Washington, DC: The World Bank (PREM), June.

_____. 2001a. *World development report 2001.* Washington, DC: World Bank.

_____. 2001b. Decentralization and governance: does decentralization improve public service delivery? *Prem Notes: The World Bank* 55 (June).

_____. 2002a. Implementing anticorruption programs in the private sector. *PREM Notes: The World Bank.* Washington DC: World Bank.

_____. 2002b. *Brazil rain forest pilot program success story: new environmental control system helps reduce deforestation by one-third in Mato Grosso.* Washington, DC: World Bank, Rain Forest Pilot Program.

World Health Organization. 1988. *Ethical criteria for medicinal drug promotion.* Geneva: WHO. Available at <http://www.who.int/medicines/library/dap/ethical-criteria/ethicalen.htm>.

_____. 1998. *Guidelines for the international procurement of vaccines and sera.* Geneva: WHO, Global Programme for Vaccines and Immunization, Vaccine Supply and Quality.

World Health Organization Expert Committee on the Use of Essential Drugs. 2002. The selection and use of essential medicines. In *Report of the WHO expert committee. World Health Organization technical report series.* Geneva: WHO.

World Wildlife Fund, Forests for Life Programme. Available at <http://www.panda.org/about_wwf/what_we_do/forests/problems/forest_crime.cfm>.

_____. n.d. *Socioeconomic root causes of biodiversity loss in the Philippines. Summary.* Washington, DC: WWF publication. Available at <http://www .panda.org/resources/programmes/mpo/library/download/philwp50.doc>.

_____. 2002. *Russia 2001 Report.* Washington, DC: WWF.

Yatskevich, O. n.d. *Corruption in education in Belarus.* Available at <http:// www.10iacc.org/download/m2–04.pdf>.

Zartman, I. William. 1989. *Ripe for resolution.* New York: Oxford University Press.

Zucker, Lynne, and Michael Darby. 1999. Comment on 'the quality of government': why do some governments have better institutions than others? *The Journal of Law, Economics, and Organization* 15 (1): 280–282.

Index

Also from Kumarian Press...

Development, Corruption, Public Administration

Better Governance and Public Policy
Capacity Building for Democratic Renewal in Africa
Edited by Dele Olowu and Soumana Sako

Building Democratic Institutions: Governance Reform in Developing Countries
G. Shabbir Cheema

Governance, Administration & Development: Making the State Work
Mark Turner and David Hulme

Managing Policy Reform
Concepts and Tools for Decision-Makers in Developing Countries
Derick W. Brinkerhoff and Benjamin L. Crosby

Reinventing Government for the Twenty First Century
State Capacity in a Globalizing Society
Edited by Dennis A. Rondinelli and G. Shabbir Cheema

Running out of Control: Dilemmas of Globalization
R. Alan Hedley

War and Intervention: Issues for Contemporary Peace Operations
Michael V. Bhatia

Where Corruption Lives
Gerald E. Caiden, O.P. Dwivedi, and Joseph Jabbra

Civil Society, Humanitarianism and Human Rights

Creating a Better World: Interpreting Global Civil Society
Edited by Rupert Taylor

Globalization and Social Exclusion: A Transformationalist Perspective
Ronaldo Munck

Human Rights and Development
Peter Uvin

The Charity of Nations: Humanitarian Action in a Calculating World
Ian Smillie and Larry Minear

Worlds Apart: Civil Society and the Battle of Ethical Globalization
John Clark

Visit Kumarian Press at **www.kpbooks.com** or
call **toll-free 800.289.2664** for a complete catalog.

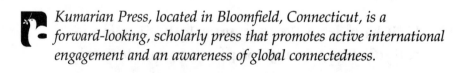